D0204619

# SOCIAL PROBLEMS AND INEQUALITY

*Shattering the old disciplinary limits with an unabashedly progressive approach John Alessio bares the underlying interconnections shaping the issues that confront us all, from everyday troubles to global disasters. His crisp, provocative analysis points the reader to examine their own role in social issues and most importantly how we can move from being part of the problem to becoming part of the solution.*

R.A. Dello Buono, Manhattan College, USA

*A masterful introduction to the sociological perspective that turns the illuminating power of the discipline onto important contemporary issues – including the oppression of animals. This powerful political-economic analysis is a compelling argument for rejecting an unsustainable system and working for justice for all the residents of the planet.*

David Nibert, Wittenberg University, USA

# Solving Social Problems

Series Editor:
*Bonnie Berry, Director of the Social Problems Research Group, USA*

Solving Social Problems provides a forum for the description and measurement of social problems, with a keen focus on the concrete remedies proposed for their solution. The series takes an international perspective, exploring social problems in various parts of the world, with the central concern being always their possible remedy. As such, work is welcomed on subjects as diverse as environmental damage, terrorism, economic disparities and economic devastation, poverty, inequalities, domestic assaults and sexual abuse, health care, natural disasters, labour inequality, animal abuse, crime, and mental illness and its treatment. In addition to recommending solutions to social problems, the books in this series are theoretically sophisticated, exploring previous discussions of the issues in question, examining other attempts to resolve them, and adopting and discussing methodologies that are commonly used to measure social problems. Proposed solutions may be framed as changes in policy, practice, or more broadly, social change and social movement. Solutions may be reflective of ideology, but are always pragmatic and detailed, explaining the means by which the suggested solutions might be achieved.

# Social Problems and Inequality

## Social Responsibility through Progressive Sociology

JOHN C. ALESSIO
*Minnesota State University, Mankato, USA*

ASHGATE

Published by
Ashgate Publishing Limited
Wey Court East
Union Road
Farnham
Surrey, GU9 7PT
England

Ashgate Publishing Company
Suite 420
101 Cherry Street
Burlington
VT 05401-4405
USA

www.ashgate.com

**British Library Cataloguing in Publication Data**
Alessio, John C.
Social problems and inequality : social responsibility through progressive sociology. -- (Solving social problems)
1. Social problems. 2. Applied sociology. 3. Social conflict. 4. Responsibility. 5. Alienation (Social psychology) 6. Social action.
I. Title II. Series
361.1-dc22

**Library of Congress Cataloging-in-Publication Data**
Alessio, John C.
Social problems and inequality : social responsibility through progressive sociology / by John C. Alessio.
p. cm. -- (Solving social problems)
Includes bibliographical references and index.
ISBN 978-1-4094-1987-7 (hardback) -- ISBN 978-1-4094-1988-4 (ebook) 1. Social problems. 2. Equality. 3. Sociology. I. Title.
HN17.5.A445 2011
305--dc22

2011012347

ISBN 9781409419877 (hbk)
ISBN 9781409419884 (ebk)

Printed and bound in Great Britain by the MPG Books Group, UK.

# Contents

# List of Figures

# Foreword

When I was a beginning instructor in large-lecture courses on the sociology of social problems, I often lamented, with like-minded colleagues, about the paucity of good textbooks available for use in the course. Our main complaint was that most current books placed heavy emphasis on individual pathologies like alcoholism, crime, or mental illness, and while many of these chapters were excellent treatments of the subject, they gave much less attention to the institutional structures that contributed to or created these problems. So I solved the problem by joining with a colleague to develop our own social problems book. We focused on three interdependent and reinforcing changes in American society that we considered to be revolutionary: technological militarism, labor-displacing cybernetics, and the human rights revolution that was an oppositional voice that would no longer accept war, corporate domination, and poverty as normal features of a healthy society.

I suspect that John Alessio also found many existing social problems textbooks to be wanting, and instead of lamenting, he acted and wrote his own book. *Social Problems and Inequality* confronts established taken-for-granted institutions and presents a critical sociology perspective that breaks the mold of social problems books in several important ways. First, and foremost, he has focused on the interconnections among social problems rather than treating them as separate entities. Many of the conditions discussed in the book are interrelated and the result of a common set of institutional factors. Second, he uses contemporary theoretical perspectives to analyze the institutional basis of social problems, and to consider different solutions to remedy systemic problems. Using this approach provides students with a working understanding of a number of theoretical perspectives including conflict theory, structural functionalism, social exchange theory, and feminist theory. Third, the discussion of social problems keeps the spotlight on dominant institutions and corporations that are the source of social and economic inequality and responsible for their continued maintenance. Fourth, the book presents for analysis real public organizations (CIA, Enron) and high-profile historical events (Iraq War, 2008 financial crisis), thereby encouraging readers to apply the sociological way of looking at the world to their own lives and to public events.

John Alessio is passionate about his subject and he consistently challenges the reader to consider important applications of the sociological perspective to the task of positive social change. There are many memorable sections and passages in this book, but here is one that stayed with me:

What this chapter tells us is that the people of the United States and the world in general need to democratically create and control their own economy and their own media and airwaves or they will continue to let the media, and hence, the economy, control them.

Robert Perrucci
Purdue University

# Preface

Solving social problems has been the goal of Sociology since its inception in the mid-nineteenth century. Much has been investigated, analyzed, and written about Sociology and its various subfields since that time. Sociologists and other social scientists have contributed a great deal toward an improved understanding of how the social world works. Many social organizations have been assisted in their efforts to achieve their goals. While sociologists have done a good job of writing about social problems as isolated individual entities, we have not done a good job of analyzing and writing about their interrelationships and common sources. Consequently, we have not been able to effectively offer credible and practical guidelines for resolving the world's most serious social problems.

This book is designed to offer a relatively new direction for social problems—one that moves toward a greater understanding of the interrelationships between the various issues commonly referred to within the social problems literature. Moving toward that goal, there are a number of primary objectives pursued.

**Integration of Theoretical Perspectives**

One objective of this book is to provide the reader with an understanding of how theory can guide one's thinking about social issues and possible solutions to social problems. Theoretical perspectives are integrated around certain issues to show their interrelationships. This process allows one to see the common sources of some of the ideas within different perspectives. For example, conflict theory and structural functionalism, while quite different in important ways, both represent responses to the systemic problems of the industrial revolution. The approach of integrating perspectives begins to be revealed within the substantive chapters where it becomes clear that no one theoretical perspective has the one true way of seeing social reality. Perspectives are discussed primarily in terms of their strengths and, therefore, what they have to offer citizen students of social problems.

The references to some of the weaknesses of theoretical perspectives are intended to caution the reader to not become overly committed to, or dogmatic about, any one perspective. Like churches, theoretical perspectives are created by humans and none of them can lay claim to the ultimate truth. Together, however, the theoretical perspectives of Sociology provide a powerful tool for helping people more fully understand the root causes of social problems. Once the somewhat artificial boundaries of the various perspectives in Sociology are overcome, it is easier to appreciate what the theoretical perspectives have in common and what they offer one another. It is unfortunate that this way of viewing sociological perspectives is often lost in the territoriality that sometimes characterizes Sociology as a discipline.

## Integration of Micro and Macro Levels of Analysis

A second objective is to challenge the reader to see the interrelationship of social problems from both a micro and macro perspective, and understand how the two levels interact with one another. The difficult task of bridging the traditional boundaries between micro Sociology and macro Sociology is addressed. I did not set out with that explicit purpose in mind when I first started thinking about writing this book. However, the first semester I spent collecting notes to begin my writing I was teaching both a Social Psychology course and a social problems course where I found myself drifting back and forth between macro and micro applications of Social Psychology. This interconnection within Social Psychology began to impact how I saw social problems content and Sociology in general. A fuller understanding emerged of what is lost by keeping macro and micro bodies of sociological literature separate. Dispersed throughout this work, the reader will find a considerable amount of interplay between what is happening at the interpersonal level, and what is happening within the larger social entities of the social world. The more I allow the micro/macro boundaries to drop in my own thinking, the more confident I am that greater integration of the micro and macro levels of analysis is needed if we hope to use sociological theory and practice effectively.

## Integration of Social Problems Issues

The third objective is to show that many of the individual social problems, currently treated as separate silos, actually stem from the same sources: root causes that work together in a complex interrelated fashion. Numerous mechanisms are in play to create and maintain various types and forms of social and economic inequality. The social construction of inequality is critical to the operation and maintenance of Western economic policies—commonly known as laissez-faire economics or free market capitalism. Inequality manifests itself in a variety of ways. One of the more common ways in which inequality is created is through the social construction of group identities. These group identities lead to in-group and out-group behavior, which is then rationalized and maintained through stereotyping, scapegoating, blaming the victim, and frequently demonizing the excluded groups.

The excluded socially constructed groups then become available for low cost labor, marketing-induced overconsumption, high interest loans, and eventual acts of desperation as people struggle to support their families and maintain some semblance of self respect and cultural/sub-cultural integrity. The globalization of the "free market" economy has moved this process to all parts of the world, forcing group identities onto entire nation-states. Dissent and deviation from the heavily prescribed economic-based norms are punished locally with imprisonment and are punished around the globe with military force and acts of genocide. People responsible for the decisions leading to the creation and maintenance of these complex social problems processes hide behind the powerful shield of corporate personhood and the corporate resources that control political systems and courts of law.

Understanding and eventually unraveling these complex processes requires first understanding human vulnerabilities, social psychological responses to vulnerabilities, and how the human condition is vitally connected with the rest of existence, including the existence of other forms of life. Those who play key roles in the perpetuation of social problems may or may not be aware of the full extent of their participation and/or the history and long term consequences of their behaviors. Notwithstanding, this book is not about demonizing those who demonize others, but is more so about understanding the processes behind the resultant social problems that occur when humans systematically create inequality for economic benefit. It is only through that understanding of the complexities and interrelatedness of social problems that long term solutions can be effectively proposed.

## Practice

Fourth, this book is as much about sociological practice as it is about sociological theory. The last two chapters address important applications of Sociology, beginning with a chapter that examines the efficacy of free market economic responses to systemic world problems. The contradictions embedded in the free market approach are analyzed and their inadequacies discussed. The final chapter outlines approaches that can be taken by citizens to be actively involved in applying Sociology in their everyday lives. There are explicit recommendations about what course(s) of action could to be taken in order to bring about positive social change. In addition to the final chapters, however, there are dispersed throughout the text, suggestions about how certain identified problem situations might have been handled differently if a progressive sociological approach had been taken.

In the study of social change, one often finds historical records of violence and, sometimes, the sociological prediction of such activities. The reader should not confuse discussions about violent revolutions and predictions of violence with condoning violence. The preferred option from the standpoint of this book is always a non-violent option and one that does the least harm relative to living beings. There are, however, revolutions that need to occur that are not necessarily violent. I say "not necessarily violent" because one can never be sure what others are going to do when they are not achieving their goals. Additionally, it is not the sociologist's place to judge the actions of severely oppressed and desperate people, or anyone for that matter.

My father was a union organizer for the coal mines in Western Pennsylvania. When the coal miners struck in an effort to organize themselves into unions, the violence was most often started by the companies who called upon local police and private security thugs to harass and even attack the striking workers. In more modern times, the National Guard, the FBI, and provocateurs have been used for the same purpose. Gandhi, influenced by the work of Leo Tolstoy (1899b), espoused complete non-violence, but that did not prevent him and the people who followed him from being attacked. How people respond to violence perpetrated against them should be first determined by their own principles about how they want to live their lives, and secondly by strategies for achieving their social goals.

# Dedication and Acknowledgements

I dedicate this book to my Italian immigrant parents, Maria Femia and Paolo Alessio, who had no formal education, but whose peasant wisdom and intelligence were extraordinary.

I would also like to acknowledge: Commissioning Editor Neil Jordan for his guidance, the anonymous reviewers for their helpful suggestions; Series Editor Bonnie Berry, whose detailed editing and encouragement were invaluable; and my life partner, Julie Andrzejewski, for her many suggestions, but most importantly for affirming and helping me rekindle my progressive peasant roots.

# Chapter 1
# The Systematic Study of Social Problems

## Personal Troubles vs. Public Issues

Perhaps the most often cited work when defining the concept "social problems" is that of C. Wright Mills' "The Sociological Imagination," originally published in 1959. In "The Sociological Imagination," among other goals, Mills endeavored to draw a distinction between personal troubles and public issues. Some social problems authors have used Mills' arguments and examples to make the point that social problems are not to be confused with personal troubles. Others have used Mills' writings to emphasize the idea that personal troubles and social problems are inextricably connected. Indeed, when we look at "The Sociological Imagination," we find evidence to support both positions. Support for the former position can be seen in the following quote:

> *Troubles* occur within the character of the individual and within the range of his immediate relations with others; they have to do with his self and with those limited areas of social life of which he is directly and personally aware …
>
> *Issues* have to do with matters that transcend these local environments of the individual and the range of his inner life. They have to do with the organization of many such milieu [sic] into the institutions of an historical society as a whole, with the ways in which various milieu [sic] overlap and interpenetrate to form the larger structure of social and historical life. (Mills 1993: 51)

As an example of a personal trouble, Mills identifies one person in a city of 100,000 being unemployed. Under these circumstances we are permitted to examine the person's character and skills for possible explanations of their unemployment. As an example of a public issue, he identifies 15 million people being unemployed out of a population of 50 million. Here we are permitted to examine the political and economic institutions of society for the sources of unemployment.

Support for the latter interpretation of Mills, i.e., that the personal and public are inextricably connected, can be seen in the next quote.

> What we experience in various and specific milieu [sic], I have noted, is often caused by structural changes. Accordingly, to understand the changes of many personal milieu [sic] we are required to look beyond them. (Mills 1993: 52)

The above quote is preceded by examples of large numbers of individuals experiencing hardships because of broader social structural problems. Regardless of which interpretation one chooses to give Mills' work, it seems clear that a purported fundamental distinction between personal troubles and public issues is the number of people involved. The importance of having a lot of people involved to constitute a public issue continues to be reflected in many of the text book definitions of social problems. Some examples are as follows:

> *A social problem exists when an influential group asserts that a certain social condition affecting a large number of people is a problem …* (Zastrow 1996: 3)

> Social Problems can be defined as situations, policies, or trends that are (1) distressing or threatening to large numbers of people … (Glynn et al. 1996: 3)

> A *social problem* is a condition affecting a significant number of people in ways considered undesirable … (Horton et al. 1997: 2)

> Sociologically, a *social problem is a phenomenon regarded as bad or undesirable by a significant number of people or a number of significant people who mobilize to remedy it.* (Heiner 2010: 5)

And most recently:

> *… an alleged situation that is incompatible with the values of a significant number of people who agree that action is needed to alter the situation.* (Rubington and Weinberg 2011: 3)

A version of Heiner's approach is the definition offered by Joel Best: "That is, the study of social problems should focus on how and why particular conditions come to be constructed as social problems" (2008: 14). A constructionist approach presumes a public awareness of a problem, which implies someone with a claim goes through a process of making others see reality in the same manner as the claim-maker. According to these definitions there are no true external benchmarks for social problems analysts to study—only the process by which events come to be seen as social problems. Under this approach there are no social problems until there is a certain level of social consciousness of a problem, which can only emerge through an effective social construction of that problem.

One could, however, work backward from Best's model to discuss what the common events are that provoke individuals to engage in the process of making a claim, or what conditions prevent a claim from being effectively made when serious harm is being done to someone or some group of people. Indeed, from a social constructionist point of view, the more relevant question might be how social reality is effectively controlled to publicly deny the "existence" of social problems. Therein lie the serious social problems, and that is the focus of the definition of a social problem in this book.

## A Definition of Social Problem

If there are conditions and circumstances under which individuals cannot be held responsible for their negative predicament, however undesirable or seemingly isolated that predicament, it would seem to be important to recognize such predicaments as part of what constitute a social problem. We look to causal sequences of events to understand how the individual's behavior or negative situation is part of a broader social fabric and not simply the outcome of a personal decision. A definition of "Social Problem" should reflect the important issues discussed in the middle chapters of this book. The definition I use may have been influenced by a combination of definitions I have encountered over the years. If it is influenced by an existing particular definition, I am unaware of the source:

> *A social problem is a condition that involves harm to one or more individuals and/or one or more social entities, has at least one social cause and/or at least one social effect, and consequently has one or more social remedies.*

The actual reason for the importance placed on large numbers by some authors is not clear. While on the surface, as sociologists, it makes intuitive sense that we would be dealing with large numbers of people, Mills' seems to fall short of a logical explanation. Others tend not to address the matter. Since I raised this issue in a paper I presented at a conference a few years before writing this book, I have noticed some changes in the definitions of a social problem. It seems there is a movement toward greater inclusion, but texts still fall short of a clear explanation of why a single individual cannot experience a social problem. Leon-Guerrero (2009) is somewhat of an exception and comes close to seeing social problems in the same manner as presented in this text.

## Framework of the Definition

On the one hand Mills indicated that personal troubles are a function of characteristics in the individual or local milieu. On the other hand he allowed public issues to consist of aggregated personal troubles. The argument seems to be that when a lot of people have a particular negative experience, it is a function of something happening in society. When few people have the same experience, it is a function of something wrong with the individual or the individual's immediate circumstances.

*Understanding blaming the victim*

From the above discussion we are cast into an interesting and challenging debate surrounding the concept of "blaming the victim." As stated by Ryan, "Blaming the victim is an ideological process, which is to say that it is a set of ideas and concepts deriving from systematically motivated, but unintended, distortions of reality" (1996: 61). The blaming the victim ideology (BVI), in its least harmful form, essentially identifies people who are different from mainstream normative standards, and asks the question, "how can we fix these individuals so they can be like everyone else?" That question implies two assumptions: 1) that the difference is intrinsically undesirable or problematic; and 2) that the difference is a result of something that is wrong with the individual. Ryan's formulation of the BVI does not include identification of genetic or innate qualities. He suggests that belief in the importance of "innate" qualities is from an earlier conservative era. His original work on this issue was in 1976. I would argue that BVI today includes the belief in genetic and innate qualities as determinants of an individual's behavioral and corresponding social characteristics.

The "bell curve" research is perhaps one of the most evident examples of attributing social status to genetically based qualities. The bell curve research refers to scientifically flawed research that was conducted and published to demonstrate the superior intelligence of some social groups and the inferior intelligence of others. This type of research is conducted and published every few years to assert White superiority over most other racial and ethnic groups.

*Whose intelligence?*

Suppose you want to be the most intelligent person in the world. What can you do to accomplish that goal? Your first thought might be that you could read and study everyday all day long until the day you die. Would you be successful? What would you choose to read? What would you choose to study? Could you possibly even come close to covering everything there is to know? Then how would you know if you covered the right topics that qualify as intelligent subject matter? Who would you ask?

There is a much easier way to achieve the status of most intelligent being on the planet. Sit down for a couple hours, with a refreshing beverage of your choice if you like, and write up a test that measures intelligence. If you are serious about your goal, you will be sure to ask only questions you can answer. If it is a good test, it will contain many questions that Research Methodologists call highly discriminating questions. That is, questions that most other people will not know how to answer because they are not you and consequently have not had the exact same experiences you have had. You may want to label this test "The Final IQ Exam" in order to maintain your preeminence as the most intelligent person in the world.

As you administer your IQ test to others, which people are most likely to do well and which people are most likely to do poorly? If you have done your job, as instructed above, the people most like yourself are the people who will tend to do the best on the exam. These are the people who grew up in your hometown, went to your schools, participated in the same activities, read the same books, traveled to the same places, and so on. As you continue to administer the test, and the population circle using the exam widens to include greater numbers of people from backgrounds increasingly more different than yours, your test will successfully ferret out the truly dumb people—that is, those people who happened to grow up in an extremely different social and physical environment.

*Not a universally testable phenomenon* The primary point being made should be pretty obvious by now. Intelligence is measured with tests. Tests measure what the test-makers believe is important, which just happens to be what the test-makers know. The information contained in any single IQ test is a very small amount of possible knowledge about the universe. A completely different test could be constructed about subject matter totally foreign to the IQ test-makers, which would evaluate them as lacking in intelligence. Even the notion of testing itself, especially as it is done in a timed written form, is a culturally biased phenomenon. That basically means that some peoples' backgrounds and socio-physical environments are more conducive to the activity of IQ test-taking than are the backgrounds of others.

People who do exceptionally well on IQ tests are mostly people who come from backgrounds similar to the people who constructed the tests. This does not mean that there cannot be exceptions. There are exceptions to most circumstances in life. With the proper training a person can now learn how to more effectively take IQ tests. There are practice IQ tests which, if taken often enough, give one a good idea of what kinds of questions to expect. Other similar achievement tests serve the same purpose. Educated people in some cultures quite different from the West where IQ tests were developed, learn the material covered on IQ tests almost in a caricature form. That is, they have focused their educational system predominantly on the areas covered by western IQ tests, and may have ignored valuable knowledge related to their own culture.

So how do we get from scores on culturally and regionally biased tests to genetic inferiority or superiority? We don't in any sensible manner. Even the best argument for attempting to do so is flawed. It is quite likely that people do have genetically different neurological systems that respond differently to various kinds of stimuli. On the basis of this point, one might argue that such differences in neurological systems are the basis for developing higher and lower levels of intelligence. We have seen, however, that decisions about which types of stimuli are most important represent a bias critical to the invalidation of IQ tests. One neurological system might be more responsive to one type of stimuli and another neurological system more responsive to another type of stimuli. The value placed on those two types of stimuli is socially determined by who controls that particular definition of reality. Furthermore, there is no evidence that there are more neurological differences between socially defined groups of people than there are within socially defined groups of people.

What about when there are neurological differences? For example, non-human animals have different neurological systems from humans and often do not respond to stimuli in the same manner as humans. On the basis of these different behavioral responses humans typically assume that animals are less intelligent than they are. Such an assumption might reflect a shortcoming in human intelligence more so than a short coming in non-human intelligence. We do not have a sufficiently common set of criteria for judging the intelligence of non-humans. Similarly, our IQ tests are insufficient for measuring intelligence in people who are from backgrounds different from the IQ exam content source.

### *Genetics agenda*

Presumably, if we can attribute "undesirable" behavioral tendencies to genetic characteristics, we open the door to implement our powerful new genome research technology to "correct" those behavioral tendencies. A long-term underlying assumption here is that if we genetically alter fetuses to make everyone behave in a certain way our social problems will disappear: no more crime and so on. There are too many ethical and philosophical problems related to this line of thinking to be able to address genetic manipulation effectively in this chapter. There are many moral and practical reasons for humans to avoid manipulating one another's genetic makeup.

As will be discussed in Chapter 9, as long as there are human differences and laws there will continue to be people defined as criminals. The economic function of human differences will also be discussed later in this book. Under an economic system focused on short term profit maximization, the demand for low cost labor will always require the social construction of human group differences. In other words, the macro-economic function of identifying some people as inferior and some people as superior might curb tendencies toward trying to genetically shaped people into having the same mental and physical characteristics. In order for people to not be channeled into superior and inferior groups under the current socio-economic norms of behavior, humans would have to be perfect clones of one another. Until that happens, and let us hope it never does, some people will find ways of defining others into particular social categories for their own purposes.

### *How many victims does it take?*

Ryan tells us that BVI is responsible for explanations that attribute conditions, such as unemployment, to characteristics and/or the decision making of the individuals experiencing those conditions. Ryan does not, however, tell us under what circumstances, if any, conditions such as unemployment, may actually be the responsibility of the individual. Mills, and numerous social problems texts following Mills' lead, tell us that the answer is somehow related to the number of people experiencing a particular condition, but most social problems scholars avoid indicating how large or small that number should be. Hence, the question that begs an answer from the available social problems literature is, *"How many 'victims' does it take to make a social problem?"* Note the reference to "victims" now instead of people. It could be argued that in a complex world such as ours we are all victims of some sort or another, and even perpetrators suffer. Notwithstanding, some circumstances are far more serious than others. How do we know if we have enough victims to constitute a circumstance serious enough to be considered a social problem?

Rubington and Weinberg (2011) ask this same question regarding the number of people it takes to make a social problem, but address it from the standpoint of how many people it takes to get an issue recognized as a social problem. The answer then becomes based on how much social power people have who want to identify something as a social problem. Most critical sociologists do not accept the notion that social problems have to be publicly recognized as such in order to be considered social problems. Hence, sociologists are not bound to accept, as given, social problems proclaimed by those who have the power to do so. The question remains unanswered: how many victims does it take to make a social problem? If sociologists cannot answer this question in a meaningful way, how can we claim that a social problem requires "large numbers of people?" I take a different approach. I propose the answer to the above question is that a social problem can involve any number of people—even one.

## When the Cause is the Problem

While sociologists who take the "large numbers" approach do not typically ignore causation, they tend to be focused on the effects of social problems. Rather than define the existence of a social problem in terms of the numbers of people suffering some particular condition, it would seem to make more sense to focus on the circumstances that lead to certain conditions. Are the circumstances that lead to "small numbers" having a certain condition different than the circumstances leading to "large numbers" having a certain condition? If there are differences, are they qualitatively different, quantitatively different, or both? For example, are the circumstances that result in one person out of 100,000 being unemployed different than the circumstances that lead to 15 million out of 50 million people being unemployed? Or, is it possible that we are dealing with the same circumstances, but with a greater magnitude in the latter instant? If the answer to the last question could be "yes" it is also the case that social problems can exist with small as well as large numbers of victims. If the circumstances that lead to the individual's undesirable condition are social in nature (consequences of some characteristic(s) of social arrangements) then one must conclude that, indeed, a social problem exists. Pursuing this line of reasoning, it would follow that one person out of

100,000 being unemployed could constitute a social problem if, indeed, the forces leading to that unemployment were social in nature.

While critical and other contemporary sociologists do not believe that power should determine what is seen as a social problem by sociologists, they understand that power does impact whether the public recognizes social problems. People in positions of power are able to control the public perception about what is a social vs. private problem. Sociologists know this well, and that knowledge should be reflected in how we define our terms. Furthermore, it is not logical to infer that social circumstances are acceptable simply because few rather than many have experienced negative consequences of those social circumstances.

Going back one more time to Mills' example, one person in 100,000 who is unemployed may be experiencing the same difficulties and lack of control of external social forces as 15 million out of 50 million people unemployed. There does not seem to be a convincing argument for requiring large numbers of people experiencing the same condition in order to say we have a social problem. The implication of requiring large numbers of people in order to consider a problem social, is that at some arbitrary number of individuals the responsibility for those individuals' negative condition shifts from the social to the personal. The definition of a social problem used herein is designed to avoid that dilemma.

### *Social cause and/or social effect*

For a problem to be social it is reasonable that it have either a social cause or a social effect. This position is not new and can be identified in the works of a number of other contemporary social problems authors, such as Lauer and Lauer (2007), and Feagin et al. (2006). If a social problem has a social cause, it would seem that the social cause should also be considered a social problem. There can be lengthy chains of cause and effect conditions representing social causes, social problems, and their effects. For example, the cultural characteristic of greed contributes to capitalism (and is a product of capitalism as well) which leads to the accumulation of wealth, which requires cheap labor, which requires unemployment and underemployment, which results in poverty, which results in homelessness, which results in various forms of suffering and premature death. While often these days we see reference to capitalism and greed as causes of many of our social problems, we seldom see them identified as social problems themselves. It is not surprising that students of social problems issues are overly focused on effects rather than causes, when professional sociologists seem to have the same tendency.

The following is an exercise designed to accomplish three important tasks: 1) challenge the myth that most problems that individuals have are personal and not social in nature; 2) integrate the blaming the victim concept into the social problems literature and show how the BVI phenomenon is used to maintain status quo thinking; and 3) think of social problems equally in terms of cause and effect.

This exercise makes the social problem definition I use more meaningful and understandable.

## Personal or Social: An Exercise

I sometimes ask students to write down three serious personal problems of which they are aware ("personal problems" used here as Mills used personal troubles). They are asked to simply rely on their current understanding of what constitutes a personal problem. I then ask for volunteer responses that I can put on the screen for the rest of the class to see. They usually come up with items like the following: being unemployed, poverty, low self esteem, not doing well in school, drug addiction, depression, long term mental illness, and long term physical illness. There are also typically a variety of other more unusual responses. For example, I had one student who was a fairly large person identify "finding shoes that fit." I typically display the first five or six volunteered items that are mentioned. The results of one particular class (the big shoe class) appear in Figure 1.1.

unemployed
low self esteem
drug addiction
depression
can't find big shoes

**Figure 1.1 Identifying personal problems**

*Effects of personal problems*

I then ask, "What effects, if any, do these personal problems have on other individuals or the social world in general?" Numerous consequences are typically identified: people who are unemployed draw unemployment which is a tax drain; people who are unemployed can't take care of their families properly so their families suffer, and also end up on welfare; unemployed people are more likely to commit criminal acts which negatively impact people who do work and crime also costs everyone else a lot of tax dollars and so on. I display these responses to the right of the corresponding personal problem item, using an arrow to indicate a causal relationship. The identified consequences tend to be similar for many of the mentioned personal problem areas.

After following the above process with each of the personal problem items, we arrive at a diagram that typically looks something like Figure 1.2 as provided below. This process tends to reveal feelings based on what most people have

**Figure 1.2 Identifying effects of personal problems**

been taught throughout their lives: that people should do a better job of managing their personal problems because their problems are costly to others and society. The issue of personal responsibility usually emerges within this context. There is a strong belief communicated that people should be held accountable for the decisions they make, because their decisions impact others as well as themselves. This is an important and delicate issue.

*Causes of personal problems*

The next step is to ask students to identify what causes the personal problems first listed in Figure 1.1 and subsequently appearing again in Figure 1.2. Invariably, most of the responses are like the following: 1) unemployment and poverty are caused by laziness, welfare, failure to attain an education, lack of ability, lack of intelligence, lack of motivation; 2) low self esteem is caused by having a bad attitude, having too many negative thoughts, not being good at the things one does; 3) drug addiction is caused by people making bad decisions, hanging around with the wrong people, partying too much, biological predispositions; 4) depression is caused by a chemical imbalance; and 5) not finding large enough shoes is caused by not looking in the right places.

When I first started doing this exercise these responses were somewhat surprising since by this stage of the exercise some students were realizing that the process I was leading them through was somewhat of a trap. At about this point it starts to become clear that one can think of social as well as non-social explanations for the problems previously identified as "personal." Indeed, some students will now provide such explanations, recognizing the apparent contradiction: that it is illogical to consider a problem entirely personal if it has a social origin. However, socialization toward BVI, and a "personal problem" way of viewing the social world has become so powerful in the United States that it is difficult for some people to grasp the point being made in this exercise.

*Searching for causes*

Is it possible that people might be unemployed because of a lack of jobs in their community that are consistent with their background? It is difficult to deny this possibility. Some will argue that one can always find a job if one wants to work badly enough. Others will respond to those comments, however, with examples from their own families of fathers, mothers or other relatives who could not find a job (once they were laid off) sufficiently adequate to support their families. These responses require that we write "lack of jobs" with an arrow pointing toward "unemployment."

Is it possible that some people may be unemployed because their company was downsized or moved to another country for cheaper labor? It is one circumstance if a community has never created sufficient employment opportunities for its members, and yet another circumstance to have existing jobs taken away. It should not be difficult to relate to this distinction and identify examples of plant relocations and job outsourcing. These factors can be added to the diagram with causal arrows as well.

In addition to a lack of education as a possible reason for unemployment, there are other possible causes: insufficient resources provided K-12 schools to properly educate everyone, one's social class, how much money a family has, and the extent to which higher education is actually available to everyone?" These issues are, of course, related to other issues, such as taxation. We can move on to the other "personal problem" items identified in Figure 1.2, and go through the same process. The result is what appears in Figure 1.3.

*Effects can also be causes*

You will notice that some of the items in Figure 1.3 are identified as effects and then again as causes. It is not uncommon for such to be the case in many situations in everyday life. Sometimes the causes and effects can be interchangeable in the same situation. This is what is known as a feedback process or a reciprocal relationship. Marital dissatisfaction can cause depression which can then turn around and cause even greater marital dissatisfaction. What is a cause in one situation may be an effect in another situation. Low self esteem may cause drug addiction in one situation, but in another situation low self esteem may be the effect. For example, low self esteem may be caused by a person doing poorly in school or losing a job.

The more general and more important point is that social life is very complicated, and it takes a great deal of skill and thought to understand the extensive fabric of variable interrelationships in the social world. If one becomes too focused on one particular issue one runs the risk of overlooking the most important causal factor in a complicated social situation. What are the causes of the causes? Figure 1.3 only begins to scratch the surface of the network of factors involved in the identified social problems. If the analysis is taken back far enough in the causal sequence, the causal factors may narrow again to the most significant root causes. Many of the causes identified in Figure 1.3 for example, when traced back to yet earlier causal factors, end up in the same place. This book will demonstrate how many of the social problems typically listed by students and social problems texts alike, can be traced to a similar root cause—if not entirely, at least in part.

## Personal vs. Social Responsibility

I briefly alluded to the commonly raised question of whether people should be held accountable for their decisions. After all, don't people ultimately make decisions themselves, and don't those decisions have consequences for their lives and the lives of others? "Making bad decisions" is somewhat of a contemporary buzz phrase. Discussions about juveniles who get into trouble of some sort often

**Figure 1.3 Identifying causes of "personal" problems**

include statements to the effect, "well, he is just not making good decisions." It is certainly true that we make our own decisions. It is not the case, however, that we make those decisions independent of a complex fabric of environmentally contextualized experiences. Much happens to us and around us before we make a decision, and everyone's circumstances are, more or less, different.

Some people have little latitude with respect to improving their own condition, or correcting their own behavior. Others have a great deal. Everyone has a responsibility to do the best they can to bring about positive change within whatever parameters of freedom are available to them. It is important to emphasize, however, that people who have access to and/or control over a lot of resources are far more able to change their conditions and behaviors than those who have little, and who consequently find themselves trapped in a very limited set of behavioral alternatives. When those who have abundant resources use them to further deny opportunities or greater choices to those with few resources, they are participating in the oppression of others. The people who are being oppressed are, indeed, victims. To make them responsible for their predicament under these circumstances is to blame them unjustifiably.

## Social Responsibility

The typical decisions that an affluent suburban juvenile makes are going to be quite different than the typical decisions that a poor inner city ghetto juvenile makes. Those two sets of decisions will most likely have significantly different consequences for themselves and for others. This is not a new revelation. The impact of one's social and physical environment on one's behavior is information that sociologists wrote extensively about during the 1960s and early 1970s. It is the basis for numerous aggressive social reconstruction programs in the United States: programs designed to equalize opportunities so that the decisions people make are from within similar sets of real choices. Decisions are based on the choices people have, and those choices can be manipulated in real terms or simply in terms of the perceptions of the individuals making the decisions. Both real and perceived choices are quite different for different groups of people who are from different physical and social backgrounds.

When apparent choices are not real choices the need for personal responsibility is superseded by the need for social responsibility. That is, people who are victims and people who understand the social constraints placed on victims, can decide to organize around sound theoretical principles to actively bring about positive social change. This book is not just about important ideas. It is also about using ideas to make improvements in the world—putting theory to practice. C. Wright Mills' concept of the sociological imagination is useful in facilitating desirable social activism, or what is sometimes called sociological practice. Creating positive social change typically means, among many other things, placing pressure on the people who have considerable resources, and corresponding behavioral latitude, to eliminate their exploitative and oppressive practices. If successful, socially responsible policies and practices follow. Making changes last is another issue that needs to be discussed later.

### Abandoning Social Programs: Social Irresponsibility

The reconstruction programs that were initiated in the 1960s (some earlier) have been abandoned for the most part, or exist with insufficient financial support. As does any significant program, social reconstruction programs cost a lot of money. The social programs were not perfect. No program is. But through the 1980s, 1990s, and first decade of the twenty-first century (at the writing of this book), social reconstruction programs have been under severe attack. Rather than finding ways of improving them, they were systematically dismantled. The motivation behind this dismantling, which received its greatest impetus under the Ronald Reagan presidency, was to channel the money from those programs into other programs. The primary targets for re-channeling the money taken from social programs were wars and tax breaks for the wealthy. What are some of the programs that have been dismantled or under-funded to the point of incapacitation? I will list only a few: busing, free/low cost state education, unemployment compensation and other related welfare programs, subsidized housing, affirmative action, environmental protection, social research programs, alternative energy research and development, health care support, retirement programs, publicly funded and maintained utilities/infrastructure, public works initiatives, worker safety protections, and consumer protections. Social Security is continually targeted for reduction, elimination or privatization. It has been borrowed against and then labeled an unsustainable program. The 2008 crash of the global economy created a political opportunity to reestablish support for some of these social programs. President Barack Obama has tried to move the United States back toward a common good public policy orientation, but with marginal success. He established some useful public works initiatives, passed a modest national health care policy and reinstated some weak corporate and consumer protection regulations. There is, however, concern about his disposition toward public education and Social Security as he continues the corporate war legacy of his predecessors.

The dismantling of social programs was done precisely to move the social world in the opposite direction of what those social programs represented. That is, tax breaks for the wealthy create more choices for people in the United States who already have a lot of choices, and fewer choices for those people in the United States whose choices have already been heavily restricted. Increased military spending, in a similar way, increased choices for the United States-based corporations by exerting dominance over other militarily weaker nation-states, and thereby reducing the choices of the people in those weaker nation-states. Reduced choices under these circumstances often mean a lack of freedom for local people to organize their social life. Hence, when looking at the topic of wealth distribution in Chapter 6, it will not be surprising that the gap between the wealthy and the rest of the population, both in the United States and in the world, has dramatically increased over the last 30 years.

*Why is socialization slanted toward a focus on the personal?*

There are numerous reasons for the various socializing agents within the United States and within many other Western nation-states, promoting BVI and a corresponding belief that personal rather than social conditions determine an individual's life circumstances. What are some of those reasons?

If there is public recognition that people's problems are predominantly social rather than personal, much money and attention would have to be spent improving social conditions to alleviate the social problems—programs such as those mentioned above. Such expenses require high taxes from those who can most afford to pay high taxes. People who have a lot of resources don't want to give up part of them by paying taxes. Ironically they pay a great deal of money to legislators and legislative lobbyists to prevent social programs legislation, and to repeal or cut funding for existing social programs.

Through direct ownership and control of the media, wealthy people are able to establish certain social agendas and censor others according to their own financial interests. Helping to pay for a healthy social environment is not viewed by wealthy people in general as being consistent with their financial interests. This is not true of all wealthy people, but it is true of enough wealthy people for the wealthy in general to control politics and public policy. Looking at the portion of the United States government tax base that is paid by large corporations shows a consistent decline from about 28 percent in the 1950s to about 10 percent or less in recent years (Klahsen 2008, Friedman 2003). Some estimates show a more dramatic decline (eRiposte 2010). Tax breaks for corporations are tax breaks for the wealthy. Additionally, tax breaks directly to wealthy individuals in the United States have followed the same pattern as tax breaks for the corporations: not only eliminating support for our social programs, but also contributing significantly to our national debt as we cover whatever programs are left and pay hundreds of billions continuously on the corporate military and their wars.

*What about charities?* There are numerous institutions and social processes for protecting the BVI ideology. Most forms of charity are a tax write-off for wealthy people, and/or a means of influencing important non-profit organizations. "Charities" as a social institution is based on the assumption that the problems of people are to be treated as unrelated to the forces that caused the predicament of the people receiving the charity. Concepts like "stereotyping" help us understand the relationship between blaming the victim as an isolated individual and blaming the victim as a member of an oppressed group.

## Summary

This chapter lays the foundation for the remainder of this book, which deals with root causes and possible sociological solutions to social problems. The reader should come away from this chapter with an understanding that individuals are not necessarily to blame for their predicament or even their "decisions" in all instances. Without such an understanding, there is not much point in studying Sociology, since the intent of Sociology is not simply to understand how the social world operates, but also, based on that understanding, to find ways to make the social and physical world a better place for all living beings. Subsequent chapters, where appropriate, will have intermixed short term or partial solutions suggested relative to the problems referenced in that particular chapter. Long term macro and micro changes will be discussed in Chapter 12.

# Chapter 2
# Macro Sociological Theory and Analyzing Social Problems

The numerous theoretical perspectives in Sociology have been categorized in a variety of ways. In this book theoretical perspectives are divided into macro and micro approaches since the relationship between macro and micro social problems is very important. The first approach covered is the macro perspective, which deals with the influences of social structures on people's lives. It is based on the notion that the whole is greater than the sum of its parts, and that human experiences and behaviors are largely determined by the nature of social institutions like churches, political organizations, and even smaller institutions like the family. Two of the most commonly discussed macro theoretical perspectives are structural functionalism and conflict theory, but other perspectives will also be included.

## Structural Functionalism

Structural functionalism is the perspective that most directly reminds us of the influence of Biology on Sociology. The nineteenth century thinking of Auguste Comte, and even more so of his follower Emile Durkheim, was heavily swayed by the images of biological organisms, which have clear structural boundaries and easily identifiable functioning parts. From the structural functional perspective social entities are viewed as relatively stable structures that have stable and clearly identifiable interconnected components. The concepts of role, structure, function, and dysfunction are relevant terms when thinking about social structures, and their interrelationship makes up the crux of the structural functional perspective.

The image that we are given by this perspective is one of an organic whole. The human body, for example, is made up of identifiable parts that are connected interdependently, thereby creating an organic whole. The heart, lungs, liver, kidneys, and other organs all come together to constitute a single human being. Each of the component parts has a function within the biological structure that contributes to the maintenance of the whole organism.

It is easy to see the application of this model to social structures once we introduce the concept of role. In the case of human social structures, roles take the place of the various component body parts that we see in biological structures, and are activated by the implantation of a human being into each role. The activation takes place as the human being carries out the expectations associated with the role. The various roles of the family are what make the family a social structure.

Each role (for example, the mother role), through its interaction with the other family roles (for example, the roles of daughter, brother, and father), fulfills a function toward the successful maintenance of the family containing those roles.

*Small and medium sized social structures*

The family is one of the oldest social structures and the most important socializing agent among social institutions. It is also one of the smallest social structures in existence. There are others, such as friendships and dyadic love relationships. There are also medium sized social structures, such as small businesses, local governments, school districts, and universities. All small and medium-sized social structures tend to have clear roles within them that make up their working parts. The working parts give the social structure its form and keep it operating and identifiable as a separate entity, which then becomes a working part of yet a larger social structure.

*Large social structures: nation-states*

Nation-states are one of the largest social entities in existence in the social world. When examining social structures of this size one quickly sees how complicated the social world can be. Nation-states are multilayered social entities containing social structures within social structures within social structures. Oftentimes, the social structures are overlapping in complicated ways. The overlap results in certain roles having a great deal of confusion associated with them in terms of which social structure is primarily served by each role. A good example of this kind of confusion is the role of a politician who serves a number of constituents. Technically, there should not be confusion about the role of a politician because technically they are supposed to serve the government within which they are elected, which technically consists of the people that make up that particular geographical location. However, politicians must win the support of their party in order to be nominated to run for election. Once they are nominated, politicians must win the support of external funding agents who provide them with their campaign resources so that they may be elected.

So are the expectations associated with being the President of the United States, for example, actually for serving the people of the United States, as is supposed to be the case? Alternatively the president could be serving the expectations of a political party, or possibly the expectations of major campaign funding sources. Once within the realm of high stakes large-scale social structures the roles within social structures become complicated and sometimes very confusing. This does not mean that they cannot be complicated and confusing in smaller social structures as well, but the tendency is far greater in large-scale social structures such as large government units, large religious organizations that span multiple nations, international governmental organizations, and multinational corporations. These massive social entities have complicated social structures and the roles that maintain them are oftentimes extremely complicated and difficult to identify clearly as separate roles. Indeed, they often literally overlap from one large-scale social structure to another. There are many examples of this overlap in politics and in the corporate world. Interlocking boards of directors across corporations is an important example from a social problems perspective.

### *Dysfunction: the lost concept*

The influence of biology on structural functional thinking within the discipline of Sociology cannot be overstated. When a biologist examines the parts of the biological organism, the question asked is not typically, "what harm are these parts doing to this organism?" On the contrary, the biologist is most likely asking what positive contribution this part makes to the maintenance of this organism. This is not a completely safe approach to take when studying the social world. It is a reasonably safe bet that a component within a biological entity is making some positive contribution to the maintenance of that entity. There are occasional exceptions to this claim but they are pretty rare. The same cannot be said for the components of social entities.

Under what circumstances, therefore, might a biological component of an organism be considered dysfunctional rather than functional? Typically, dysfunction does not apply to the components of biological organisms unless the biological organism is damaged in some particular way. For example, if a kidney is cancerous it has become dysfunctional to the survival of the body that contains it, and it will most likely have to be removed. This issue is more complicated within larger biological structures that contain many organisms, like an ecosystem. Here we see greater similarity between Biology and Sociology. As humans increasingly interfere with the evolving biological world, biologists have had to more frequently look for dysfunction within biological systems, as well as function.

Sociologists employing structural functional thinking must also learn to do the same. That is, they must look for dysfunction at least as much as function within social structures. For example, one might ask if certain foreign policy programs are functional or dysfunctional to the maintenance of the social entities contained within the social structure of the United States. A parallel question is whether accommodating multinational corporations with our international policies is functional or dysfunctional to the security of the people contained within the United States? Are tax breaks for the wealthy functional or dysfunctional to the well-being of the people who make up the vast majority of the United States? If the Central Intelligence Agency (CIA) is engaging in activities on behalf of multinational corporations that result in generating extreme hatred towards the United States, is the CIA functional or dysfunctional to the security of the people of the United States? These questions and many others like them can be and should be examined from within the theoretical perspective of structural functionalism. The tendency in Sociology, however, has been to focus predominantly on function as biologists might focus on the function of a part within a single organism. For structural functionalism to be useful to the study of social reality, especially social problems within social reality, that tendency should be changed.

*What causes what?*

The tendency to focus on function tends to result in a neglect of causation. When looking at a total social structure with many interdependent parts, it is sometimes difficult to know how those parts are affecting one another. When thinking only in terms of functional interdependence this problem does not seem to be very significant. However, once the concept of dysfunction is introduced, the issue of causation becomes one of glaring importance. It is important to know for example why a particular component of the social structure has become dysfunctional. This is an important issue within small social structures as well as within large social structures such as nation-states. If an individual within a family structure is not fulfilling role expectations within that family, a positive change in that individual cannot be expected without knowing the cause of the undesirable behavior. By understanding the cause of a person's behavior, change can more effectively be initiated that will positively impact that behavior, which will in turn positively impact the social structure containing that person. Social and behavioral scientists who identify as behaviorists do not agree with this analysis, but the nature of that disagreement is tied into principles of behaviorism covered in the next chapter.

Oftentimes, social components of social structures that were initially designed to have an important social function end up being dysfunctional to the social entity within which they reside. When this happens, it is important to know why it is happening, what are the causal forces behind making it happen, and what is the particular causal order of events that explain the situation in its current form? Whether we agree with the original intent of the CIA or not, the intended function of the CIA was to improve national security for the nation-state of the United States and thereby make the people within the United States more secure. If that has not happened as expected, it is not sufficient to know that the function of the CIA was not fulfilled. We must also know why it was not fulfilled, and the answer to that question involves understanding certain motivations behind the actions of the CIA.

Like most terms used in Sociology, causality is a construct. It does not serve us well to think of causality as something that is easy to determine. Causality is not something that can be seen or touched. It is something that is inferred from circumstantial evidence. Determining causal order requires sociologists to be clever about piecing together information that reveals a pattern of behavior that fits the earlier description of "cause." The notion of causality is no less abstract in the other sciences. Yet we do not expect other scientists to abandon this important construct. Because sociological subject matter tends to be more abstract than the content of the other sciences, it is far more difficult to demonstrate causal connections in a clear and highly defensible manner.

*Committing to a non-causal world: post modernism* Through the 1980s and most of the 1990s a theoretical perspective closely related to Structural Functionalism became prominent in the United States and Europe. This theoretical perspective grew out of what was originally known as French Structuralism and later became known as Post Modernism. While Post Modernism was initially and quite indirectly influenced by Durkheim, Post Modern thinkers attempted to incorporate the later works of Karl Marx, who is discussed briefly below under the topic of conflict theory. This particular perspective is mentioned simply because it epitomizes deliberate avoidance of causal thinking. Even prominent economic post modernists such as Lash and Urry, "… disavow causal sequences preferring to speak of preconditions and ideal-types" (Turner 2003: 238).

The era of post modernism coincided with a peak in conservative politics in the West: the rollback of social programs, international trade agreements that negatively impact the poor, and a step-up of international espionage by Western nation-state powers to destroy grassroots peoples' movements wherever they occurred. The rise of this theoretical movement in the United States seemed to represent a sophisticated way of talking about the many terrible things happening in the world without attributing any responsibility to anyone or anything, and doing so in a coded language completely unavailable to the average world citizen.

A sarcastic summary of the post modernist view of the world might go something like: "life happens, it is complicated, some suffer, some don't, and there is nothing we can do about it." A non-causal view of the social world does not give concerned citizens, social activists, and other serious students of Sociology much hope for a better future, since social problem remedies require some understanding of the factors that cause the social problems. As stated by Feagin and Vera, "Given the life-threatening problems created by a globalizing capitalist system on planet Earth—such as global warming and its threats to the atmosphere, biosphere, and sociosphere—the larger-scale emancipatory theory and research projects cannot be abandoned to a postmodern malaise" (2001: 222). Some post modernists are seeing the limitations of their perspective and are moving back toward causal sociological thinking.

Taking the position that causation does not exist, or that it can never be adequately demonstrated, is a way of absolving oneself and others from any sense of social responsibility. The intent behind studying Sociology is not to assign blame in a punitive sense, but to identify primary sources of problems so that appropriate social remedies may be developed. This sometimes means that people have to recognize their own role in contributing to the world's problems. People from a dominant nation-state or even from the more privileged groups within an oppressed nation-state, are benefiting from the suffering of others. There is logic to this phenomenon that is not too difficult to track. Causes and corresponding effects do exist. Actions bring about other actions and so on. In this important respect, this book is patterned in general principle after the excellent work of John Mirowsky and Catherine E. Ross, *Social Causes of Psychological Distress* (2003). Their work does exactly what the book title suggests: identifies social causes of individual problems. Social structures can and do impact the individual and individual relationships. Their work also represents a good example of the importance of Social Psychology for understanding social problems.

*Humans have motivations, body parts do not*

Human beings as activators of social roles bring with them individual motivations. Sometimes those individual motivations are consistent with the welfare of the larger social entity, and sometimes they are not. It is probably rarely the case that human beings fulfilling roles within social structures are doing so from a position of personal motive neutrality. One might also question the extent to which humans as activators of roles consistently have the interests of the whole social structure in mind as they are fulfilling their role expectations. This point represents the most significant difference between structural functionalism, as it applies to social life, and structural functionalism as it applies to biological life. The absence of indifference (as typically characterizes the parts of a biological structure) or the absence of complete social altruism in human role fulfillment, is the critical point that brings us to a discussion of a second important macro theoretical perspective.

## Conflict Theory

Conflict theorists, like structural functionalists, view social reality in terms of social structures: parts making up a social whole. Such a view of the social world includes an understanding that social facts exist, and this is true of conflict theory as much as it is true of structural functionalism. Common ground notwithstanding, conflict theory and structural functionalism are also dramatically different in one important way. When conflict theorists view a social structure they do not see interrelated parts necessarily working together for the good of the whole. While the parts may indeed be interrelated, existent role behavior cannot be characterized as selfless cooperation. From a conflict perspective, such thinking about social life is Pollyannaish and unrealistic.

*Struggle trumps cooperation*

Rather than viewing a social structure as being made up of cooperating parts, conflict theorists view a social structure as being made up of competing parts. Hence, the most pertinent question is not what does an individual do for the good of the whole, but how will that individual's role eventually serve his/her own interests. Consider the example of the university. When students pay tuition are they being thankful for the opportunity to make a contribution to the ongoing maintenance of the entire university? Are they making this tuition contribution out of pure goodness or perhaps as an act of charity? For the most part, albeit not entirely, the appropriate answer is probably "no" in both instances. People attending the university expect to get something in return. Students are not offering tuition as a contribution to the good of the whole.

When conflict theorists look at the university they see continuous struggle. Students are often struggling with faculty members to get the grades that they want. Faculty members are sometimes struggling with students to win their compliance in remembering the information they believe is important. Faculty members are struggling with the administrators to attain the resources they believe they need to adequately maintain their programs and teach the courses that need to be taught. Administrators are struggling with faculty members to accept lower pay than faculty members believe they deserve, and there are other related conflicts within the university. Additionally the university is in continuous struggle with external agents. Administrators within a state university must lobby state politicians to attain the resources they need to keep the university operating at a sufficiently high level of performance. Administrators within a private university must be in continual contact with private donors in their efforts to convince them to give more money to the university, which sometimes involves important educational compromises.

### *The haves and have-nots*

From a conflict theory perspective the world is made up of those who have a lot of resources and those who have far fewer resources. Those who do not have many resources are behaving in ways that they hope will give them access to the resources of others. People who do have resources, however, are typically not satisfied to simply keep the resources they have, but want more. The struggle becomes complicated because those who have many resources oftentimes are finding ways of getting still more resources from those who have little, as well as from others that also have a lot of resources.

Karl Marx, the founder of conflict theory, and his co-author Frederick Engels, saw the industrial revolution as a way for wealthy people to use their resources to gain still more resources from the labor of poor people (Marx and Engels 1969). The early writings of Karl Marx portray the industrial worker as a person being alienated from meaningful life sustaining activities that contribute to the well-being of the worker as a total person (Marx 2008). Contemporary conflict theorists do not believe that the industrial revolution marked either the beginning or the end of the struggle between the wealthy and the poor. According to conflict theorists, the struggle between the haves and have-nots continues to this day and permeates all aspects of social life.

### *Tools of social power*

If you are a wealthy person and you would like to get other people to work for you in a way that will produce still more wealth for yourself, how should you proceed? What tools do you, as a wealthy person, have available to make this happen? What obstacles must you overcome? The first and most obvious challenge for wealthy people in their effort to generate more wealth for themselves from the labor and resources of others is a "reasonable" explanation for why they deserve to have their wealth, and so many other people deserve to have very little or nothing. When one has control of a vast amount of resources there are many tools that can be purchased to help one overcome this challenge. In general, the most important tool that a wealthy person can have is control over information. If one can control information then one can also control public perceptions.

Information is controlled in a variety of ways, and some of those ways will be discussed in other parts of this book. It should be safe to assume that wealthy people will not want the public to have a favorable view of labor unions and other grass roots organizing activities that challenge their privileges. Have the wealthy been successful in controlling information? How one responds to that question will most likely depend on one's propensity for seeing the world from a conflict theory perspective or from a structural functionalist perspective.

*A bridge of flowers* It is within the context of information control that the notion "false reality" becomes important. When profit motivated information becomes widespread and a false reality prevails, what happens to the true reality? Marxists view this circumstance as a dual reality state of existence. The prevailing false reality is sometimes referred to by Marxists as a superstructure, and the reality that is now hidden from sight, is referred to as the infrastructure. The purpose of the superstructure is to normalize the existing state of wide gaps between the wealthy and the remaining population, and to do it in a way that makes people feel good and feel hopeful that they too may someday be wealthy. It is important that the general public view the significant gulf between the resources of the wealthy and their own resources as perfectly "logical" and, therefore, not only acceptable but also laudable. Most often this process works for the wealthy to an amazing degree. Wealthy people are even given awards for their ability to accumulate wealth.

The infrastructure, or the true reality, is the actual struggle for the control of resources. The more unaware the general public is of the existence of this struggle the easier it will be for the wealthy to increase their wealth at the expense of others. Suppose you are walking down a country road, and in the distance you see a beautiful bridge made out of flowers. As you approach the bridge you marvel at its beauty and accept without question that indeed this bridge is made out of flowers. However, once you are standing on the bridge and are able to touch it, you move away the flowers and see the cold hard rusty steel that is truly the bridge upon which you are standing. If not for the steel beneath the flowers, you would have fallen into the river below the bridge. The flowers are analogous to the superstructure in social life, and the hard rusty steel is analogous to the infrastructure in social life. The flowers certainly looked nice and made you feel good, but it was the truth of the steel that ultimately kept you dry. The lesson of this metaphor is that searches for truth, and the realities of truth's approximations, may not always look nice or sound nice, but they represent the best chance of keeping one's head above water.

From a Marxist standpoint, the truth, or infrastructure, is the reality of struggle. It is the realization that huge differences in wealth are not logical or acceptable, and that the only way to prevent such differences is by doing whatever you can to expose and keep the struggle out in the open. By so doing, one increases opportunities for others to participate in working toward eliminating the conditions that create the uneven resource distributions within social entities. This is not an easy task. Sometimes the truth is buried deeply beneath a sophisticated superstructure.

### *W.E.B. Du Bois*

W.E.B. Du Bois was a conflict theorist long before he associated himself with Marxism. Even as a teenager Du Bois was educating others on the plight of African Americans. At an early age he began to propose Black separation from Whites and the eventual return of Blacks to Africa. Earning a PhD from Harvard, when Ph.D.'s were not all that common in general, was a remarkable accomplishment for an early twentieth century Black person with such radical leanings (Foner 1970). The brilliance of Du Bois, however, dwarfs the significance of the Harvard degree.

Du Bois' work paralleled and was influenced by the early empirical studies conducted by Jane Addams and others who were part of the Hull-House movement to help the poor. Holding a position at Atlanta University for several years, Du Bois taught Sociology and did systematic empirical research on many aspects of Black life and Black oppression (Du Bois 2003, Foner 1970). In the early 1900s this kind of systematic sociological research was not common, since Sociology was still a relatively new discipline.

*Discrimination has economic roots* From the standpoint of this book there are two pieces of Du Bois' work that are most relevant: 1) Du Bois was the first sociologist to identify the connection between capitalism and racism, a connection extended to all of the isms in this text; 2) he believed that Sociology had a greater responsibility than to simply do research and put forward ideas. Hence, Du Bois was as much of an activist as he was an intellectual and scholar. He organized the first Pan-African Congress, which was attended by representatives from fifteen countries. He also fought his entire life for racial justice and justice for all oppressed peoples. His research informed his convictions and he moved forward based on both without hesitation (King 2003).

### *Critical theory as a subarea of conflict theory*

Wealth and corresponding power are used to create and maintain the superstructure. From the standpoint of the wealthy, the ideal is for the superstructure to eventually become the only reality. This point raises an interesting philosophical question, which is whether a reality can exist if nobody knows about it. It is conceivable that a sufficiently sophisticated and powerful information control program could eliminate, from everyone's consciousness, an existing reality. Multiple generations of information control could conceivably accomplish such an amazing goal.

There are a number of interpretations of Marx's writings. Critical theory focuses on that aspect of Marx's work that portrays social reality as having multiple layers. One of the areas best known for the application of critical theory is Critical Criminology. An early Critical Criminology study revealed the hidden profit motive behind the vagrancy laws (Chambliss 1964). Now contemporary prisons are being looked at with a similar critical view, showing how the profit motive perpetuates racism in the criminal justice system and motivates the construction and crowding of prisons (Davis 1998, 2003).

*False realities as only realities* What prevents a false reality from becoming the only reality? There is no guarantee that a false reality will never become the only reality. Indeed, as information control becomes more sophisticated and corporations increase their influence and control within the schools, it becomes increasingly more difficult for the average person to sort out fact from fiction. But long before anything close to modern technology existed, the false reality of the inferiority of women prevailed as the only reality in most parts of the world. The exposure of that false reality by the emergence of feminism is a recent development in human history.

Critical theorists tell us that false realities invariably become awkwardly entangled and thereby create a distorted image of what they are supposed to represent. In an oscillating manner the distortion becomes increasingly apparent as greater numbers of people are negatively impacted by the inaccuracies of prevailing "information." The entangled false realities oftentimes represent contradictions between what people were taught to believe is true and what they are actually experiencing, as well as what they observe to be the experiences of others. "Contradictions" is an important term frequently used by critical theorists to describe the inconsistencies between a veneer status quo version of truth and a radical (root based) emergent version.

An analogy sometimes used in conjunction with critical analysis is that of peeling away the layers of an onion, whereby the critical researcher, in search of the true reality, is peeling away the onion layers one at a time. Each layer of the onion represents a layer of reality. Sometimes the truest reality is one layer deep. Sometimes it is many layers deep. The intent behind this book is not to make social life look simple or one-dimensional. Sociologists are challenged to recognize the complexity of social life, come to a reasonably accurate understanding of that complexity, and help others make decisions about what problems can and cannot be remedied.

*A critical look at the American dream*

Most of us were taught in school, and most children are still taught, that regardless of their background, if they work hard enough, they can achieve the highest levels of success. Theoretically, this means that if one wants to become a senator, the CEO of a multinational corporation, or the President of the United States, all one has to do is work hard enough. At the very least, the American Dream suggests that one will achieve a high status education, a high status job, and have a big house in the country with two kids, a dog, a cat, and three goldfish. The American Dream tells us that it doesn't matter: if your skin is black; if you're a woman; if you're poor; if you're openly gay; and/or if you attended an inner city ghetto elementary school or high school. The veracity of the American dream is called into question immediately by the above human categories, since until 2008 no president in the last 100 years, and few United States senators, has had any of those characteristics. When the president of the United States gives his state of the union address and the television viewer is given a scan of the audience (the United States Congress) from behind the president, what does the television viewer see? Indeed, it is a pretty solid wall of affluent gray haired White men.

One does not need to watch the President's state of the union address, however, to know that the American dream does not apply to most people within the United States. Looking back on one's educational experience helps one understand how the American dream is derailed. Children start elementary school with advantages and disadvantages based on the socioeconomic status of their parents. Highly educated parents are more likely to give their children a head start by teaching them to read and learn math skills early. It all begins with the little magnetic letters and numbers on the refrigerator. Once in school one finds oneself in a competitive environment. Not everyone can be in the high reading group. Not everyone can win the spelling bee contest. Not everyone can win the prize for completing the math problems the fastest. The result is that some students advance and others stay behind, so that by the time they reach middle school children are already tracked into high and low achievement groups. This is more so the case in the large public schools than it is in the smaller private schools, a distinction which is a function of wealth and status differences in itself.

By the time students from multiple middle schools converge on a single high school they have been carefully sifted so that a select group of students make up what is known as the advanced standing category. Out of a graduating class of 400 students the advanced standing group may be as few as 30 or 35 students. These are the students who are selected for the accelerated college credit courses, and are, therefore, the students targeted for college admission. Indeed, at this point these students still hold firmly to their American dream, whatever the dream may be. But only ten of these students can be ranked in the top ten of their class, and that can be a determining factor as to whether they are able to enter the university of their choice. Even being ranked in the top ten of one's class of 400 students does not assure one of entrance into the university of one's choice, particularly if a person is attending a public high school.

*Some make it?* Supposing an individual achieves the rank of seventh in their class out of a public high school class of 400 students, and is fortunate enough to be admitted into a first choice university, how is this person going to pay for this expensive education? Imbedded somewhere in the American dream is the notion that if you do well enough in school you will receive a scholarship. Typically the scholarships that students receive today are quite modest in light of the overall cost of attending the university. There is also a common misunderstanding that scholarships are readily available for students of color, regardless of their level of academic achievement. This simply is not true. As an academic Dean at a private university that had a goal of increasing its campus diversity, I found myself quite frustrated by our inability to give scholarships and other forms of financial support to even very high achievement level students of color. Now that I am a dean in a large state university, the same frustration applies.

*Most don't* Notice that we have been talking about how difficult it is to achieve the American dream for the top ten students out of a class of 400 from one public school. What about all the rest of the students? If some of the top ten students struggle to achieve their American dream, what can we say about the remaining 390 students? If they attend the university at all, it will probably be while they are working two or three part time jobs, or possibly a fulltime job. They will be attending the local state university or perhaps a community college, which does not mean they will be receiving a low quality education necessarily. It does mean that their education will not be as powerful a ticket in the job market and for entrance into graduate programs later on, as a degree from a high status private university or a prestigious land grant university. By working long hours and multiple jobs to pay for their education, students are oftentimes not able to fully access the education for which they are paying. They find that they must miss classes; they do not have time to go to the library to work on projects; they do not have time to read the assignments. Oftentimes when they do attend class they find it difficult to stay awake, and they find it difficult to pay their bills because they have to own a car to travel to their various jobs and to school.

At what point do individuals ask if the American dream applies to them? It could be at any one of the various steps mentioned in the above example. For children growing up in urban ghettos, especially young boys of color, the realization that the American dream does not apply to them occurs early in their lives. Under these circumstances, why should they be interested in doing well in school? Indeed, some public high schools are graduating less than 60 percent of the students (Kozol 1991). A majority of the students in many of these impoverished schools are people of color. A statistic that may be even more surprising to some people is that less than 28 percent of the total adult population of the United States has a four-year undergraduate college or university degree (US Census Bureau

2004). If you are among that estimated 28 percent and are still unable to achieve the so-called American dream, you must consider what it is like for the remaining 72 percent? Certainly we can all think of examples of people with little education who work hard and are highly successful, but these people are the exception to the rule. Furthermore, it typically requires far more than hard work to achieve high levels of success. For the average person within any social structure, hard work is necessary for success but rarely sufficient. For people who come from high levels of privilege, success may be attained without hard work, or without working much at all.

*Could this happen to you?* Perhaps one of the best and most striking examples representing the last sentence in the above paragraph is George W. Bush, President of the United States 2000–2008. Mr. Bush was, at best, an average student when he was growing up. Yet, because of the wealth and status of his father (who had also been a United States president), he was admitted into Yale University (the same school his father had attended), where he earned a record of academic mediocrity and a reputation of basically just having fun most of the time. He was denied admission into the University of Texas law school and went to Harvard where he received an MBA degree. Once he completed his education, Mr. Bush went from one failed scheme to another—schemes oftentimes funded by friends of his father who are in the oil industry. He finally became co-owner of a baseball team, which was his only successful venture prior to being elected governor of Texas. I say "successful" generously because the success of the baseball team had little to do with Mr. Bush owning it. I believe it is safe to say that being Governor of Texas was the first notable full time job that Mr. Bush held. The Presidency of the United States was the second.

Could this happen to you, or anyone you know? Most likely it could not. This example serves as an important illustration of how the American dream, as part of the conflict theory conception of superstructure, is exposed as a false reality of everyday life within the United States. If George W. Bush grew up in any of the vast majority of American families and displayed the same behaviors, he would not have become President of the United States. He would far more likely have been unemployed, or at the very least, underemployed.

### *The irrepressible infrastructure*

When one observes success associated with privileges, and failures associated with hard work, one recognizes the contradictions inherent in the American dream. When people work hard all of their life only to find their jobs moved to another country in order to increase profits for people who already have great wealth, those people are going to start asking questions. Those questions will be based on the apparent contradictions between what they were told their entire life and what they are now experiencing. According to conflict theory, when enough people begin to see the contradictions between what they have been taught through the media and through their education, the infrastructure or true reality becomes exposed. Many people in the United States are at the time of this writing standing on the bridge touching the cold hard rusty steal, and realizing they have been deceived. According to conflict theory, when enough people come to this realization the foundation for revolution has been laid.

Today we recognize that revolutions can come in a variety of shapes and forms. Yes, they may still be violent in nature, but they may also be nonviolent. The advancements in electronic communication have made communicating with millions of people almost instantly part of everyday life. The internet, for example, is increasingly being used to expose false realities and bring people together for social action. There are probably hundreds of examples of this kind of revolutionary internet activity taking place at this very moment—not the least of which is WikiLeaks, a non-profit organization that has disseminated large amounts of leaked classified government and military documents via the internet. Some are, indeed, calling these activities a revolution. While the wealthy have purchased and now own nearly all of the mainstream media in the United States, they have not yet found a way to keep the general public from communicating with one another on a massive scale through the internet. Efforts to curtail general public internet use will most likely become more serious and direct than they have been so far.

According to Marxism, and hence conflict theory, exposing the infrastructure is the primary catalyst for revolution. It is through revolution that the have-nots take back the resources that have been extracted from their labor and their communities under false pretenses. There have been many failed revolutions throughout history, but there have also been successful revolutions. For example, India, under the leadership of Gandhi, eventually freed itself from British rule; the United States freed itself from British rule via the revolutionary war; and the Cuban people successfully revolted against the oppressive Western supported Batista regime to establish their own political and economic systems. Marx's theory of social change predicted cycles of new superstructures, new revelations of infrastructures, and new revolutions, all leading toward an eventual classless social world. While there is much to be said for Marx's ideas in general, there is little evidence to substantiate the idea that the world is moving increasingly toward classlessness. The closest we have come to seeing any evidence to this effect is most likely the Cuban revolution. Indeed, when we look at the evidence relating to wealth distribution throughout the world we see that the opposite has occurred, and is continuing to occur. The wealthy have continued to become wealthier and continue to separate themselves economically farther from the rest of the population of the world. This increasing gap between the wealthy and everyone else has also continued to occur within individual nation-states.

### *The role of fear in maintaining social control*

Students of Sociology must overcome their instilled fears of thinking about such things as Marxism and revolution. One does not have to start a revolution to understand it. Nor does one have to be a Marxist to appreciate the value of his ideas and the application of some of those ideas to everyday life. There are few social thinkers, past or present, who understood the nature of social reality more fully than did Karl Marx. As we can see from Marx's prediction of a classless world, however, he was not perfect. It is our responsibility as applied sociologists to effectively sort out what we can and cannot use. Whatever one may think of the various socio-economic and political attempts to apply Marx's ideas, he himself was a brilliant social theorist. Sociologists should not let contrived ideological and political spoofs prevent them from doing their work either as professionals or as informed public citizens.

Likewise, structural functionalism, through the ideas of people like Comte and Durkheim, has some important insights to offer the analysis of social reality. Durkheim insisted that social structures and other social facts are sufficiently real that they can be identified and studied. This viewpoint has been a valuable tool for analyzing the social world and for recommending possible solutions to social problems. It is important to make full use of structural functional notions like: social structure, function, and dysfunction. Dysfunction has not played a notably prominent role within structural functionalism, and for Sociology to be fulfilled as a useful applied science, it must.

## Feminist Theory

There is some debate about where feminist theory belongs in terms of major paradigms. Often times it is included as a subfield of critical-conflict theory, which is where it is being placed in this book. Wherever it is located, its importance in the social sciences should not be overlooked, for it is a theoretical perspective that has revolutionized the way most of the world now sees women, and the realities surrounding women. The irony of that statement is that feminist theory accomplished its successes related to how the world now sees women by first changing the way women see the world, and then eventually changing the way many men see the world as well. This critically important step in the liberation of women, which is still an incomplete process, is now sometimes lost in the non-causal, motivation-free thinking prevalent among some third wave feminists (Finley and Reynolds Stringer 2010). The social science of women's liberation and feminist theory can be traced to the work of Mary Wollstonecraft, who lived and wrote in London during the late 1700s. Rarely mentioned in the women's liberation literature in the United States, Wollstonecraft made important contributions to feminist thought. Her highly controversial 1792 work, *Vindication of the Rights of Women* (2004), stands out as a major breakthrough in the way women might want to see themselves and the world around them if they expect to be equals with men.

Feminists of color and feminists from other excluded groups bring still other unique perspectives to the analysis of the social world. The experiences of

Black feminists stand out in contrast to White feminist women and Black men (Washington 2007, Collins 1998).

Feminist thought in the United States was also fueled by the women's suffrage movement, during which time strong independent minded women such as Susan B. Anthony and Elizabeth Stanton dedicated their lives to winning the right for women in the United States to vote: ultimately the 19th amendment of the United States Constitution, which was passed in 1920. People in Western nation-states tend to overlook that the right of women to vote or run for public office was a world-wide movement that took place roughly over a period of 150 years.

There were many great nineteenth century and early twentieth century social thinkers and researchers who were women, and most of them were feminists in some important respect. It is unfortunate that they were left out of Sociology textbooks for so long. Some played leading roles in important areas of discovery and application. Their work is still downplayed and students of Sociology continue to miss the full benefit of their contributions. Some will be referenced later in this book.

### *Betty Friedan*

The person often credited with being the contemporary founder of feminist theory in the United States is Betty Friedan, who became quite famous for *The Feminine Mystique* (1963), a book I read as a college sophomore many years ago. Friedan's work set the stage for enabling, first women and then women and men, to see the hidden world of Women's oppression. Feminist theory is based on some basic questions related to inequality. How does a social circumstance look from the woman's standpoint? Is there a double standard governing the role expectations of women and the role expectations of men? Are current social arrangements working to the systematic advantage of men as compared with women? Would men prefer to have the social status and role expectations of women: if not, why? Do women have the same depth of social choices as do men in terms of lifestyles and social roles: if not, why?

These, and other questions like them, create a filter that can be attached to one's observational lens to determine whether sex discrimination is present within social entities. Hence, feminist theory becomes a means by which one exposes the underlying reality of female exploitation, a reality that previously was buried beneath the flowers of the socially idealized female martyr. The ability to see hidden realities related to the oppression of women requires a great deal of training in order to be able to see past what we gradually, over a long period of time, have come to believe is natural.

Some social scientists believe that gender inequality as derived from sexism is the oldest form of inequality known to humans. If this is true, it tells us something important about what is possible: both in terms of the potential for creating a false reality that can become the only reality, and in terms of the never ending hope of eventually exposing false realities in order to create more just living arrangements.

## Max Weber

Max Weber was what George Ritzer refers to as a "paradigm bridger" (Ritzer 1975). We need paradigm bridgers today more than ever in the study of social reality. Weber understood more fully than most the importance of having a broad disposition toward studying social life. One of Max Weber's important contributions to Sociology is the legitimacy he brought to subjectivity as a tool for understanding social life. Rather than squeeze objectivity beyond what it has to offer, Weber quite logically argued that an advantage humans have in studying human social life is the ability to subjectively understand social reality based on personal experiences within the social world—hence his use of the notion verstehen (subjective understanding). Verstehen is an important concept for bringing together qualitative data from many disciplines that can contribute to a better understanding of Social Problems and how to solve them.

### *Value neutrality? Not possible*

There have been debates about Max Weber's position on value neutrality. I am in agreement with the interpretation of Feagin and Vera (2001). Max Weber did not believe that value neutrality was possible. In Weber's view all humans have values and cannot separate those values from the way they see reality. His greatest concern regarding values was to guard against, to whatever extent possible, allowing personal gain or the gain of others, politically or economically motivated, to influence one's research and ideas. Additionally, Weber encouraged sociologists to state their values and then let them guide their work openly, rather than through a veil of objectivity.

Weber was a believer in the importance of causation—so much so that he defined Sociology accordingly. He defined Sociology as, "that science which aims at the interpretative understanding of social behavior in order to gain an explanation of its causes, its courses, and its effects" (Turner 2003: 358). While this might not be a sufficiently broad definition for contemporary sociological work, it is clearly consistent with the causal thinking and language used throughout this book.

## Anarchist Theory: What is It?

Everyone knows what anarchism is … right? I have found very few people who know anything at all about anarchism. People are often surprised to learn that the famous author and pacifist Leo Tolstoy was an anarchist, and that someone as widely respected as Noam Chomsky has at times identified as an anarcho-syndicalist (Chomsky 1976).

The censorship of anarchism in the United States has a long and unpleasant history. Until about 1970 Italians were the largest immigrant group in the United States. The early Italian immigrants, who were recruited for their labor by United

States based companies, were mostly peasant people from Southern Italy. Many of them were anarchists, which is something corporations and the government didn't bother to find out when they were looking around the world for cheap labor they could import. Once the United States government discovered that the Italians were anarchists the government began a program of severe harassment of Italian immigrants. There were raids on Italian neighborhoods. The Italian immigrants tried to retaliate against the government, but were unsuccessful. The disposition of the government toward Italians increased hatred and fear of Italians among other people in the population. The result was that Italian immigrants were killed in a variety of ways by government and non-government people, including KKK hangings. Eventually many of them were deported. One of the culminating moments in the history of the United States government's attack on Italian immigrants was the famous Sacco and Vanzetti case, which resulted in the arrest and eventual execution of two anarchist Italian men widely known to be innocent.

The censorship of anarchism is so thorough that it is virtually excluded from the discipline of Sociology. This is an amazing statement when one realizes how many Sociology conferences there are across the country, how big these conferences are, and how seldom, if ever, one sees a session on anarchism on a Sociology conference program. This is not to say that the discipline of Sociology has itself censored anarchism. It is to say that anarchism has been so thoroughly purged from public discourse that even Sociology, as a discipline that deals with social life issues, cannot pick it up on its radar screen. There are no high school courses that deal with the subject, few if any university courses, and no mention of anarchism in the mainstream media except to occasionally blame anarchists for any violence that occurs during demonstrations.

*Why the fuss?*

The most fundamental tenant of anarchism is that people do not need nation-state governments to tell them how to run their communities. This seems like a pretty radical point of view until we come to realize that, given the history of humankind, nation-states are a fairly recent development. At one time the vast majority of the world's people were, by default, anarchists without necessarily applying that term to themselves.

*Major assumptions of anarchism*

There were a number of anarchist leaders during the mid to late 1800s, and it is difficult to know who to credit as the founder of the contemporary movement. Pierre Joseph Proudhon is most often referred to as a founder of modern anarchism, but he is not a favorite choice of many contemporary anarchists. His sexism and racism eventually became widely documented and he was close friends with Mikhail Bakunin who, unlike most true proponents of anarchism, supported revolutionary violence. Proudhon was also associated with the 1848 French revolution that he did not fully support (Nettlau 1996, Sonn 1992).

Emma Goldman is probably a much better representative of what anarchism stands for among most anarchists. She was born in Russia in 1869 and lived for many years in the United States. She, like many of the Southern European anarchists living in the United States, was deported for openly expressing her anarchist ideas, for helping to organize labor unions, and for organizing against United States military involvement in other countries. Within two years Goldman was also deported from Russia (by that time the Soviet Union) for opposing the violent revolutionary activity there (Shulman 1996).

The anarchist movement of the mid-nineteenth century and early-twentieth century grew out of the same concerns as did socialism. Both ideological perspectives saw the industrial revolution from the standpoint of the alienated worker, whose labor was being coercively extracted to make a few people extremely wealthy. While anarchists and socialists saw the same problem and agreed on the common connection with industrialism, they were quite different on their views regarding the role of the nation-state. For socialists, the problem was not the *existence* of the nation-state as much as who controlled it. For anarchists nation-states were the problem and it didn't make sense to replace one with simply another of a different kind, as was the goal of socialism.

*Nation-states and human labor*

First and foremost, anarchism tells us that the nation-state is a contrived entity for the purpose of enabling wealthy capitalists to more effectively control the earth's natural resources and to more effectively control human labor. When the largest political entities were city-states, capitalists had to work through too many political layers to extract resources, organize large labor pools, and easily move their goods about without concern for safe passage from one place to another (Weber 1958). To anarchists, nation-states are tools for the wealthy to help them gain control and maintain control of (through the use of violence) natural resources and human labor so that production and trade can be facilitated (Goldman 1996a, 1996b, 1996c, Sonn 1992, Chomsky 1976, 1986).

From the anarchists' perspective, they were puzzled by the socialists wanting to take the nation-state from the wealthy capitalists, and then turn around and impose it upon themselves. Emma Goldman supported the Russian Revolution thinking that when victory was won the state would be dismantled. She obviously was wrong, and she eventually came to regret her support for the Russian Revolution, because it violated her commitment to non-violence as well as her commitment to human freedom (Shulman 1996, Sonn 1992).

### *(Dis)Organizing and controlling humans for labor*

With the development of nation-states much of human social life, similar to non-human social life, has been removed from the control of the people experiencing it in their local communities. From an anarchist perspective, we either work directly for corporations or work indirectly for them through the corporate controlled nation-state. Anarchists also maintain that the largest portion of the taxes Western nation-states collect from their citizens is used to pay for wars that help corporations control labor and resources in other countries (Chomsky 1993 2005), a view shared by critical political economists as well (Parenti 1995, 2011). Citizen taxes also support job training programs of various levels of sophistication, which primarily benefit the corporations. The work experience of humans in industrialized nation-states is more aversive than work required to simply maintain oneself, such as when one lives off the land or has a trade (Fourier 2005). This is an important area of similarity between anarchists and Marxists who focus on Marx's early work on alienated labor (Marx 2008).

### *Is anarchism realistic?*

Anarchism is not what most people think it is. Anarchists believe that it is within the nature of humans to be able to organize themselves into social entities around the local resources available to them, just as many indigenous communities of people continue to do. The key to making anarchist thinking useful is information. People need an accurate understanding of the circumstances surrounding their lives. Anarchists promote organizing locally as needed through participatory democracy—democracy that is ongoing and not just based on periodic elections. They also call on people to have their own vision of social reality and work toward that vision. This could involve local economies that have localized means of exchanging goods and services. Many people across the United States are living in a way that approximates an anarchist lifestyle—albeit most often not intentionally as anarchists. They are doing it out of the need to survive at a time when they, as individuals, are no longer very useful to the multinational corporations that control the nation-state. Their labor has been replaced by cheaper labor in other countries or by technology. Greater focus on the local community has also been spurred by a decrease in support from state and federal governments to cities and counties.

Misperceptions about anarchism are difficult to overcome because the federal government and corporations do not want people to focus on their local living arrangements. The same was true of Communism under the Soviet Union. Local institutions such as the family were targeted for elimination because they weakened allegiance to the nation-state. Anarchism is thus portrayed by national and some state governments as an ideology that promotes violence and bombings during disruptive demonstrations. These activities are typically the work of provocateurs labeled anarchists by government authorities.

Most people who read about anarchism come away thinking that the world could not possibly be organized according to anarchist principles. Who would protect us from outside invaders? What would we do about crime? There are anarchist answers to these questions, some of which will be addressed later in this book. For now it is important to realize that anarchism is not a state of chaos perpetuated by people bent on making trouble, as portrayed in the corporate mainstream media. Neither is Anarchism a utopian idea. It is simply a set of assumptions about the nature of humans as potentially relatively free beings: beings that, like other beings, have the capacity to create livable grassroots social entities. There is no way of life among any beings that does not have problems. The challenge of humans in the modern world is to minimize the problems they create for themselves, others, and future generations of life. Anarchism, like the other sociological perspectives, has an important role to play in understanding viable solutions to social problems. Those solutions must be based on the reality that nation-states currently exist and are not likely to completely disappear within the near future.

# Chapter 3
# Micro Sociological Analysis of Social Problems

## Introduction

Social arrangements in the form of institutions, communities, and other social structures have important implications for human and non-human experiences. Social Psychologists would argue, however, that social life must also be understood from the standpoint of the encounters and relationships people have with each other and other beings. While Chapter 2 focused on macro theoretical perspectives or the broad structural aspects of social reality, Chapter 3 addresses micro perspectives, which are best represented through the work of social psychologists. Including both macro and micro perspectives will facilitate inclusion of a full range of variables and provide insights for both short term and long term remedies when solving social problems.

## Symbolic Interactionism

Symbolic interactionism has its roots in the thinking of the pragmatic philosophers of the nineteenth century. It was initially brought into Sociology through the work of Charles Horton Cooley (1902). Cooley's work was followed by that of George Herbert Mead, who is most often credited as being the founder of symbolic interactionism and the author of one of the most meaningful descriptions of the concept "society" (Mead 1934). This is a complicated theoretical perspective with multiple schools of thought within it and important applications at both micro and macro levels. I will focus on a few concepts most pertinent to social problems.

Out of the interaction process the self emerges and people learn how to control their identities, impact the identities of others, control situations, and socially construct and control reality. These are not minor accomplishments and they have great implications for numerous social problems issues.

## Social Construction of Reality

An important part of conflict theory is the notion that people in positions of power and wealth use that power and wealth to control public perceptions about reality. A goal of the wealthy is to get the people who do not have wealth and power to accept, without question, the extreme difference in resource distribution between themselves and the wealthy. Symbolic interactionism helps us understand more fully how wealth and power combine to actually create a preferred reality for the privileged few.

The term "social construction of reality" is often used within macro contexts involving large social entities such as communities, states, very large organizations, or nation-states. It is one thing to impact how a person's family and friends see that person, but controlling how an entire population views some aspect of reality, such as high unemployment, poverty, war, diminished social services, national debt, free trade, or the decisions of a president relating to these issues, is another matter altogether. Is a superstructure actually possible i.e. a socially constructed false reality? The macro social construction of reality is not easy or cheap, but it is possible and happens routinely.

In an earlier discussion under conflict theory, it was mentioned that controlling reality on a scale as large as a nation-state requires controlling the media and the educational system. What is the symbolic process that employs media and schools in the construction of social reality?

### *Media control*

In 1973 two young reporters for the Washington Post broke a story about criminal activities that were traced all the way to the President of the United States. With the certainty that the president was about to be impeached, he was forced to resign. This was a president, Richard Nixon, whose agenda served the interests of wealthy people. Just prior to the breaking news of the Watergate crimes the famous Pentagon Papers were leaked to the press and published in the mainstream media. It is not likely that either Watergate or the Pentagon papers would be published today if the sitting president favors the wealthy. Nixon's resignation was a short-term loss for the wealthy people he represented, and a source of humiliation for his political party. This presidential scandal is what became known as the Watergate affair. The question that emerged in the minds of those who invested a lot of money in getting President Nixon elected was, "how could we let this happen?" The answer was really quite simple. They neglected to buy all of the newspapers, and all the other important public sources of communication. That is how they let it happen.

The above mentioned "mistake" of failing to own the media has since been remedied by people with wealth and power. There have been presidents since Watergate, such as Ronald Reagan and George W. Bush for example, who have been implicated in far worse crimes than those of President Nixon. Extensive senate hearings occurred to investigate President Reagan's involvement in criminal activities; yet, nothing even close to an impeachment occurred. Ronald Reagan and the two Bush presidents since Reagan were open protectors of the wealthy and enjoyed mainstream media protections accordingly. Not only have the wealthy gained monopoly control over the media, they have also learned the importance of using those media effectively. Presidents and other representatives of wealthy interests now know that they cannot go before the public on matters that may involve implicating them or their administration in wrongdoing without considerable preparation and media coaching.

### *How it works*

In 1974 President Nixon, the subject of congressional impeachment hearings at the time, went on national television and with notable agitation specifically declared he was "not a crook." He might as well have been wearing handcuffs. Such careless disregard for the importance of image in the public eye would never take place today. High profile public figures, like presidents, and other politicians, need to be able to project a public image of honesty, trustworthiness, strength, confidence, and competence regardless of what they might actually be doing. Hence, they are taught how to project these images so that the public will respond to them via polls, public gatherings, and elections, with affirmation of the projected image. It is the same process that takes place when a person wants to be viewed by friends in a particular way. Ultimately the question is, "who controls the situation?" By projecting a consistent and tightly controlled image to the public, using all of the most sophisticated media tools available, a president can prevail in the interaction process and gain control of the situation, creating the reality of being an effective, honest, strong, hard working, straightforward person who deserves to be president.

The relationship between politicians and the populations they represent is no longer a distant arrangement. The various highly controlled media have made it a close relationship. We see the president of the United States more often than we see many of our friends and relatives, and the situation is always perfectly controlled by the President's staff via the media. Through daily White House press releases the public sees, either via the newspaper or television, a daily image of this strong, friendly, honest person who is doing everything possible to protect them and look after their interests. It is a daily handshake. The public doesn't have an opportunity to have the last anticipation, because most of the interaction is one directional. Public opinion pieces help represent the public's ability to try to have the last anticipation, but opinion pieces and letters to the editor, unlike the president's image, are not on the front page and are often so heavily countered that they are neutralized even within the opinion section of the paper itself. As will be discussed later in this book, not all media are the same and not all presidents are treated the same by the media.

### *Changing the subject*

Through various polls and other information gathering approaches, politicians know how the public is responding to them. When ratings start getting dangerously low or no confidence petitions start gathering hundreds of thousands of signatures against them, public leaders, such as presidents, can now employ standard policy/media responses. A senator can announce a new bill, a governor can announce a new highway construction project, and a president can announce a dramatic intervention in another country. These actions divert the public attention away from the failings of the politician and bring attention back to those general qualities of strength, honesty, competence, protectiveness and so on. The act, whatever it is, creates a media event that can be spun into the image needed to control public perception.

This process is no different than the process that is used in everyday life by people in their interactions with their co-workers, friends, and family. If a conversation is starting to expose a person's shortcomings and that person begins to feel uncomfortable at their possible loss of standing with the person with whom they are interacting, what will that person do if sufficiently prepared to deal with the situation? Changing the subject of the conversation to a more comfortable topic is the likely preferred response. This is a skill some people learn more effectively than others, and it can make a significant difference in how a person is perceived by those with whom one communicates. Exercising this skill is also a dynamic oscillating process. The more positively others see you, the more positively you see yourself, which enhances your future communications with others, which in turn enhances your self image further … and so on and so forth. The oscillation can also work in a negative direction however. When this begins to happen, dramatic intervention in the interaction process is needed: changing the subject, or changing the people with whom one interacts. Or in the case of a president who is losing public affirmation because of, for example, public concern about the faltering national economy, it might mean announcing a new anti-crime program, or opening talks with another country with which we have not previously had diplomatic relations, or possibly invading another country.

It is important that the reader understand the process behind the social construction of reality at both micro and macro levels. With the sophisticated development of electronic mass media, and greater sophistication in how to use the mass media, the distinction between macro and micro processes becomes increasingly blurred. People are controlled through individual interactions with others. They are also controlled through political media events and activities that "inform" populations of what they are to expect of one another in their individual interactions. These expectations of one another include interpretations of the activities of political and other social leaders, as well as judgments about which ideas are acceptable and which are not.

### *Constructions need foundations*

The censorship of ideas, while governed in the short run by the media, is more effectively controlled in the long run by the schools. If we want a lesson on the role of schools in the social construction of reality all we have to do is investigate how the indigenous peoples were treated after the communal land they lived on for centuries was privatized by Europeans, thereby forcing them off their land. Once the indigenous peoples were under control, their children were taken away from their families and forced into English speaking schools for re-socialization, stripping them of their language and the symbolic representations of their cultures. The goal was to remove the resentment these children naturally had toward the hostile invaders from Europe, and develop within them loyalties to the newly emerging nation-state. Their own ways had to be viewed as primitive and uninviting, while the ways of the invaders had to be viewed as new and exciting. Some indigenous people escaped this oppressive program and still others were able to re-socialize themselves back again to their traditional ways, thereby saving their way of life from complete annihilation. However, the re-socialization of the Indians through the use of schools was largely successful for the invaders. It created tremendous havoc for Indians that is still felt to this day.

It was known, therefore, over 150 years ago, that the purpose of schools was not simply to educate children about the wonderful phenomena of the earth, but to indoctrinate them based on fairly narrow political purposes (Illich 1971). The primary responsibility of the schools was to insure that children would be loyal to the nation-state in which they lived, and just as importantly to insure they would be prepared to serve the nation-state with their minds and their bodies. In the United States the function of the schools now is little different than it was for the indigenous children taken from their families many years ago. The trauma is not nearly the same because most of the contemporary children's parents and grandparents went through a similar educational system (Andrzejewski and Alessio 1999). An ongoing dilemma that people of all nation-states face is whether the schools are actually helping socialize children into a long term slowly evolving culture of a given community of people, or whether the schools are being used by powerful people via giant corporations to control and manipulate a culture in support of financial interests (Illich 1971).

Schools, therefore, serve a very important social function in the social construction of reality. As discussed under conflict theory and critical theory, building a superstructure requires having young people accept false information as truth. When children encounter the various superstructure media symbols, those symbols must seem sufficiently natural to be acceptable without question. Hence, wealthy people benefiting from a socially constructed reality have much to gain by investing money into schools in order to further assure that they deliver, overall, the "right" message. Based on this realization, corporations have increased their involvement in the schools. Donations of money, electronic hardware and software, building wings onto buildings, and the funding of specific programs, typically come with a price tag. That price tag is the willingness of schools to compromise on definitions of what is real and what is not real. Schools will be discussed further in later chapters dealing with the concepts of socialization and re-socialization.

The primary point of the above discussion is that the social construction of reality is a controlled process, and those with the greatest amount of social power win in the struggle for that control. The Symbolic Interactionist perspective is enhanced greatly by an understanding of the importance of social power and conflict. Conflict Theorists have much to benefit from a good understanding of the symbolic processes that make prevailing power distributions "real." A sociologist must be able to effectively use knowledge of social process and symbolic communication, in conjunction with other theoretical perspectives, to analyze and understand social reality.

## Behaviorism

Behaviorism, clinically referred to as operant conditioning or behavior modification, has been demonstrated to work in various clinical and applied settings and has a logic to it that is difficult to deny. Without going into great detail, there are some behavioral concepts that will facilitate the study of social reality and thus social problems. Behavioral conditioning can and does work in certain highly controlled situations: child rearing, some types of rehabilitation, some aspects of schooling, commercial and political advertising, and military training, to name just a few. How far one wants to take behaviorism with respect to analyzing everyday life is another matter, and a journey filled with complications.

### *Positive and negative reinforcers*

A positive reinforcer is an experience that, by its presence, increases the likelihood of a particular behavior occurring. Hence, a piece of candy is a positive reinforcer to a small child for successfully walking across the room, assuming the child likes candy. A negative reinforcer is something that increases the likelihood of a behavior occurring when it is removed. If I make strange and obnoxious noises until I see you pick up this book, and then quickly discontinue the obnoxious noises, I have reinforced your tendency to pick up this book. Negative reinforcement is used in everyday life far more often than one might think. For example, "intimate" partners sometimes yell at one another until the other person does what the yeller wants: takes out the garbage; gets dinner ready at five and so on. The removal of the yelling reinforces the behavior.

Politicians use negative reinforcement strategies when they are campaigning. They frighten the public about some particular issue: terrorists, drugs, crime, and so on, and then present themselves as the antidote to that scary issue. "Vote for me and I will hunt down the terrorists and kill them." Hence, the anticipation of the removal of an aversive experience (which may or may not be real) is a reinforcer for voting for a particular candidate. Soldiers training for war experience a great deal of negative reinforcement. They are continuously yelled at and threatened. Well-timed removal of those aversive stimuli becomes a powerful reinforcer for the soldier continuing the training program. Negative reinforcement is often times confused with punishment, which is the act of following a behavior with an aversive stimulus so as to decrease, not increase, the likelihood of that behavior occurring again.

*Criminal and international punishments*

Punishment, or the threat of punishment, to deter criminal behavior and/or to deter other countries from certain activities is ineffectual. In addition to being timely, punishment must be certain, strong, and perceived to be justified by the recipient if behavioral change is to occur. With respect to criminal behavior, the punishment is usually long after the crime occurred. Further, few crimes actually result in a legal conviction and sentence. Punishments frequently do not match the nature of the crime, and often times the punished do not believe they were doing anything wrong. To make matters worse, criminals frequently plea bargain their way to lighter sentences by admitting to crimes they didn't commit. So there is sometimes confusion about exactly for what the person is being punished: not to the court perhaps, but certainly to the individual as a behavioral organism supposedly responding to stimuli.

The situation is even more confusing when it comes to punishing and threatening to punish other countries, a strategy that has been an important part of United States international policy. Punishing Vietnam for challenging colonialism turned out to be devastating, not only for Vietnam, but for the people of the United States as well. The George W. Bush administration's threat to punish North Korea for having a small and relatively insignificant nuclear program has resulted in North Korea accelerating its nuclear program to several times its previous size. Being bigger and stronger does not guarantee that one will have exclusive punishment rights indefinitely.

The people of other countries that the United States has attempted to punish for not "cooperating" with colonization continue to organize against the United States and invent creative ways of challenging the massive military violence inflicted upon them. Hence, suicide bombings are increasing in the Middle East, killing many United States soldiers and civilians. With an international policy so heavily based on punishment, the United States will most likely see more of these unusual kinds of violence. Invariably, violence begets violence, and the biggest and strongest don't always win—whatever winning means under such circumstances. The wars of Vietnam, Iraq, and Afghanistan serve as painful examples of wars without winners. The punished become punishers, only to be punished more severely in the future, and so it goes. Effective international polices, as in effective interpersonal relations, are healthiest and most productive in the long run if they involve positive reinforcers rather than punishment.

## Social Exchange Theory

Social exchange theory was brought into the social sciences initially by Anthropologists (Frazer 1919, Malinowski 1922), and was later adapted for Social Psychology (Homans 1961, Blau 1964). Exchange relations can be quite complicated in terms of the vast number of items that can be exchanged in a relationship and/or in terms of the number of social actors involved in exchange relations—the later is sometimes referred to as network theory. The most basic concept within social exchange theory is the norm of reciprocity, and successful reciprocity is often a matter of perception rather than objective value. As stated by Homans, "The open secret of human exchange is to give the other man behavior that is more valuable to him than it is costly to you and to get from him behavior that is more valuable to you than it is costly to him" (1961: 62).

The norm of reciprocity tells us that if someone does something for another person, the recipient will normally feel a sense of indebtedness to the benefactor and want to reciprocate in some way. The principles of exchange can only be applied to relationships where the social actors are free to participate or not participate. Any form of external coercion nullifies the application of exchange theory principles.

### *Involuntary exchange: coercion*

Ultimately, if voluntary reciprocity cannot be maintained based on what a person has to offer the relationship, then that person might be tempted to resort to coercive or manipulative means of getting what is wanted from the other in the exchange relationship. This issue is critical for understanding the failure of free market capitalism, which is theoretically based on the principle of voluntary exchange relations.

Suppose I am the leader of a small country and you are the CEO of a multinational corporation. The way it is supposed to work is that if I have no need for your product at all then you will simply have to initiate an exchange somewhere else. Or if I don't like your price, I can go somewhere else to get what I need for a better price. In reality, however, it does not work that way. If I don't like your price I can say I am going somewhere else with my product, but what I might find is that you have access to powerful social forces, like the military or the intelligence agency of a nation-state which you can use to block my exchanges with others. Nation-states can, and often do, threaten to withhold essential products from other nation-states or social entities so as to force an involuntary exchange. If I still refuse to exchange on your terms I might then discover that your nation-state is organizing an embargo against me so that I cannot get the basic necessities for my survival from anywhere else either. If I refuse to give in to your demands under those circumstances, you might instigate a revolt against me, replace me with someone who will be more "reasonable" and "cooperative," and thereby attain what you want at your price. Finally, if the corrupt person you chose to replace me decides to deal with someone else, you might influence your government to invade or bomb my country and simply take what you want.

### *Demand creation*

Similarly, if I have no need for your product at all and don't want it, rather than taking it somewhere else, you might, instead, spend billions of dollars creating advertisements that will make me want the product that I don't really need. You will then add the cost of the advertisement to the price of the product you sell me. Or, if it is a product that I need but already have, you might instead decide to create a need for *your particular* version of the product by making sure that I no longer have access to the product otherwise. An example of this is the process of companies like Coke and Pepsi taking water out of rivers or aquifers in various places around the world and selling it back to the people who used to be able to get the water for free as a public resource.

*Are free markets free?* "Free market" capitalism is anything but free, for it does not ordinarily operate as a voluntary social exchange process. Macro level free market capitalism, that involves the use of nation-state militaries, operates in a manner similar to an abusive relationship. For example, a man might abuse his intimate female partner to obtain favors or behaviors he received willingly during courtship through an exchange process. The abuse of women by male partners is typically a control process to avoid the inconveniences of maintaining a voluntary relationship. Free market capitalism is the same control process, but on a much greater scale. From a Social Exchange perspective truly "free" market capitalism cannot be implemented based on current international relations policies. Laissez-faire capitalism would have greater potential as a workable economic system if it followed one of the most fundamental principles of social exchange theory, which is that exchanges should be free of coercion.

### *Exchange theory and oil*

Humans are depleting the earth's oil supply so we can drive our cars every time we want to go someplace and store our goods in plastic containers. As oil becomes an increasingly scarce commodity, countries with high dependency on oil don't want to pay the real market price for it, which is whatever price the oil rich countries would ask for it if they were free of threat and coercion. Would the United States have attacked Iraq in 2003 if Iraq were not rich in oil? The answer to that question is most likely "no." None of the stated reasons for bombing Iraq in 2003 were ever substantiated by evidence. Western nation-states in particular have created a way of life so heavily dependent on oil that it is hard to imagine life without it. While people express most concern about gasoline, few people stop to think that most plastics are made from oil, and plastic is everywhere. Many fabrics are also made from oil.

For Social Exchange Theory to be useful under conditions of controlled and/or fabricated markets, the controls and fabrications must be built into the analysis process. For example, the United States purchase of a barrel of Iraq oil can be viewed as an exchange. However, it may not only be the money that is exchanged for the oil, but also the condition to not bomb or occupy Iraq. Negative reinforcement, the removal of harm, then becomes the primary variable in the exchange process. If compliance does not occur, aversive stimuli (bombing, embargos, political interferences, and so on) can be resumed to create a condition conducive to future negative reinforcement.

One of the greatest ironies of the lassie-faire capitalism movement is that the contemporary champions of the movement, Milton Freeman and the Chicago School of Economics, could not successfully assert their ideology in the country of Chile during the 1950s. Despite massive support from the United States government and the training of hundreds of Freeman economists to be advisors in Chile, the population of Chile still voted for a highly controlled economy, one that would assure a distribution of wealth that protected the interests of everyone rather than a few. Upon discovering that there was insufficient market for lassie-faire capitalism to be successful in Chile, the proponents of the free market ideology began a process of physical intervention, advocating for United States military and covert operations to destroy the successful Chilean economy and the political democracy that supported their economy (Klein 2007).

This example illustrates how complex exchange processes can be to analyze. Negative reinforcers are difficult to measure and assess in terms of their impact on the exchange process. Yet, the analysis is incomplete without them. The example also provides us with a demonstration of how weak the notion of free market capitalism is as a means of contributing to free and balanced exchange relations.

*How much is enough?*

Social exchange theory also tells us that social actors tend to try to gain as much as they can in exchange relations, and they particularly want to gain more than they give. The ideal is what Homans expressed in the earlier quotation: that exchange relations are most satisfying if both actors in the exchange relationship feel they are receiving more than they are giving. Such an exchange relation is not easy to achieve. Gift exchanges in various cultural circumstances, such as holidays, anniversaries and birthdays, suffer from this dilemma, which is why many people set exact amounts that can be spent on the gifts to be exchanged. This way the exchange is at least even and perceived to be fair.

## Balance Theory

While space limitations reduce the extent to which micro perspectives can be discussed, it is important for the reader to understand that social exchanges that do not follow fundamental social mores, or that incorporate conflicting social mores, have consequences for individual psychological responses to those exchanges. Those psychological responses determine future behaviors relative to the subject matter of the exchanges, and possibly subject matter tangentially related to the exchanges as well. Predicting behavioral and mental outcomes of different kinds of exchange distributions brings one into the theoretical domains of equity theory and balance theory (Alessio 1990). Herein the focus will be on Balance Theory.

One might ask what individual reactions to social situations have to do with social problems; isn't an individual's response really a personal issue? One of the best examples of why the answer is "no" can be found by looking at over-consumption, a serious social problem. Product marketing strategies are frequently based on an understanding of how to manipulate and distort individual cognitions so as to create a perception that the only way to achieve mental balance in a situation is to buy a particular product. Famous public figures are often used in advertisements as key pieces of the cognitive puzzle. It isn't just one individual buying that product as a result of being mentally manipulated, but it is thousands if not millions doing so—hence, the continual purchasing of unneeded, environmentally destructive, wasteful, and sometimes personally harmful products.

Information and misinformation are used in the same manner for the same purpose in political campaigns. Key pieces of "information" are carefully and strategically placed relative to other key pieces of "information" to force a thought pattern that maximizes a particular outcome: voting for the candidate who sponsored the ad. Hence, the social problems of overfunded campaigns, and political victories based on false information, become very much connected with the micro world of individual cognition. Perceptions of what is fair or "equitable" as a means of controlling public opinion on a policy issue can be manipulated using the same strategies. Sociologists need to understand the significance of these social psychological processes if we are going to be able to deal effectively with social problem solutions.

According to Heider (1958), and most balance theorists, humans have a need to maintain consistency in their thoughts and in their actions. Whenever we see inconsistencies within our thoughts, or within our thoughts and actions, we experience what is known as cognitive dissonance. Cognitive dissonance does not have a specific symptom associated with it, but it can manifest itself as a source of stress and consternation—a feeling of unease. The experience of dissonance causes individuals to want to realign their thoughts or actions until they are consistent with one another in order to remove the uncomfortable experience associated with cognitive dissonance. Hence, the notion of cognitive consistency is basically another way of saying "balance."

Cognitive dissonance and cognitive consistency are psychological concepts that, by themselves, have little to do with Sociology. However, cognitive dissonance and cognitive consistency are caused by, and in turn have an impact upon, social reality. The social impact of these seemingly simple processes can be quite profound and far reaching. How humans mitigate or resolve dissonance based on apparent contradictions is an important part of breaking the corporate owned media information barriers. Likewise, it is important for humans to be able to easily recognize and deal with dissonance based on cleverly constructed false contradictions. Balance theory examples related to social problems will be examined later in this book using the Heiderian three point structure model.

## Bridging the Macro and Micro Perspectives: Humanistic Social Psychology

### *Human needs*

The primary message of Humanistic Social Psychology is that humans have needs that must be met if they are to grow, remain healthy, and have healthy social relationships. Fulfillment of these needs depends, for the most part, on relations with other beings. Identifying those needs and how they might be related to one another, particularly in terms of how they are fulfilled, is an important piece of the puzzle of understanding social reality and social life. Most of the other theoretical perspectives have an underlying implicit assumption of the existence of needs, but never explicitly say what they are or what their behavioral and social significance might be relative to humans trying to have those needs fulfilled. Behaviorism comes close, but in a strikingly different way.

According to Humanistic Social Psychology, the type of need one has at a particular time in one's life can determine behavior patterns for that person. How external factors, such as other people or social entities, respond to the needs of individuals plays an important role in determining how individuals relate to the outside world.

### *Maslow's hierarchy*

While it would be impossible to enumerate every specific need that people claim to have, Abraham Maslow developed a set of need categories that he argued were hierarchical in nature. Hierarchical in this case means that before one can move to concentrate on seeking fulfillment on a "higher level" need one must find fulfillment on the "lower level" needs. "Lower" means more primary to the physical survival of the individual, and hence first in terms of fulfillment priority. Lower needs are also sometimes referred to as the more basic needs. The typology of needs as suggested by Maslow, from lower to higher, is as follows: physiological needs; safety needs; sense of belonging need; self esteem need; and self-actualization need (Maslow 1954). The need for creativity was added much later and is often excluded from Maslow's theory.

### *Self-actualizing people*

While the steps toward self actualization are not formulaic, it is clear that people cannot move toward self actualization if preoccupied with lower level needs. Some of the well known role models of this unusual quality have been: Albert

Einstein, Susan B. Anthony, Emma Goldman, Mohandas Gandhi, and Martin Luther King. Important characteristics of highly self-actualized people are: the ability to take risks on matters of high importance; the ability to stand alone in every sense of the word; the ability to see through false realities and behave accordingly (despite severe costs to oneself); the ability to do what is in the best interest of others over one's own interests; typically not acting out of personal ego or self-aggrandizement. These characteristics reveal the relevance of Humanistic Social Psychology to the study of social problems and to solving social problems. The greater the number of self-actualized people there are, the greater the potential for both avoiding and solving social problems. Furthermore, the higher the level of self-actualization within a population, the lower the likelihood that population will be easily controlled by false realities. This relatively simple statement demonstrates Humanistic Social Psychology's propensity for bridging macro and micro levels of analysis.

### *Socialization and over-socialization*

Humanistic Social Psychology also enhances our understanding of the importance of socialization, particularly as it relates to over-socialization. The value position of Humanistic Social Psychology—that individual freedom should be protected to the maximum extent possible—is a driving force in understanding the social, as well as individual costs of over-socialization (Fromm 1941). Effective socialization creates social order and mental health. Over-socialization, driven largely by the efforts of socializing agents to satisfy the labor demands of potential employers (corporations in capitalist nation-states, and government in communist nation-states), creates stifled individuals and social units with limited tolerance for diversity of thought and action. Over-socialization results in an oppressed individual, but also an oppressive social environment that further restricts freedom, creativity, and tolerance for human differences. Over-socialization is largely a function of labor supply and demand, which in capitalist nation-states is largely controlled by the wealthy through corporations. Over-socialization will likely increase during periods of high unemployment when corporations are reducing production, and when hoarding wealth is increasing.

Throughout this book the issue of socialization will emerge periodically. A primary social problems question from the micro perspective is, "how do we socialize or re-socialize people toward greater self-actualization, and thus toward a disposition less oriented toward wealth accumulation and more oriented toward healthy social order community living?"

## Summary

What are the most serious social problems and what are the root causes of those problems? The theoretical perspectives we have discussed make important contributions toward answering those questions. Most people don't need to be told what the serious problems of the world are, but few people understand what causes and maintains them. This is the work of sociologists: identifying why social reality is the way it is, where it needs to be changed for improvement, and how that change can be brought about.

# Chapter 4
# Probable Roots and Current Manifestations of Inequality

What is "inequality?" To answer that question one should start with what it means to be equal. In mathematics we refer to one value being equal to another value through an expression like: $2 + 2 = 4$, or $X = Y$. It is easy to see that what is on the left side of the equation is not the same as what is on the right side of the equation. It would serve no purpose to say that $2 = 2$ for example, since 2 is 2. Likewise, when we think sociologically, we must avoid thinking of equality in terms of sameness. One person is never exactly the same as another.

## Equal in Value

When we use the term equality, therefore, we are really saying that units are comparable, and particularly comparable in value. This is true in math and it is true in the application of sociology. $2 + 2$ is of the same value as 4, and one human being is of the same value as another, or one group of humans is of the same value as another group of humans. Humans are not the same, but they are of the same value. Animal rights activists would extend that argument to suggest that all forms of animal life are of the same value, even though there are many striking differences among the species of the earth (Regan 2004, Nibert 2002). It is difficult for many people to accept that humans are of the same value. Applying that notion to all species is far more difficult.

During World War II the United States fought the Germans and in so doing denigrated the moral character of the German people. This always happens during war. Soldiers are indoctrinated to believe in the inferiority of the "enemy" to make it seem reasonable and right to kill them. We now know that what we assumed about the Germans as humans was incorrect. The same might also be said of the Japanese, the Koreans, and the Vietnamese. Most likely we will someday realize the same about the Iraqis and the Afghans with whom we are currently at war.

The point is that there is no real basis for determining greater or lesser value of humans. Yet, such differential values are continually being invented and applied to human groups and populations. People are equal in the sense that they have equal value, and there is no objectively true way of actually knowing anything different. To whatever extent those who control a situation successfully construct and assign a different value to different individuals, human groups, or human populations, is the extent to which inequality exists in a sociological sense. Inequality, therefore, is when people who should be treated as if they are equal are actually treated as if they are not equal. Treating some people as less valuable than others serves numerous social functions within many large and small social entities around the world. Keep in mind that when something is functional to the maintenance of a social structure, that does not mean that it, and/or the structure it serves, are intrinsically good or have a positive impact on other social structures or social entities. Sociologists are challenged to identify the dysfunction imbedded in social structures built on inequality. Oftentimes, dysfunction is masked by the constructed reality of those who benefit from the social structure being maintained in its current form.

## Survival without Surplus: Need Fulfillment

What are the root causes of inequality? Perhaps we can address that question by first analyzing the possible evolution of modern day economic greed? There are no longitudinal data sets tracing greed back to its origin. However, if we tax our imaginations a bit we should be able to come up with a scenario that seems to make sense. Let's go back to Maslow's hierarchy of needs. What are the first needs that all humans, and most likely all beings, must fulfill? Of course, it is one's physiological needs: nourishment, water, sufficient warmth and so on. It is not difficult to imagine a time when people who evolved within, or migrated to, climates with limited growing seasons faced a great deal of uncertainty about their survival through the winter. How does one respond to this circumstance? Most likely, at some point someone figured out a way to successfully store food, and this was the beginning of surplus.

### *Surplus: how much is enough?*

Now if you are the person who makes this incredible discovery, how do you decide how much to store? Do you store just enough to get you through the winter? Do you store a little extra, just in case the winter is longer than normal? Or should you store as much as you can, not knowing exactly what the future holds? This last option would surely be tempting. Observe a juvenile who starts collecting sea shells. How many is enough? There is no predetermined answer to that question—not for sea shells, and not for most things in life.

Others that see that you have plenty of stored food may ask you to share so that they may survive also. How do you respond to such a request? Most likely you cannot supply everyone with all the food they need. How do you decide who gets the food and who doesn't? It is quite likely that you will work out some sort of exchange relationship with other people. Perhaps you will provide others with food if they will help you collect it and store it in the future. Now you not only have far more than you need to survive, you have an amount of food that has little to do with your survival. Your surplus has exceeded any logical amount based on the need that provided the motivation for accumulating the surplus in the first place.

*Surplus as the beginning of wealth*

If your accumulation of greater and greater amounts of food is creating a scarcity for others who do not work for you, then you will most likely want to be working on your security needs. You may have to give a little more food to those who help protect you … and so it goes. What once belonged to everyone in your area now belongs to … you. Of course, your claim of control over all of the surrounding berries and nuts is so you can "generously" provide food for some of the others in order to help them make it through the winter. Isn't that what you would convince yourself and others? Never mind that the accumulation is making it more and more difficult for the remainder of the people to survive—even as long as they did before you began your hoarding activities.

If you are storing more food than you could ever eat, you are well protected from harm. You also know you are accepted by your family and community, so what could possibly be the motivation for continuing to gather more and more and more food? Yes, it is the way others respond to you. You now feel important, as reflected in the deference that others show toward you. Your surplus for survival has now turned into wealth for self esteem. You have now moved to a preoccupation with a higher level need. This is not to say that you didn't have self esteem before you started your wealth accumulation. It is simply that you could not focus on self-esteem as a primary motivation for your behavior when you were worrying about whether you were going to make it through the winter. This, according to Maslow, is the hierarchical nature of human needs.

## Laissez-Faire Capitalism

The above hypothetical illustration of how greed may have evolved into what Marx referred to as surplus value (Mandel 2010), economically addresses some important issues. What are the possible motivations behind drives such as greed? When does need fulfillment become greed? How would the above description regarding surplus and self esteem be related to the way capitalism works in the world in general? That is, does capitalism create jobs and wealth for some at the expense of others, particularly through the private control of public resources? Should people be able to do whatever they want with public resources if their behaviors deny others of basic rights such as clean air and water, healthy food, and adequate materials for clothing and shelter? In 1776 Adam Smith answered this question with an astonishing "yes." He laid down the foundation for what is known as free market economics (Smith 1777). As developed, this concept suggests that capitalism will work to everyone's benefit if allowed to operate without external regulation. Supposedly, the wants and needs of everyone will create magically balanced markets all over the world that will fulfill everyone's expectations harmoniously. Smith was not a proponent of greed and did have some sense of the importance of a public good, but his commitment to free market capitalism, and what he thought it would do for humans, created problems beyond what he could have imagined in 1776–77.

Markets are created in a lot of ways, and may or may not have a lot to do with people's actual needs and wants. Notwithstanding, free market economics is still taught in universities as something that could work. Some actually claim it is working now. The early twenty-first century near collapse of the global "free market" economy demonstrated that it cannot effectively work, except for the very wealthy who create and benefit from the so-called "free markets."

Through the 1980s, 1990s, and the early part of the twenty-first century, there was a dramatic movement toward fully implementing free market economics. Nearly all economic regulations were removed so the market (what Adam Smith called the invisible hand) would be uninhibited. Corporations, already too large, were allowed to become larger without protections for the smaller entrepreneur (Reback 2009). What happened? One major financial institution after another collapsed as a result of unregulated competition leading to massive corruption and unchecked criminal activities. Millions of people's fortunes, retirement programs, and jobs were lost. The United States government stepped in on one occasion after another, starting with the massive Savings and Loan scandal of the 1980s, to bail out the failing financial institutions with public money. The massive government bailouts of financial institutions in 2008 and 2009, while millions of individuals suffered unemployment and home foreclosures, exposed the myth of "free markets."

There is no such thing as a "free market." Products are made by investors and marketed to people using whatever methods possible to make them want ("need") to buy the products. The exploitation and oppression that are part of the process of creating "free markets" result in many people suffering and dying around the world. To avoid confusion, the term laissez-faire capitalism will be used as a label for the current United States economic system. The terms free market economics and laissez-faire capitalism apply to the same processes and belief systems.

Laissez-faire capitalism conveys the notion that people who control sufficient resources are permitted to use those resources to do whatever they deem necessary to maximize their own profits. There is no expectation of consideration for the masses of people who have few resources at their disposal, or to environmental degradation. Somewhat contradictory, but still consistent with Adam Smith's philosophy, is the notion that using the tax supported United States government and its military to further enhance one's profit maximization is a fair and reasonable maneuver.

With an economy built on laissez-faire capitalism, a system based on the notion of unregulated business opportunities, it should not be a surprise that massive inequality has been created within the United States and around the world where multinational corporation interests operate.

### *The self esteem imperative*

People with a lot of wealth do not continue to accumulate wealth in order to satisfy basic needs; nor can such desire for endless wealth accumulation be motivated by the need for self-actualization. Hoarding and excessive wealth accumulations are considered antithetical to the typical behavior patterns of self-actualizing people. People who have self-actualizing tendencies strive to help others at their own expense, and typically have a strong sense of social justice. Wealth accumulation is not a priority for self-actualizing people. If hoarding and endless wealth accumulation are not motivated by basic need gratification or self-actualization, the only remaining motivation is self esteem.

There is an inherent flaw in the logic of trying to fulfill a higher level need, such as self esteem, with activities designed for lower need gratification, such as accumulating material wealth. The nature of material wealth is that it satisfies material needs, which are our basic needs of food, shelter, clothing and so on. According to Maslow, higher needs should be satisfied with higher level activities. If people who have their basic needs satisfied move on to higher level activities to satisfy their self esteem, the ground work is laid for self actualizing tendencies as well. By promoting a logical hierarchical progression of need satisfaction activities within all socializing venues, it should be possible to prevent basic need gratification from turning into greed and the corresponding irrational endless hoarding of resources.

Deriving high self esteem from material gain has become increasingly possible as greater numbers of people in the world accept material wealth as an important part of a person's value, and hence, one's status. People who have material wealth are treated with higher regard than people who do not. As the connection between human value and material worth strengthens, it becomes ever more difficult to move people beyond a preoccupation with material gain. The more focused people are on material gain, the more likely it is that inequality will continue to occur … not only because self esteem has become viewed in Western cultures as something derived relative to the status of others, but also because accumulation of wealth by one person is usually dependent upon others having less wealth.

### *Greed: positive or negative value?*

According to Maslow's notion of hierarchical needs, satisfying higher level needs should result from activities that are other directed rather than self directed. Public response to accumulations of wealth should not necessarily be approval. Since "greed" has historically been considered a negative characteristic, the public response to wealth accumulation should not be positive. If one looks up greed in a dictionary, thesaurus, or religious text, one finds that greed is considered an undesirable characteristic. The Catholic Church, for example, considers greed one of the seven deadly sins. Yet, we see that people who accumulate large amounts of wealth through greedy behavior are most often admired, given awards, and treated in a privileged manner. In other words, the socialization process, influenced by elites in industrialized countries has a built-in flaw. Friends, relatives, and generalized others actually respond favorably to greedy behaviors, which in turn enhances a greedy person's self esteem. As stated by Perkins in his critique of the United States economic system, "We have placed sociopathic CEOs and politicians on false pedestals, glorifying their excessive wealth, multiple mansions, megayachts, and luxurious private jets. For years we've empowered these people (almost exclusively men) to create a system that is scandalously wasteful, overtly reckless, and—we now know—ultimately self-destructive" (2010: 1). How far will people go to protect the greed-based identities described by Perkins?

### *Changing the value of greed*

Throughout most of the history of capitalism efforts were made to hide its greed-based foundation. Earlier socially constructed reality projected the idea that wealthy benevolent capitalists were trying their best to provide a decent way of life for the "less intelligent" and "less enlightened" poor people of the world. Yet, laissez-faire capitalism is based on the imperative of maximizing profits. An important part of maximizing profits is maintaining the lowest possible expenses, a big part of which is labor. To keep labor costs low laborers have to accept a low personal value. Hence, wealthy capitalists, through their corporations, influence the public to believe that laborers are greedy if they try to organize for better wages. Unions are projected as obstructionist organizations run by greedy thugs. Capitalists, on the other hand, are portrayed as benevolent philanthropists who take all the risks by investing their money while laborers basically enjoy the ride.

With the gap between the wealthy and non-wealthy population dramatically increasing each year it has become obvious that this socially constructed reality can no longer be fully sustained. As the difficulty of disguising the greed basis for capitalism increases, one has to choose between viewing capitalism as bad or viewing greed as good. The investment in a capitalist system is so great that it would be extremely difficult for economists to view capitalism as a negative social force. The alternative seems much more feasible: change the valence of greed.

A few years ago, as I was searching for information about greed, I found an article in *Capitalism Magazine* titled, "The Virtue of Greed" by Walter Williams. At first I thought it was a joke, but then quickly realized that the author was completely serious. It represented, in effect, an unintentional caricature of the ideas of Adam Smith. The article starts out with the sentence, "YOU CAN CALL IT GREED, selfishness or enlightened self-interest, but the bottom line is that it's these human motivations that get wonderful things done" (Williams 2001: 1). It continues a paragraph later with the following:

> There's probably widespread agreement that it's a wonderful thing that most of us own cars. Is there anyone who believes that the reason we have cars is because Detroit assembly-line workers care about us? It's also wonderful that

> Texas cattle ranchers make sacrifices of time and effort caring for steer so that New Yorkers can enjoy a steak now and then. Again, is there anyone who believes that ranchers who make these sacrifices do so out of a concern for and feeling the pain of New Yorkers. (Williams 2001: 1)

This is an important paragraph for a variety of reasons. First, it includes a negative inference about Detroit assembly line workers. That is, that they do not care about us. That choice of wording is revealing. The language regarding Texas ranchers (property owners) is softer. One might question why the car example refers negatively to the assembly line worker and not the people who own and run the auto companies. Would it not serve the writer's interests to say that the corporate owners don't care about us? It is one thing to be greedy, but another matter entirely to not actually care about other people. We see in the above quote, among other issues, the importance of carefully constructing symbolic communications to control reality.

### The Environment?

The most important aspect of the above quote by Williams, however, is not the facetious questions being asked, but the statements preceding them. They were worded as if they are undeniable truths. A more careful look at those statements is in order. First look at "There's probably widespread agreement that it's a wonderful thing that most of us own cars." If such an agreement exists, it is a badly misinformed agreement. Cars are a source of many of our most serious environmental problems. Motor vehicles emit carbon dioxide that contributes to the destruction of the earth's ozone and raises global temperatures at rates that will soon make many parts of the earth uninhabitable by humans and other forms of life. Dramatic effects of this accelerating process are increasing rapidly: ice melting in the Arctic and Antarctic; the warming of the oceans and earth's atmosphere; extreme weather; increased diseases related to climate shifts; increased respiratory problems related to declining air quality; and severe loss of species. It should not be surprising that Williams denies human impact on the environment; claiming that the scientific evidence is a hoax (2008b, 2010).

Additionally, the massive highway construction (to accommodate the trucks and automobiles) that has taken place since the 1950s (led by the United States) has destroyed the habitat of many humans and non-human forms of life. This may seem insignificant to those who are used to the highway system as it currently exists and grows, but entire neighborhoods of large cities have been destroyed to make way for the massive highways and clover leaf intersections. United States dependence on oil, much of which is used for gasoline and components for our cars, is the cause of international conflicts, wars, and millions of deaths.

*How did this happen?*

When Williams asks whether anyone believes we have cars because Detroit assembly-line workers care about us, he should be asking instead whether the auto company owners have ever cared about us, the environment, or even what constitutes efficient and effective transportation. They are responsible for the absence of efficient and effective public transportation in most parts of the United States.

It is true that most people enjoy driving their car, but there are important reasons to conclude that cars are not wonderful. They are one of the most polluting and dangerous of all human creations. Approximately 43,000 people are killed every year in automobile/motorcycle wrecks in the United States (US Census Bureau 2010: 1). Train accidents are relatively rare (infoplease 2007). Even airplane deaths are only about 1,000 per year (Wikipedia 2010a). One might rightfully ask, "If cars are so bad why did they become so popular and win the support of the general public?" The answer to that question is not as complicated as one might expect. Cars were made the primary mode of transportation in the United States through an elaborate and sophisticated conspiracy spearheaded by General Motors. The conspiracy included Standard Oil of California, Firestone, and National City Lines, a company secretly funded and controlled by General Motors. The process was quite lengthy and involved many prongs. The objective was to destroy public transportation and replace it with highways, cars, and trucks.

Among other important strategies, the president of GM became Secretary of Defense in 1953 and declared an elaborate system of highways necessary for national security. The result was the passage of the Federal-Aid Highway Act of 1956 worth 25 billion dollars (Motavalli 2003). In 1956 one seldom saw the word "billion" within any context—let alone within the context of money. The United States was under no threat of being invaded, and if it had been invaded, a good rail system would have been just as effective as a highway system—possibly more effective, given the amount of cargo that can be transported by rail and the comparative costs.

As for public support, a poll conducted in Los Angeles, one of the cities most negatively impacted by cars, highways, and pollution, showed that 88 percent of the public favored expanding the electric rail system following World War II (Motavalli 2003). Instead, through the use of GM controlled National City Lines, the electric rail system was shut down. Whether you are inclined to believe in conspiracies or not, they do sometimes exist, and this one was proven in federal court. Antitrust violations and conspiracy convictions were found against General Motors for its systematic destruction of public transportation systems for its own financial benefit. The company was fined only $5,000, and the costs of the conspiracy continue to mount to this day.

Community planning and democratic decision-making, if allowed to be properly executed, would have led the United States in a different direction from where it is now in terms of transportation. European countries that have for so many years relied on a good public transportation system, are now giving in to the same kinds of corporate pressures that brought the massive congested highway system to the United States. Notwithstanding, with only four percent of the world's population, the United States contributes twenty-five percent of the carbon dioxide that is rapidly deteriorating the earth's ozone.

*The dilemma of steak*

Williams also stated that "It is also wonderful … that New Yorkers can enjoy a steak now and then." Over one billion people are suffering from hunger (The Telegraph 2009) and millions die each year from starvation, especially children (Poverty.com 2010). The United States is not an exception since over 14 percent of adults and 22 percent of children do not have enough food to live healthy lives (FRAC 2009), owing to the United States having the highest poverty and working poverty rates among the 18 most affluent countries (Brady et al. 2010).

Starvation among humans is not yet caused by a global food shortage; although if our current environmentally destructive practices continue, that day will almost certainly come. People are starving today because food is produced and distributed based on greed-based profit maximization rather than on a logical plan designed to sustain human and non-human life. Access to food and water should be the most fundamental right of all people everywhere. Yet, even in a country as rich in food production as the United States, food is not made available to all of its citizens. Some people in New York can have a steak now and then, but it is also the case that many children in New York, and Detroit, and Chicago, and Los Angeles, and East St. Louis and Cleveland … go hungry. Is greed really wonderful? Greed is an emotion that causes one to lose control of their reasoned judgment, just as strong physical attraction or fear might. Human and environmental sustainability require reasoned, rather than emotional, decision-making.

There is ample information from a variety of sources that shows meat-based diets require far more land than plant-based diets (Pimentel and Pimentel 2003, Robbins 2001). Just as the United States was cleared to accommodate British cattle culture (Rifkin 1992), multinational corporations are clear-cutting old growth forests to feed cows. Cows require more vegetation for survival than would humans on a plant-based diet. A large portion of the beef produced is used for fast food, which is particularly problematic for the health of consumers (Schlosser 2002). Old growth clear cutting not only destroys irreplaceable forests, but also displaces thousands of species of life, including many humans (McCarthy 2009). One might think lightly of the displacement of other species, a tendency known as speciesism, but reckless destruction of the complex fabric of life will have serious long term consequences (Mason 1993). There is growing evidence that some of the relatively recent diseases in the world are related to displaced viruses adapting to new environments and, hence, new hosts (Maheshwari 2001, Lean 2000), including the e coli bacteria which consequently creates the deadly e coli

O157H7 (Brown 1997). The primary source of e coli O157H7 for humans is cow feces, since humans eat a lot of easily contaminated beef.

*And the cows?*

Cows currently exist, almost entirely, for human consumption or milk production. Their total aggregated weight is greater than that of humans and, like cars, they are a major contributor (via methane gas production) to global warming. One might say, "Don't cows have a right to eat also?" Of course they do, but cows are bred and raised specifically for meat or milk. Cows no longer have anything approximating a natural social arrangement. They are produced and reproduced solely for their economic contribution to their owner. Their reproduction is neither controlled by the cows themselves nor by a natural environment containing the cows. Most cows now have no life other than a feedlot or a body sized stall that minimizes their movement. They are given various kinds of chemicals: to grow, to stop growing, to get fat, and to not get diseases (because their living conditions are so unnatural and unhealthy). The food they eat is heavily contaminated with herbicides, pesticides, and slaughterhouse waste. The chemicals put into cows, medicinal or otherwise, are passed on to humans through consumption of the milk and meat. While the cows themselves do not typically live long enough to experience all the negative effects of the chemicals, the people in New York, eating "a steak now and then," do. The result is that the most current and reliable information we have about meat is that it contributes significantly to heart disease, cancer, and diabetes, three of the greatest causes of human death (along with auto crashes) in the United States and other Western heavy meat eating countries. Further, the massive use of antibiotics decreases their effectiveness against diseases in the animals and the humans who consume them.

People don't eat meat because it is good for them; albeit many may think that it is good for them. Many United States residents are suffering from health problems related to too much protein, fat, and cholesterol, and the many diseases caused directly or indirectly by eating meat. People in the United States eat large amounts of meat because they inherited the practice from the British, who colonized the United States in part to expand their cattle production (Rifkin 1992). United States corporations continue to spread cattle agribusiness throughout the rest of the world, heavily promoting the consumption of meat to expand the profitable beef industry.

Following World War II advances in agriculture resulted in notably high grain production in the United States. In 1949 a congressional decision was made to find ways of encouraging increased production and consumption of meat in order to avoid excessive surpluses of grains (Winders and Nibert 2004). The balancing process continues to oscillate out of control: more grain, more cows, more meat eaters, more grain, more cows, and so on. Sixty to seventy-five percent of the destruction of old growth rainforest today is to accommodate the beef industry.

The United States meat and dairy industries have powerful lobbying groups and have infiltrated the lives of people in many important ways. Remember the basic food group chart that you were shown in grade school? That was a gift from the meat and dairy industries. They provided the information and the chart, and for many decades nobody ever questioned it. Recently, as a result of a considerable amount of evidence, the basic food groups have been changed. Meat and dairy products no longer play such a prominent role. Unfortunately, this modest change has not yet affected the production and distribution of meat around the world. In addition to the cruelty to animals taking place through factory farming, the environmental degradation that goes with the meat industries, and the many health problems related to eating meat, there is also the matter of mad cow disease (Bovine Spongiform Encephalopathy), identified as Creutzfeldt-Jakob's disease in humans. Everything possible is being done by the beef industry to hide the presence of mad cow disease, also found in elk and deer (Lyman 1998, 2006).

Williams' irrational arguments notwithstanding (2008a, 2009, 2010) greed is not wonderful and does not bring the world wonderful things (Korten 2010). It may bring moments of pleasure and immediate gratification to those who successfully practice greed, but it is not a positive force for good in the world. To the contrary, it ultimately brings chaos and destruction to all forms of life and the earth. Our grandparents and religious leaders had it right when they assigned a negative valence to greed. What part of a person's socialization would lead one to have such a distorted view of reality as to argue that greed is positive?

## Summary: Envisioning and Planning Solutions

A contemporary analysis of social inequality does not end with the knowledge that some people have more resources than others, or even with an understanding of the causes of the unequal distribution of resources. Understanding social inequality requires knowing also how it relates to the entire fabric of life. How does inequality relate to environmental issues? How does inequality relate to health issues: for both wealthy and poor people? How does inequality relate to interpersonal violence and wars between nation-states? How does inequality relate, as cause and consequence, to the way social life is organized?

By studying historical and current events, and analyzing them as social processes, inequality can be understood, not as something that just happens and thus requires assistance through charitable deeds, but as something that is systematically and sometimes deliberately created for reasons of personal gain, with many residual interrelated effects.

It is utopian and counterproductive to think that inequality can be completely eliminated. Efforts to create such socioeconomic environments have failed, partly because of interference from capitalist countries that were threatened by non-capitalist economies, and partly because such efforts were by necessity oppressive forms of social organization. By understanding the social forces and processes by which inequality is created, however, it is possible to envision plans and corresponding policies that will reduce inequality to a point where everyone has a reasonably comfortable lifestyle within a healthy cultural and environmental context. The mythical notion of an invisible hand that will magically make everything right in the end, as promoted by laissez-faire capitalists, is a groundless ideology that protects those who control resources from those who do not. Solutions for creating a better world require encouraging people to collectively plan their social and economic policies rather than convincing people that a mysterious invisible hand will somehow take care of their problems.

# Chapter 5
# Inequality and Social Disorganization

Social disorganization is a term used by sociologists to identify circumstances where the parts of a social structure are not operating together in a reasonably balanced and coherent manner for the good of the whole. For example, if a parent is removed from a family there may be a period of social disorganization within that family until it can readjust to the change in its form. Hence, there may be a period of some chaos where members of the family unit are not sure what they are supposed to do since one of the roles of the unit is no longer in operation. Slight shifts in role behavior over time, however, typically allow the family to re-stabilize into a reasonably well organized unit. It is possible that the family could emerge better organized than it was before the loss of the parent. Structural functionalists and conflict theorists will disagree on the extent to which social disorganization is prevalent within a social entity, and will most likely also disagree on the cause of the disorganization. Both perspectives, however, will agree that social disorganization is a serious problem at all levels of analysis.

The reader might recall the discussion in Chapter 2 about the misperceptions frequently promulgated about anarchism. One of the more obvious of those misperceptions is that anarchists promote chaos. Contrary to that misunderstanding, anarchists believe that humans have the capacity to self organize without the need for external coercion. There is, however, an important irony associated with the just noted misconception. The most vigilant promoters of the idea that anarchists seek and create chaos are also the most vigilant promoters and protectors of the chaos that comes with laissez-faire capitalism, or what John Perkins refers to as "predatory capitalism." Laissez-faire capitalists believe that nothing should get in the way of a person's (or corporation's) ability to maximize profits, including collectively agreed upon laws. Hence, laissez-faire capitalism systematically and vigilantly denies the right of people to democratically plan their future and make decisions based on what is best for entire communities, including what is best for future generations. Carefully planning and creating healthy social and physical environments interferes with the ability of people motivated by greed to do what they want, which is to amass ever greater amounts of surplus wealth using whatever methods necessary to accomplish their goal.

Most of the world circumstances surrounding and impacted by laissez-faire capitalism are kept in a state of social disorganization as a means of accommodating plans that wealthy people and corporations want to actualize—even at the possible expense of the health and safety of all life throughout the world. Created or fostered social disorganization has become a major source of many of the world's systemic problems, and is, therefore, a significant problem in itself.

## Planned Social Disorganization and the Shock Doctrine

It would seem facetious to claim that the creation of social disorganization is somehow deliberate on the part of a particular group of people. However, there is ample documentation that, indeed, indicates that proponents of the most rigid form of laissez-faire capitalism maintain a strategy for taking advantage of chaotic social situations (Klein 2007). This strategy is sufficiently effective that chaos opportunities are, not only welcomed, but also sometimes encouraged or created. Who are the people that have enough power to actually create social disorganization? There are think tanks, people appointed to government agencies, members of quasi government agencies (for example, "The Enterprise" of the Iran-Contra affair), corporate lobbyists, and sometimes elected political leaders, who represent the wealthiest and most powerful people of the United States: people who stand to gain millions or billions of dollars by taking advantage of, or facilitating, social disorganization opportunities. The Central Intelligence Agency is a primary tool of those who have enough power to control or influence the United States government into action on their behalf. The existence of a common cause shared among a relatively small group of powerful wealthy people has been well documented (Klein 2007, Perkins 2004, Webb 1999). The people to whom I refer are what C. Wright Mills identified as the power elite. As Mills stated, "The power elite is composed of men whose positions enable them to transcend the ordinary environments of ordinary men and women; they are in positions to make decisions having major consequences" (1973: 270).

### *Economic hit men*

John Perkins, a former corporate banking consultant (known inside the business as an Economic Hit Man), whose responsibility it was to disrupt local economies and help make third world countries "ready" for Western corporations, demonstrated the connection between the power elite and the deliberate creation of social disorganization when he stated, "Economic hit men (EHM's) are highly paid professionals who cheat countries around the globe out of trillions of dollars. They funnel money from the World Bank, the U.S. Agency for International Development (USAID), and other foreign "aid" organizations into the coffers of huge corporations and the pockets of a few wealthy families who control the planet's natural resources" (Perkins 2004: ix). "… I was stunned by the magnitude of what we EHM's had accomplished, in so many places. I tried to concentrate on a few countries that stood out, but the list of places where I had worked and which were worse off afterward was astounding" (Perkins 2004: 179).

### *Milton Friedman*

Naomi Klein (2007) credits Milton Friedman, the famous champion of free market economics for what she refers to as disaster capitalism. Disaster capitalism is the spreading of laissez-faire capitalism through the exploitation of disasters. Some, such as Klein, argue not only are disasters exploited for the purpose of spreading free market capitalism, but they are sometimes facilitated or even created. Friedman argued that proponents of free market capitalism should be ready to move in with privatization activities once a disaster occurs. Hence, the hurricane that devastated New Orleans in 2005 was immediately followed, not by systematic disaster relief to restore public order, but by privatization experts who took over the public schools for profit. These privatized schools are referred to euphemistically as charter schools. This type of action was specifically recommended by Friedman in a statement published in the Wall Street Journal. As stated by Klein, "Before Hurricane Katrina, the school board had run 123 public schools; now it ran just 4. Before the storm, there had been 7 charter schools in the city; now there were 31. New Orleans teachers used to be represented by a strong union; now the union's contract had been shredded, and its forty-seven hundred members had all been fired" (Klein 2007: 5). Klein gives several other examples of disaster capitalism including the 2004 Sri Lankan tsunami, the 2001 attacks on the World Trade Center, and the 2003 Iraq war.

The Friedman belief that free market capitalism can best be spread following a disaster is based on the accurate understanding that people are most vulnerable and thus malleable following a shock of some sort, such as a disaster. Out of the social disorganization of a disaster comes the opportunity for control and exploitation. This philosophy, established by Friedman and followed by many world leaders directly influenced by Friedman, is what Klein refers to as the Shock Doctrine. Once laissez-faire economics is solidly established in a location, it perpetuates, in a slow burn state, the social disorganization upon which it was built. Laissez-faire capitalism is the antithesis of community self-governance through democratic practices. A true democracy has the capacity and motivation to override and control individual extraction of wealth from communal resources and human labor extraction at the expense of the majority of citizens. Yet, such extraction and exploitation of citizen rights are what happen routinely almost everywhere in the United States and across the globe. Herein lies the long standing modern day connection between inequality and laissez-faire economics. Inequality is not something that just somehow happens. There are structural and motivational causes of inequality that are designed and protected via an economic system that serves primarily the wealthiest people.

The social disorganization systematically created and maintained by laissez-faire capitalism is more obvious in some places than it is in others. For example, in many places in the United States and Europe there appears to be a fairly tranquil state of existence. Midwestern United States has a lot of rural communities that are largely economically based in agriculture and small business, seemingly never seriously touched by the industrial revolution. While many of these communities have in recent years suffered the loss of the family farm to bank foreclosures, agribusiness, and globalization, they have, for the most part, enjoyed a relatively stable and prosperous life for several generations. A glance at the Midwestern rural communities in Minnesota, Wisconsin, and Iowa would suggest that social organization can and does prevail. With the loss of family farms and the corresponding abandonment of small towns by the young, the veneer of rural stability and grass roots control is growing thin.

## The Function of Social Disorganization in Laissez-faire Capitalism

If one takes a trip to almost any major urban inner city area: New York City, Chicago, East St. Louis, and East Los Angeles, what does one find? There is usually substantial unemployment, poverty, and an underground economy that operates separately from the mainstream economy. What is the source of these conditions, and why are they maintained in their current state? How are these conditions related to similar and even more obvious cases of social disorganization in places like Iran, Iraq, Afghanistan, Columbia, and many African Countries? The social disorganization associated with the above questions is not a result of natural processes or even human negligence. It is a result of economic policies that motivate wealthy and powerful people and their corporations to systematically and purposely disrupt grass roots processes of cooperative human social organization. These economic policies, based on laissez-faire capitalism, also prevent positive human intervention to solve problems created by the systematic disruption. In sociological terms, pervasive social disorganization is functional to capitalism as capitalism is currently designed and practiced. Social disorganization maximizes one's ability to create, and take advantage of, entrepreneurial opportunities, as described above in the work of economic hit men and the implementation of the shock doctrine.

### *Confusion about "functional"*

It is easy to become confused by the sociological use of the term "functional." A part of a socially harmful structure can be functional to that harmful structure. There are many potential examples of this condition in all aspects of life. For example, a gasoline operated lawn mower that is quite functional for the purposes of maintaining a well manicured lawn is at the same time quite dysfunctional to the maintenance of a healthy environment. An intimate couple spending a lot of time with each other and very little time with their children, could be functional for their intimate relationship, but dysfunctional for the health of the larger social unit: the family. It is in this same manner that social disorganization, which is functional to a pure form of laissez-faire capitalism, is dysfunctional to the social world in general.

In places where people have managed to resist somewhat the forces of capitalism, the human capacity to create relatively well organized social arrangements can be found. Cuba, some of the Scandinavian countries, emerging South American countries, and some small communities within the United States, such as Arcata, California, and Olympia, Washington, serve as models. While these nation-states and communities have not been completely successful at avoiding capitalism, they have managed to resist laissez-faire capitalism sufficiently to mitigate the deliberate social disorganization that allows laissez-faire capitalism to thrive. People in these nation-states and communities collectively decide how their resources will be used and what kinds of businesses will be welcome: paying attention to the long term environmental, social, and economic impact of such decisions on the overall well being of most people living in those locations.

Thus, we see that the relationship between social disorganization and laissez-faire capitalism is a reciprocal one. Laissez-faire capitalism systematically creates social disorganization and social disorganization provides the optimum environment within which laissez-faire capitalism can expand. Later in this book, we will discuss how specific manifestations of social disorganization, such as crime, unemployment, discrimination, and violence, are tied into laissez-faire capitalism. Again, these manifestations are not only evidence of social disorganization, they feed back into capitalism to increase profit maximization for the few who truly benefit financially from capital investments.

### *The hidden function of "healthy" competition*

In order for advanced laissez-faire capitalism to operate as it currently does, the people living and working within the economy must be taught that competition is good. The extreme and most effective form of this understanding is that competition is actually intrinsically valuable independent of external rewards that may also be possible. That is, it is commonly believed that competition builds character, and makes one stronger. Competitive people are viewed as healthier, more balanced, and more socially desirable than non-competitive people. Anyone doubting the existence of these beliefs and/or their prevalence, can simply type "healthy competition" into an internet search engine and hit "go." The list of websites based on the notion that competition is healthy will be quite long. Competitive nonviolent games have been part of many cultures throughout history. Healthy competition is possible if all participants feel better after the game than they did before it started; otherwise how could it be considered "healthy"?

Competition is important to capitalism because accumulation, the ultimate goal of capitalism, is in large part a race. Those who can control the *most* resources, control the *cheapest* labor, sell the *most* products at the *fastest* rate and, hence, achieve the *highest* profits, win the race of accumulation. For one to do this successfully there must be laborers and managers available who automatically assume a competitive disposition toward their work. Such a disposition has to be taught at an early age, which is done through the schools, the various supporting media, and by parents who want their children to be "successful" and "normal." In other words, the competition required by capitalism becomes part of everyday life.

*Competition and militarism*

The quest for "most" and "cheapest" often intrudes into the territories of others (socio-cultural and nation-state boundaries), where a different way of life makes laissez-faire capitalism particularly unwelcome. Methods and organizations have been developed for winning control of resources and labor in "unfriendly" places. The military and the Central Intelligence Agency (CIA) are two such organizations through which innocent people of other cultures are defined as enemies, demonized, and eventually invaded and destroyed. The form of competition associated with the military and CIA is most directly related to the masculine socialization patterns typically found within a capitalist economy. Acceptable masculinity is defined early in the developmental process by winning interpersonal physical conflicts, winning at games, and ultimately winning in sports—many of which have become violent in themselves.

The competitiveness achieved through the above mentioned repetitive violent activities throughout one's youth prepares one for the competition inherent in combat: combat in the board rooms for those of higher socio-economic status, and combat in the war battlefields for those of lower socio-economic status. Both are serving the same ultimate goal of wealth accumulation. The combative board members are working primarily for themselves. The combat soldiers typically don't know the real reasons for their combat, but they too are working for the board members. Soldiers and spies are often misled by the notion that patriotism is of primary importance and that being a soldier or undercover agent is the ultimate way of expressing one's patriotism. Competition through espionage and war have also become important for controlling places where goods can be sold, euphemistically known as "opening markets" for the "global economy." People around the world must be taught to want and buy products they don't need and sometimes cannot use. A major source of tension between countries today is the deliberate devaluation of currency to incentivize people in other countries to buy products from their country. Both China and the United States have recently been accused of using this competitive strategy.

Using the language of sports is more than a metaphor. There is a direct transfer of skills, attitudes, and masculinized ways of behaving that make international aggression and invasive actions the competition known as foreign policy. In sports competition, often times the derogatory feelings and comments about and toward the "opposing" team are transferred to the fans who shout various insults at the other players—sometimes focusing on individual players. The role of the fan parallels the role of the "patriot" whose obligation is to categorically support the home military, regardless of the circumstances surrounding the military's destructive behaviors toward other beings.

*"Support the troops"*

The 2003 United States invasion of Iraq by President George W. Bush's administration is an excellent example of how the public role in the competition process works. All of the reasons provided by the Bush administration for invading Iraq were, after a long period of highly organized public deception strategies, openly demonstrated to be false by many sources inside his own administration. By the time the truth was sufficiently recognized by the public, it was too late to prevent the war. The 9/11/01 destruction of the World Trade Center was a sufficiently great disaster that an opportunity was created for illegally invading Iraq without significant public resistance.

Despite the eventual exposure of the false information upon which the Iraq war was based, people continued to support the war with many claiming, in a somewhat confused state, that they felt they had to support the troops. Hence, "supporting the troops" translates into supporting the war no matter how unjust the war or unfounded the basis for the war. How is it that people cling to what seems to be an obvious false reality in the face of blatant evidence against that reality? Like fans for the home team, the United States public is well trained to provide unconditional support no matter how much the home team violates the rules of the game or how unnecessarily aggressive the team plays. For the most part, the more devastated the opposition, the happier people are for "their" team, and the more devastated "their" team, the more they hate the opposition.

Once the war is started, the ingrained "support the home team" imperative takes over. This places an automatic positive sign between supporting the home team and the now existing war, as shown in Figure 5.1. Anyone who has ever been to a hometown football, basketball, hockey or soccer game knows that you cannot support the home team if you don't support the contest in which they are engaged.

## The Creation and Use of Public Dissonance

"Supporting the troops" in the face of blatant evidence against the need for the war becomes a cognitive trap that can be analyzed using Heider's three-point structure. Once investigative journalism was conducted (primarily by alternative presses), the reasons that were given for going to war were exposed as unsubstantiated. The relationship between that information and the existing war becomes negative as shown by a negative sign in Figure 5.1.

If individuals are exposed to the circumstance depicted in Figure 5.1, how are they likely to mentally complete the three point structure in terms of the sign between items A and B? Is that sign going to be positive or negative? Keep in mind that balance theory tells us that we strive to maintain balance among our thoughts and actions. That principle would tell us that the sign between A and B would have to be negative as depicted in Figure 5.2.

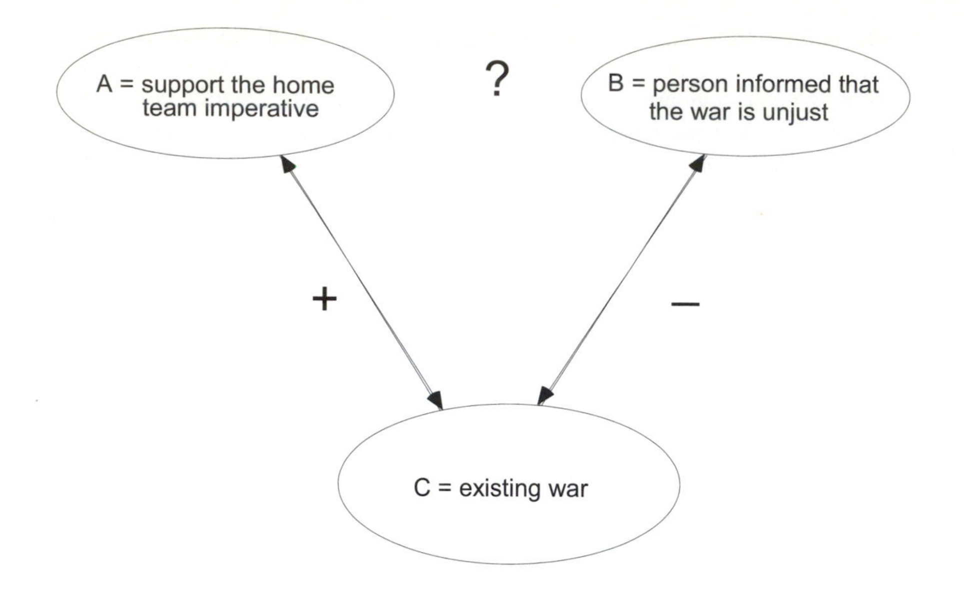


**Figure 5.1 When accurate information conflicts with past socialization**

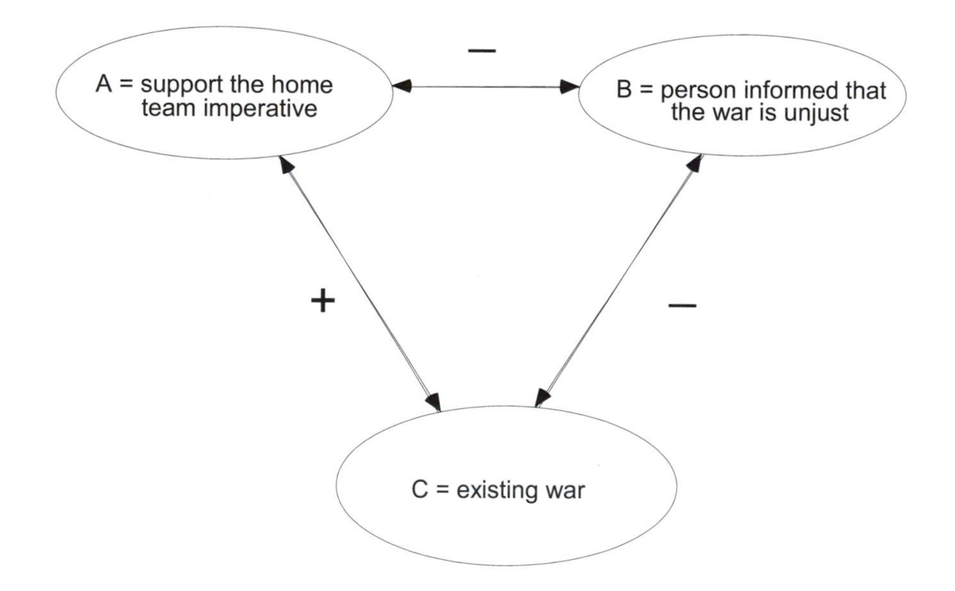


**Figure 5.2 Choosing information over past socialization**

If one multiplies the signs of the above structure (as if each sign has a value of 1) the product is positive, which conveys balance among the related thoughts. If the individual having the thoughts depicted in the above diagram commits to the belief that B is accurate, then the sign between A and B would have to be positive and the structure would be imbalanced. This imbalance would then result in cognitive dissonance for that individual based on the apparent inconsistency within the individual's thought processes. People will generally try to alleviate this kind of dissonance however they are able to do so. Social disorganization and its maintenance systematically and frequently create conditions of cognitive dissonance.

*And the survey says…*

Figure 5.2 helps demonstrate why surveys have shown so many people in the United States continuing to believe that Saddam Hussein, former ruler of Iraq, had weapons of mass destruction long after it was publicly demonstrated that he did not. Saddam Hussein was removed from power, tried as a war criminal, and executed by the United States government. He was a ruthless dictator, but the United States government put him in power. Many people continue to say they believe that Iraq was somehow responsible for the 9/11/01 attack on the World Trade Center and Pentagon, even though there is no evidence to support that conclusion. It is somewhat ironic that few people suspected the involvement of Saudi Arabia in the 9/11/01 attacks since most of the hijackers who carried out the attack were reportedly from Saudi Arabia, as is Osama Bin Laden, the supposed leader of the 9/11/01 attacks (important credible questions have been raised about what actually took place during this event: see Huff et al. 2010).

"Support the Troops" is an appeal to emotions rooted in hometown sports and jingoism. Too few people rationally consider that the best way to support troops is to keep them out of harms way. Such thinking would be akin to fans supporting their home team by telling them not to engage in the coming football game since they might injure themselves or someone else. Many parents would never think of such a thing. Indeed, many support their child's participation even if their daughter or son is already injured. An ingrained competitive spirit denies rational thought processes. What is best for all concerned in the long run (and sometimes the short run) is of little significance. Winning takes precedence over everything else. The maintenance of this disposition among all segments of the population provides the social psychological infrastructure upon which successful capitalists can build their fortunes.

## Competitiveness as a Form or Manifestation of Greed

Greed was probably not born of competitiveness, but contemporary competitiveness helps justify greed and helps individuals develop the tools to actualize greed. In terms of outcomes one must examine whether there is an actual difference between greed and competing to win at the expense of those one defeats. If competitiveness is viewed as healthy, as it seems to be in most western nation-states, and the outcome of competition is that some win and some lose (some have a lot and some have very little) then competition becomes little more than a sanitized form of greed. With competition enjoying high positive social standing, one need never think about greed if one prefers not to do so. Much of greed's work can be just as easily done under the guise of "healthy" competition. When competition becomes so extreme that it carelessly drops its "healthy" or "friendly" mask, the true reality of greed is revealed.

This is what has happened with capitalism over the last thirty years. The veil of "healthy competition" has been lifted by the extreme and rapidly growing differences in wealth within nation-states and across nation-states. Capitalism can no longer be disguised as healthy competition. Serious believers in laissez-faire capitalism, like Williams discussed in Chapter 4, must now turn to making greed an honorable motivation.

### *Patriarchy and violent masculinity*

There are only so many slots on the football team, and relatively few make it.

Unable to participate in the glorious fighting of the rival cross-town enemies, many youth experience pressure to find ways of compensating for their failure to effectively compete and for their corresponding lower status. Efforts by such individuals to elevate their status may manifest learned behaviors modeled after "heroic" media images. The identification of a group of one's peers as evil and deserving of punishment is no more difficult than attributing the same identification to the inhabitants of a distant land or even the football team of a nearby town. Scapegoat discourse is sufficiently prevalent in the media, in a young person's home, and even in the schools and churches, that it is not difficult for alienated youth, typically males, to find a target. Racial, ethnic, gendered, and class-based groups are some of the most common examples of targets.

Through movies and video games young people can experience the violent defeat of inferior losers depicted over and over again with (to the infrequent observer) staggering exaggerated imagery. To the frequent observer, such images become part of everyday life. They are normalized representations of how people relate to one another and "resolve" their differences within an environment of conquest and perpetual social disorganization.

It is important to remember that the competitive culture created to serve a capitalist economy is predominantly a masculine culture. It is men who have created and operated the capitalist system. Hence, the characteristics necessary to make capitalism work are the characteristics which define the male identity. Female identity is defined relative to the needs of the male identity. Patriarchy and masculine culture dominate in many noncapitalist systems as well—often as a means of controlling women's labor and sexuality within the immediate home environment. The competitive, tough, successful male image is particularly important for the maintenance of the imperative capitalist economy. Hence, any serious movement toward gender equality tends to involve women becoming more like men and not vice versa. Females are an obvious target group in the competitive training circles of young males. Their gender identity automatically signals their "inferiority" and vulnerability. Not complying with their expected supportive female identity role can be even more dangerous since such behaviors can be threatening to males, young and old, who are barely making it themselves within the competitive capitalist system. Sexism in general is discussed in greater detail in Chapter 7.

## Greed Reduction and Inequality?

As we listen to the mainstream corporate media news programs and read the corporate papers, it quickly becomes obvious that the economy is the all-consuming topic of discussion. The economy is presented as if it is a valuable good in itself, and as if it is independent of its effects on life and the world. The key criteria for evaluating economic exchanges should be their positive effects on all life, and the long-term future of the world. An economy is not an end in itself. It is a means by which people exchange their goods with one another and share what they need from the earth's resources. If what humans are doing is harmful to the earth and most forms of life, it would make sense that humans try something different.

It is difficult to know where to begin to bring about positive constructive change. How can cultural characteristics of competition, greed, and corresponding waste and destruction be turned into cultural characteristics of cooperation, conservation, and preservation? In other words, how do we change the norms and behavioral practices within social entities so that communities of people can plan their lives based on what is best for themselves and the future of the earth's resources, rather than on what is best for the "economy" which really means what is financially best for a few of the wealthiest capitalists?

### *Current socializing agents for greed and disorganization*

Before we can talk about re-socialization for positive social organization, we must come to terms with the current socialization process. There are three primary socializing agents within most modern western nation-states: family, schools, and media. Note the following quote about United States schools from William Boyer:

> Most twentieth century education:
>
> Trained people to become employable but not as democratic citizens
> Helped shift power to the corporations
> Ignored environmental issues

> Taught capitalist economics
> Ignored public planning
> Was nationalistic and ethnocentric. (2003: 133)

If we cannot count on schools we should still have two other socializing agents upon which we can depend, but unfortunately that is not the case. As stated by Peter Phillips, "The Americans who tune in to 24-hour TV news view the top-down stories the power elites of the world want them to hear. Consolidated media are increasingly more deeply embedded in the global corporate power structure and have become the lapdog press to agendas of inequality, globalization, militarism and empire" (2004a: 15).

If the schools are socializing us to be uncritically loyal to capitalism and the corporations, and the media has become a "lapdog press" run by and for the wealthy, that leaves only the family as a possible source of socialization that will help us replace greed, competition, and social disorganization with planned communities based on cooperation and democratic decision-making. Unfortunately, the modern western family is a by-product of the media and the schools. People socialize their children in ways that they believe will make their children most successful within the models projected by the schools and the media. Many parents today have been "educated" and misled ("dumbed down") by the same schools and media that their children are experiencing.

Hope for effective socialization and re-socialization lies within the remaining cracks left by the corporate media. The cracks of hope are known as the alternative press: those seeking and distributing information for the purpose of finding the truth rather than for personal gain or corporate profit maximization. Hope also lies with those educators and parents who have somehow escaped the full corporate socialization process and who have re-educated themselves to be able to teach socially responsible subject matter to their students and their children. Alternative media, self taught educators, and enlightened parents in the United States and around the world are creating a significant force that has the potential to create significant social chance through socialization and re-socialization programs.

### *Re-socialization programs*

One of the most maligned social experiments in the world, and yet one of the most successful, is that of post-Batista Cuba. The Cuban Revolution that began in the late 1950s is not successful just because the revolutionaries overthrew Fulgencio Batista, the ruthless dictator supported by the United States and other western countries. It was successful primarily because of the genius of Cuba's re-socialization program after Batista was removed from power. Toward that objective of re-socialization, there is no identifiable period that represents the end of the Cuban Revolution, because to most Cubans the revolution is still happening.

Under the leadership of Fidel Castro, Cuba instituted a free education system that integrated the values that most of us only lightly encounter as part of our

Sunday school lessons: greed creates problems for everyone, cooperation is the only real basis for planning, democratic planning is necessary in order to have healthy communities and avoid social disorganization, and so on. In other words, Cuba did what we do in the United States, but instead of letting capitalist economics determine the underlying curriculum, Cuba infused threads of information that would help people live healthier lives and help people better take care of the world in which they live.

Cuba is a healthier social structure overall than is the United States. How one defines "healthy" is an important issue in comparing nation-states with one another. The typical indicators are infant mortality rates, education levels, availability of health care, employment rates, and other qualities that relate to the conditions of life for most citizens.

### *The importance of schools*

The lesson learned from Cuba is that re-socialization is possible. The schools can be a powerful force in teaching people how to live in balance with other beings and the earth. Just as schools in the United States are now being used to teach students how to use the earth's resources to accumulate wealth, an alternative agenda can be addressed that benefits everyone rather than just a few. No doubt some readers will say that this is propagandizing and not educating. This response is a common control strategy. When those who are in control of information want to instill an ideology into the population it is called education. When others who are not in control of information want to provide a different way of seeing the world, it is called propaganda. The reader may want to revisit Symbolic Interactionism and Conflict Theory to further understand this process.

Controlling social reality through education has been documented by Symcox (2002), who details the strategy of the United States political administration under President George W. Bush to eliminate the inclusion of alternative perspectives within the K-12 schools throughout the United States. Our school curricula have many inaccuracies about history and about how the social world operates (Symcox 2002, Andrzejewski and Alessio 1999, Zinn 1980). In order to foster healthy social structures it is important to correct existing inaccuracies and establish curricula designed around common values that will bring people together in cooperation rather than competition. The United States education system is designed almost exclusively for the support and perpetuation of the economy, rather than for a healthy community-based lifestyle that a planned economy supports.

In addition to changing the curricula of K-12 schools to be more closely in line with the values that will build stronger communities and healthier environments (Andrzejewski et al. 2009), higher education needs to be made available to everyone. People are sometimes shocked to learn that only about twenty-eight percent (28 percent) of the adult population (25 or older) of the United States has an undergraduate bachelor's degree. Through education, especially the general education requirements that typically come with higher education degrees, people learn a great deal more about the many alternative ways of viewing the world and the realities within the world. A broad based higher education makes a person less controllable mentally, and better able to recognize the distortions created by for-profit corporate media. This is why the large corporations do not want money to go toward higher education. Additionally, corporate CEO's, boards, and think tanks want the money that does go into higher education to be put toward specialized technical programs with fewer general education requirements. In other words, they want education to be a jobs training program so they do not have to train their workers. Furthermore, corporate think tanks and corresponding lobbyists do not want workers that will question the way the corporation is run, especially if it is run in a socially irresponsible manner.

## Legitimizing Inequality

Highly educated people, as a group in general, are a threat to the agendas of the wealthy elites. California once had free higher education for all of its residents. That service was removed by Ronald Reagan when he was Governor of California. Reagan was, both as Governor and as President, an open and proud close friend of the richest people in the United States and in the world in general. His polices and decisions clearly reflected that distinction. Both as governor and president he declared war on public education, damaging the California higher education system and cutting the federal budget for education by 50 percent (Clabaugh 2004). In addition to cutting funding for education, he cut taxes for the wealthy and for corporations, and brought laissez-faire capitalism to a new level of notoriety with his trickle-down economics policies. Trickle-down economics is basically the idea that if you let corporations do whatever they want and do not require them to pay taxes, they will use their money and creativeness to find new ways of investing their fortunes. These new investments will then, theoretically, result in more jobs for the rest of the population.

Trickle-down economics is institutionalized legitimization of inequality. It is a policy that encourages rapid and highly centralized accumulation of wealth with the supposed expectation that some of that wealth will sprinkle back down on the rest of the population once the wealth is reinvested. This policy asserts that the wealthier a few people become, the more there will be to trickle down on everyone else. The popularization of trickle-down economics pushed the issue of the valence of greed a step further. Greed must be considered good if it is what drives wealthy people to become wealthier and thereby shower occasional residual benefits to others.

Aside from the problem of an explicit assumption about the right of some to be extremely wealthy and the obligation of others to be satisfied with very little, trickle-down economics does not work. It creates, instead, still greater social disorganization. The wealthy do not invest in jobs unless they absolutely have to. They prefer investing in other kinds of existing wealth. Furthermore, when the wealthy do invest in production, they invest in other places in the world where the labor is the cheapest and where there are even fewer environmental protections than here in the United States. Ronald Reagan was also an early champion of giving corporations full reign over the rest of the world. It was during his presidency that the massive exodus of corporations to third world countries began. Yet, because our population is inadequately educated, as well as misinformed by the media, most people don't realize the extent of the problems with the Reagan administration policies relative to the well being of the United States social structure. He is heralded as one of the greatest presidents in the history of the United States.

### *Education and media*

Earlier I referred to the hope that lies in the alternative media and self taught critical educators. If people learn to question the corporate owned media it will lose its socializing capabilities as a tool primarily for wealthy interests. Through greater support for better and more accessible education, people from all income backgrounds will be able to create their own grassroots forms of media. We are seeing much of this happening today with many web based forms of communication and many alternative press publications available. These forms of media are currently used primarily by the more highly educated members of the population. Increasing the number of highly educated people will bring more people into this important alternative media pool. Recognizing this potential, media giants are now struggling to seize control of the internet.

With a more cooperative based educational agenda in our schools, and with the expansion of the use of alternative forms of media, it is possible to re-socialize people away from greed and competition toward working together for a stable and safe social and physical environment. This functionally desirable outcome will not take place quickly. The current culture of greed took a long time to reach its current state, and so will its reversal. A necessary antecedent variable is a political system that recognizes education as an essential component for a healthy democratic social structure. Developing such a system is the work of many activist organizations that are currently in existence. While most social change takes place slowly, it is important to remember what Fidel Castro recognized following the removal of Batista: if you don't change the way people see the world you will soon end up right back where you started.

Without de-legitimizing greed as a basis for the way we produce and distribute the goods that we need, there is no point in doing anything else. Changing political parties, changing economic strategies, changing international policies and so forth will not mean anything without a population that understands the importance of cooperation and the social and environmental dangers of competition/greed driven policies and practices. This seemingly simple notion is a reminder of the importance of social psychology in understanding and changing social entities.

## Re-Socialization Across Socioeconomic Levels: Micro Solutions to Macro Problems

It is also the case that the children of wealth sometimes, as a result of their own re-socialization or perhaps through a liberal arts education, come to realize the problems associated with greed and, hence, the false realities upon which their family fortunes have been built. Two excellent examples of this phenomenon are Patrick Reynolds and John Robbins. Patrick Reynolds denounced his family's tobacco fortunes as a result of coming to realize the harmfulness of tobacco. He now travels the country lecturing and writing about the harmfulness of tobacco use. John Robbins, of the famous Baskin and Robbins Ice Cream Company, has completely denounced the production, sale, and consumption of, not just ice cream, but all animal products. He has become a famous author of health and environmental preservation books, and is a popular national lecturer. Both Reynolds and Robbins show the power of re-socialization. Re-socialization of the wealthy, perhaps through subsequent generations, is even more important than the re-socialization of the rest of the population because most wealthy people believe they have the most to lose by giving up their greed-based behaviors. If you listen carefully to Patrick Reynolds and John Robbins, you will find that the wealthy actually have the most to gain by giving up such behaviors.

Figure 5.3 provides a composite picture of the probable social psychological evolution of greed and its socio-economic effects leading up to imperialism through an early form of wealth expansion that involved, as Michael Parenti describes it, emperors and conquistadors mostly engaged in plunder, thief, and glory. I refer to this as a pre-capitalism state of economic greed.

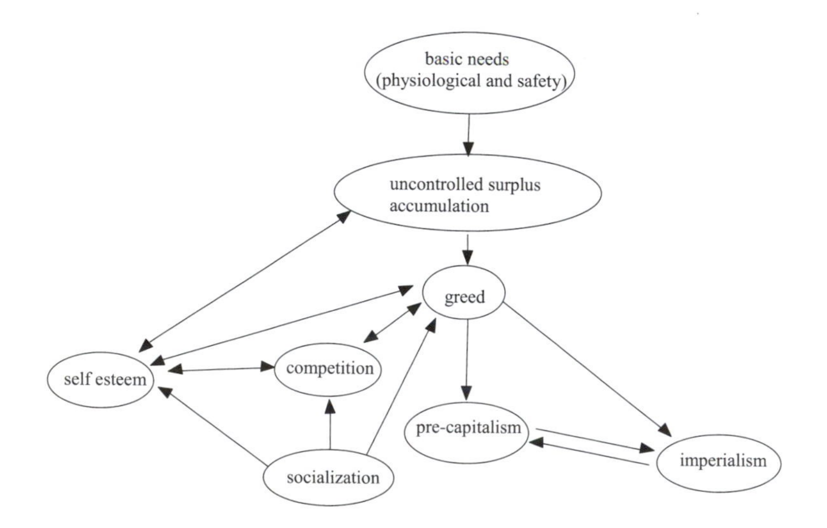


**Figure 5.3 Social psychological root causes of imperialism**

As Figure 5.3 suggests, the socialization process, carried out almost entirely through the family unit during the pre-capitalism stage, most likely included some competitiveness for survival, but not an overt form of greed. Corporate laissez-faire capitalism brings overt greed into the socialization process since capitalism, as it takes over the world, eventually becomes the primary means of survival. Positive self-regard (self esteem), however, most likely became directly associated with surplus accumulation at a very early stage in the development of human social life. The future of the world may well depend on the ability of socializing agents to socialize and re-socialize people beyond self esteem toward a self-actualizing state of existence. Such a socialization process would take as a given the negative value rightfully attached to greed and its various manifestations. Community planning and grassroots democratic decision-making will be fostered as means of replacing deliberate social disorganization with policies and programs that benefit all rather than a few.

Finally, one will notice from Figure 5.3 that the social psychological and macro socio-economic levels are still operating in relatively independent spheres of reality from what has been discussed up to this point. As the book progresses that changes and the two spheres become increasingly intertwined into one social structure.

## Chapter 6
# Social Class and Stratification

Do you ever wonder why all the nasty isms just never seem to go away: classism, racism, sexism, heterosexism and so on? These are not new problems, and it isn't that people have not been working on them for a long time. In the United States millions of dollars have been spent on anti-ism programs since the 1960s, and here we are—still talking about them. Sometimes we are led to believe that the problems are solved, and we don't need those kinds of programs anymore. I am frequently amazed at how many people with whom I speak believe that racism and sexism are no longer issues of concern for them. Yet, through a review of the data, court cases, and a discussion of personal experiences one quickly learns that such is not the case. The isms are alive and well despite continuous concerted efforts to eliminate them.

The anti-littering campaign of the 1960s and 1970s most likely cost a fraction of what the anti-ism campaigns have cost, and yet it was successful in the United States. In fact, the rather stiff fines for littering actually helped to offset the cost of the anti-littering campaign. Constitutional amendments and federal/state legislation were created to help stop the isms, while anti-littering required nothing comparable in magnitude in order to be successful. Why haven't there been similar successes with the anti-ism campaigns? Unfortunately, there is an answer to that question, and it isn't the kind of answer for which we would hope.

Conflict theory would tell us that the ability to eliminate a behavior pattern or social disposition is negatively related to the extent to which powerful people benefit from that behavior pattern or social disposition. In other words, the more powerful people have to gain from something happening, the more resources they are going to invest to make sure it continues to happen. What do wealthy powerful people have to gain from other people littering? Correct: nothing. What do wealthy powerful people have to gain from the maintenance of the isms? If you said billions of dollars you would be on the right track. It is probably trillions over an extended period of time. It is difficult to know exactly how much money is involved, but it is certainly billions per year all told. So what is the connection between the isms and wealth? What prevents the effective re-socialization of our population despite numerous programs and efforts to do so? A brief discussion of the class structure in the United States might lead toward a possible answer to that question.

The broadest separation of people into groups with variable degrees of wealth and income is what is known sociologically as the class system: a system built upon economic strata and accompanied by a complex set of sub-cultural expectations and behavioral tendencies. The class system gives stability and legitimacy to gross levels of inequality among humans, serving as the broadest human filtering process for sorting people into higher and lower status groups. All other filtering processes, commonly referred to as the "isms," are tributaries funneling people into the river of social class. This does not mean that any one ism is more or less important than the others. It means that the ultimate objective of wealthy people, regardless of the isms used, is to keep as many people as possible sufficiently far from the upper class to be able to control their labor and control most of the earth's resources. This basic idea was the fundamental principle of Karl Marx's writings that eventually became known as conflict theory, which was discussed in Chapter 2. This chapter focuses on classism (the river), and Chapter 7 will address the various other isms that feed into classism (the tributaries).

## Classism and Stratification

*Social Class* refers to specific categories of people differentiated primarily by their occupations and incomes, but also, and importantly, by the lifestyles and sub-cultural characteristics that become associated with those occupations and incomes. *Classism*, therefore, is a notion that refers to the tendency of people to judge other people, and thusly relate to other people, in accordance with their respective social classes. While people in lower classes may judge people in higher classes, problems typically only emerge in one direction, which is when people in more powerful groups judge people in less powerful groups to be inferior and less valued human beings, and treat them accordingly. The notions of "higher classes" and "lower classes" should be used with full consciousness of the purely economic basis of the "higher" and "lower" components of those labels, with "higher" meaning higher wealth and "lower" meaning lower wealth. If we do not maintain that clear awareness, there is a tendency to attach qualitative value to class level. People in higher classes are in no way better than people in lower classes. Given the power difference, there probably are more reasons to question the behavioral tendencies of people in the higher classes than the people in the lower classes, but that is not typically the way it works. It probably would be best if names were invented for the classes that do not include the notions of higher and lower. That is accomplished somewhat with the label "working class."

### *Reverse discrimination: an oxymoron*

People in lower classes, regardless of their judgments, typically have little power to create problems for the upper classes. Union organizing activities, for example, inconvenience the upper classes, but do not eliminate their huge profits, diminish their status, or harm the upper class people in any way. They do not deny them any of their fundamental rights or the material and cultural benefits they enjoy. In other words, lower power groups do not discriminate against higher power groups in the sociological sense of systemic discrimination. *Discrimination* is a systemic process by which members of a more powerful group deny members of a less powerful group equal opportunities for rewards or desired experiences, and sometimes basic rights. Discrimination is not typically thought of relative to class because social class has not been identified as a protected category under discrimination law. Sociologically, discrimination by class is extremely important. The social policies and laws protecting people from discrimination are lacking in this regard.

Since discrimination is when members of a more powerful group in some way persecute members of a less powerful group, the notion of reverse discrimination is an oxymoron. If a less powerful group were to reach a point where its members could deny more powerful group members their rights and equal opportunities, they then would become the more powerful group, which makes them the discriminators, and not the reverse discriminators. Individuals of a more powerful group can be denied their privilege as a member of that powerful group, as sometimes happens through programs like Affirmative Action, but that is not to be construed as discrimination. A privilege is not a right, and implies inequality by its meaning. In fact, programs like Affirmative Action are often times self-imposed concessions in order to avert organized rebellions by less powerful groups against the gross injustices of actual discrimination. This discussion is not meant to imply that individuals in more powerful groups cannot be mistreated in a variety of ways and by a wide variety of people from various groups. Such incidents are simply not discrimination related to their membership in that more powerful group.

## The Law and Discrimination

When looking at the confusion surrounding the notion of discrimination we see how delicate social reality can be. The sociological term of discrimination eventually found its way into the courts as a result of anti-discrimination legislation and constitutional amendments. The legal system operates in somewhat of a circular manner. It takes a concept into a trial and bounces it around the courtroom for a few days. In some important instances the winner of the trial, by virtue of the victory alone, has redefined the concept. It is in this way that "precedence" becomes a primary operating component of the United States legal system. Once a victory is won, a precedent has been set, and all relevant important concepts bend to fit that precedent. So it is with discrimination and other terms related to the isms. It does not matter how illogical the notion of reverse discrimination may be, as soon as one member of a powerful group is able to prevail in a legal case where "reverse discrimination" is claimed, the precedent creates the term "reverse discrimination" and the concept of discrimination is compromised.

The legal context of the emergence of the notion "reverse discrimination" took prominence in the University of California v. Bakke case decided in 1978, where Bakke claimed he was not admitted to medical school in order for the University to admit members of excluded groups. Bakke won his Supreme Court case on the grounds that quotas, not Affirmative Action, were illegal. But since that time there have been so many conflicting interpretations of that legal precedent that new precedents have been set and the court battles continue, with Affirmative Action sometimes winning and sometimes losing. The point is that so called "reverse discrimination" cases flourish without careful regard for the original intent or actual meaning of the term discrimination: powerful groups discriminate against less powerful groups and not the other way around. Until discrimination ceases altogether, which is unlikely in our lifetime, there needs to be ways of adjusting for its effects, and Affirmative Action is one of those ways relative to employment and educational practices.

*Classism's exclusion from affirmative action*

Affirmative Action addresses many of the isms, but does not address classism. That should not be surprising. While all of the isms contribute to greater accumulation of wealth for the upper classes, it is the class structure itself that most directly manifests the effects of the other isms toward the objective of greater profits for the wealthy. Discrimination with respect to all of the excluded group categories: peoples with disabilities; women; peoples of color; gay, lesbian, bisexual, transgender (GLBT) people; people from certain religious and ethnic backgrounds; and older people, assures the availability of predetermined criteria for maintaining and even enhancing the class structure in its current form. The world is taught, by various subtle and not so subtle means, that if you are from one of the above mentioned groups you should expect to be less employable and thereby poorer than everyone else. This does not mean that everyone that is poor is from those particular groups. It means that people from those groups are over represented among the underpaid and poorer classes.

There are also many able bodied White males who are poor. Under these circumstances the people from the excluded groups serve a double function within the class structure. They provide a ready cache of poor people for cheap labor and they provide a ready scapegoat for poor White men who are not from the excluded groups. People from the excluded groups named above are commonly blamed for taking the jobs of White men in the lower classes who are not from the named excluded groups. Not being in one of the above named groups gives White men a sense of entitlement of better treatment, and when that doesn't happen they can blame excluded group people for their plight. Scapegoating excluded group people is, unfortunately, sometimes increased by the existence of Affirmative Action Programs—programs designed to assure the inclusion of people from otherwise above named excluded groups. Since affirmative action programs were never extended to social class, affirmative action sometimes results in unsuccessful White men claiming that the jobs they would have had were stolen by "unqualified" people—that is, people from the various *other* excluded groups named earlier who fit under the canopy of affirmative action programs. Scapegoating can also take place among the named excluded groups and can be complicated, especially since some members of the named excluded groups do make it into the higher classes.

The problem does not lie in people from the lower classes stealing jobs from one another via other excluded group identities. The problem lies first in the artificially created condition that all people must hold jobs and do so within a capitalist economy in order to survive. Secondly there are not enough livable wage jobs for everyone who needs one, especially everyone in the working class and other lower classes. Because they are the victims of discrimination, people in the above named groups are often times over-qualified for the jobs they hold. Notwithstanding, when people from excluded groups do not do a good job they are pointed to as the embodiment of all that is wrong with affirmative action, and they are used as justification for future scapegoating and discrimination. The equivalent of this process does not take place when a non-excluded group person is incompetent and does not do a good job. Often times other people will try to cover for that person and make excuses for him. What is important to remember, however, is that people from the working and lower classes also suffer their own form of discrimination regardless of their status relative to the other isms. Furthermore, the primary purpose of discrimination based on non-class isms is to make sure that there is an ample supply of people making up the working and lower classes to meet upper class labor demands. Eliminating discrimination by social class would eliminate capitalism as it is currently practiced in the Western world.

### *Who is responsible?*

Lower status groups within a social setting did not and do not create the higher status groups. They couldn't intentionally create them; but why would they if they could? It is the other way around. The higher status groups create the lower status (lower valued) groups as the only means by which they can establish themselves as "higher." Once established as "higher" they then grant themselves permission to use the lower social classes for their own economic and social benefits.

Ask yourself this simple question: "Would you choose to be poor?" There are, of course, monks and religious sisters who would answer in the affirmative. There may be others, but the vast majority of the people in the world would most likely not hesitate to say "no." So then answer this question: "would you choose to be wealthy?" Undoubtedly, most people would say "yes." If you answered "yes" to this last question and you are not wealthy, that can only mean one thing. You are not in control of who gets to be wealthy and who does not. As it turns out, you are in good company because few people in the world are truly monetarily and materially wealthy. If you cannot attain enough wealth to be considered wealthy you are not directly responsible for the inequality related to classism—albeit we are all indirectly responsible to some degree. You have not created and are not maintaining the various groups that constitute social class.

On the other hand if you are wealthy, you might be able to argue that your generation did not create the class structure, but you certainly could not claim that you are not playing a major role in maintaining it. What can you do to make up for your contribution to the problems created by inequality? You could give up your wealth, but more importantly, you could recognize that your wealth comes from the labor of the people who are not wealthy and/or those who are the working poor. You could make sure that your wealth did not come from the exploitation of other people and the environment. The point is that only wealthy people truly have the power to make those decisions. Everyone else can only try to figure out ways of either convincing or forcing the wealthy to do the right thing for other people and for the world in general.

Free market capitalism is not working as promoted, and it cannot continue without doing extensive long term damage to most forms of life and the ecosystem. Unfortunately, Economics is dominated by the free market paradigm. There has been little incentive or opportunity for thinking outside the Western driven free market economics box.

## The Class Structure and Inequality

There are two components that constitute social class. The first and most obvious is the economic component: how much income and wealth does a person have? The second component, not completely separate from the first, is that of sub-cultural characteristics. The first component, economic, is the primary basis for what sociologists refer to as economic stratification. Stratification consists of the layers of a population relative to the income, wealth, and social standing (privilege) of those layers. Strata can be represented within individual countries or within other identifiable aggregates of people. Typically American sociologists refer to stratification as it pertains to the United States—occasionally referring to stratification in the world in general. Unlike strata of the earth's surface, characterizations of socio-economic stratification are somewhat arbitrary since nice neat brackets of people by income, wealth, and/or sub-cultural characteristics are not always clearly discernible in real life.

Any breakdown encountered of social classes in the United States is most likely a breakdown primarily by economic stratification, tending to ignore the sub-cultural/occupational components of social class. The issue of class sub-cultural characteristics is complicated by mid-twentieth century writings suggesting the existence of a culture of poverty. The culture of poverty concept is related to the belief that the poor lived in a culture that created and maintained poverty. This claim was first made by Oscar Lewis (1959), and was later supported by other authors, such as Banfield (1970). Identifying a culture of poverty, which is a "blaming the victim" approach to analyzing poverty, is not the same as recognizing that the various classes have sub-cultural differences. Different levels of wealth can create different lifestyles that can be transmitted across generations. This should not be surprising to anyone. The lifestyles of the wealthy contain opportunities for accumulating more wealth and the lifestyles of the poor do not. That should not be surprising to anyone either. These simple pieces of harsh reality should not be confused with how the wealthy typically attain their wealth in the first place, or how the poor become and remain poor.

The simplest breakdown that one will find is a four strata structure. Finer breakdowns are sometimes used as well. The most common four categories are: Upper Class = approximately 3 percent of the population, Middle Class = about 40–45 percent, Working Class = 35–40 percent, Lower Class = 15–20 percent. The rough estimates of the percentage of the population within each class represent acknowledgement that we do not have a completely clear breakdown of the class structure. Some people who have a lot of money and resources have low status occupations while some people with relatively high status occupations have low wealth and/or income. Sometimes this inconsistency is built into an occupation (status inconsistency) and sometimes it is due to other circumstances.

More important than status inconsistency in terms of explaining the lack of precision in the identified class structure, is the downward mobility that has been taking place in the United States over the last several decades (Leicht and Fitzgerald 2007). This downward mobility forces people from the middle class, or their children, into the new working class, which is a class that is now heavily made up of underpaid service workers. The low paying service jobs, that are not livable wage jobs, have replaced the livable wage working class union jobs that were eliminated when the large corporations moved their industries to other countries or disinvested in production. This transition has created some confusion about what actually are the working class jobs in the United States today and the extent to which there still exists a middle class. Perrucci and Wysong (2008: 29) have identified a class structure that is quite different than earlier models, containing a privileged class and a new working class. Within the privileged class are: superclass (six and seven figure incomes and large investment capital: 1–2 percent of population), managers (six and seven figure incomes: 13–15 percent of population), and professionals (lower to upper six figure incomes: 4–5 percent of population). Within the new working class are: comfort class (nurses, teachers, union carpenters etc. $35–50K: 10 percent of population), wage earners (clerical, sales, machine operators etc.: 50 percent of population), self-employed (no employees, low income: 3–4 percent of population), and excluded class (in and out of labor force: 10–15 percent of population).

For the purposes of this book I will not discuss all of the strata within the United States class structure. However, it will be useful to discuss the upper class since the upper class has the greatest amount of control over the construction of social reality. It is important to understand how exclusive and powerful people in the upper class can be. Early models of the class structure identify two general categories of the upper class: upper-upper (Perrucci and Wysong's 2008 superclass) and lower-upper.

### *Upper-upper and lower-upper classes*

The upper-upper class represents about one percent of the total population of the United States. These are basically the people who run the world. It might be more accurate to say that these are the people who keep the world in a permanent state of social disorganization for their own material benefit. That one percent roughly represents the top one percent of the income scale in the United States, but not exactly. The upper-upper class people are sometimes referred to as the old rich because typically great wealth has been in their families for several generations. There may be some people in the lower-upper class who have more money than some of the upper-upper class people but who do not have the socio-political power of old wealth. Bill Gates, considered the wealthiest person in the world for about 12 consecutive years, might be considered lower-upper class since most of his extreme wealth was created in one generation, and since his behavioral characteristics do not fit the upper-upper class profile.

Upper-upper class people are somewhat reclusive and live secluded private lives. They are not typically the people that you see on the front page of the newspaper or on the cover of a popular magazine, as is frequently the case with Bill Gates. Lower-upper class people are people of wealth without necessarily the long standing roots into socio-political power and privilege. Despite their extreme wealth, they might not have as much direct access to political power through world leaders as the upper-upper class.

The upper classes, especially the upper-upper class, have lives that are not remotely similar to the rest of the people in the world. They have private jets and can fly wherever they choose any time they want. For example, an upper class person may frequently fly to other countries to shop for a few days, or to simply spend a few days in one of their other homes located in the Swiss Alps or on the Riviera. They have private lawyers, accountants, and even physicians. Their homes are fully staffed with cooks, maintenance people, gardeners and so on. There is practically nothing they could not have if they want it. Upper class people do not work for anyone else. They do not hold jobs like the rest of the population. Some may play a direct role in managing their own investments, but they also hire others to do that for them.

### *What are our chances?*

When we come to understand how exclusive and different the upper-upper class people are from the rest of us we more fully appreciate the deceptiveness built into the American dream. What are the odds of being in the upper class of the United States? If we take a simplistic approach, they are not difficult to calculate: 3:100 (based on 3 percent of the population). What are the odds of being in the lower class? Again, it can appear to be quite simple: 20:100. But the odds are misleading because becoming upper class is not a random event. Most of the upper class wealth is inherited, and the upper-upper class, especially, maintains closed social circles.

For the average person in the United States the possibility of becoming upper class is far less than 3 in 100. The forces of upper class power repel newcomers. If they did not repel newcomers the exclusivity of the upper class social standing would be diminished, and exclusivity is an important benefit of being upper class, especially upper-upper class. Most of that three percent (one percent in the case of upper-upper class) is a function of some birth related characteristic: existing family wealth; White, male, a particular physical body type (as in tall fast athletes of which only a few "make it"); or a particular appearance (as in famous actors, of which only a few "make it"). Under these circumstances, for those who do not have a special inroad to the upper class, it would most likely be more accurate to say that a person's odds of being in the upper class are closer to 3:1,000,000. A person who is not advantaged in some particular way has a far better chance of going to jail or prison than becoming a member of the upper-class, especially if that person is from an excluded group. For every 100,000 White men in the United States there are approximately 773 White men in jail or prison. For every 100,000 Black men in the United States, there are 4,618 in jail or prison (DrugWarFacts 2008). Clearly, the chances of non-wealthy people being incarcerated are far greater than their chances of someday being in the upper class.

Unlike upper class people, lower class people do not forcefully repel others from becoming part of their class. They are, for the most part, indifferent. Furthermore, and somewhat ironically, the greater the size is of the lower class, the greater the power and wealth of the upper class. Hence, the forces of upper class power are continually pressing the rest of the population downward toward the lower class. One might say, "Well, the lower class people don't have jobs for the most part, how could they be making wealth for the upper class?" The answer is simple. The lower class is the labor pool reserve. The larger that reserve, the less everyone else has to be paid because there are many other people waiting to take each available job. The less everyone in the working population is paid, the more profits there are for the wealthy. As capitalism is currently designed, its success depends on a large section of the population being unemployed and poor. The success of uncontrolled capitalism is measured by indicators that serve the wealthy—not the rest of the population.

*With which class would you identify?* It is important, therefore, for non-wealthy people to realize that they are far closer to being lower class than they are to being upper class. Furthermore, the average person in the United States has far more in common with lower class people than with upper class people. This is not an easy piece of information to accept given the heavy socialization into the American dream, which tells us we too can become wealthy and that there is no limit to our successes if we work hard enough.

One might think, "If working hard is not going to get me into the upper class, why should I bother?" This is a good question and the answer is important. While working hard is not typically necessary or sufficient in order for someone from an upper class background to remain in the upper class, working hard is necessary for everyone else in the population to successfully avoid being in the lower class. Furthermore, hard work, while necessary for most people, may not be sufficient to avoid being in the lower class. As much as we are taught to scorn lower class people, most of them are not where they are for lack of a willingness to work (Eley 2008). It is much easier to end up in the lower class than one might think.

*Abject poverty*

People are poor when they cannot attain what their immediate social world defines as necessary for a reasonably comfortable life. There are many people who are without the basic items needed for decent health and survival: a warm house, healthy food and water, and clean air. But poverty is far more complicated than that. One can have the basic necessities of life for physical survival but live in conditions that are overly burdensome, stressful, and oppressive; conditions that communicate to a person that they are not as good as others around them and that they, therefore, must settle for a life that is always close to the edge. People living on or close to the edge never know for certain whether they will be able to continue at their current pace of work, or they are constantly reminded that their children will be disadvantaged relative to the other children around them. If a family does not have medical insurance they must worry about family illnesses to a much greater degree than if they did have medical insurance. Of course, if someone does get sick that elevates the stress tenfold again. Foregoing payment on new tags for one's car in order to buy something a little special for the holiday creates still another new worry about being in trouble with the criminal justice system. Such is the life of someone in abject poverty. It is a life of continual struggle and oppression by one's surrounding socio-economic structure; a life of few freedoms and very little control of one's external environment.

According to the Access Project (2010), the United States federal government defines poverty for the contiguous United States as anyone making under $10,830 a year. For a two person family the cut off is $14,570. Those values change slightly over time with inflation. Saying that a couple in the United States making about $14,570 a year in 2010 is not poor indicates a lack of understanding of what it is like to survive on that much money. For a family of four in 2010 the designated amount is $22,050, which shows again a lack of understanding of how difficult it is to raise children on such a meager income. It is difficult to imagine trying to nurture a family of four on about $22,000 a year today. Given the excessive pressures placed on everyone just to lead a relatively "normal" life, $22,000 a year would not even come close to keeping a family of four, most likely two adults and two children, out of abject poverty.

*Global stratification for the global economy*

As the global economy expanded, the wealthy people of the world became wealthier and the rest of the population of the world became poorer. Global stratification is a term used most often to refer to the wealth gaps between all nation-states. This way of viewing global stratification, while useful in many respects, tends to limit our view of the process of globalizing the economy, a process built on reduction/elimination of national boundaries. Globalization has a profound impact on stratification within nation-states and across nation-states.

While no population in the world has as large a gap between the rich and poor as the population of the United States, the populations of other countries like China are becoming far more stratified than they had been in the past. Furthermore, the increased stratification in countries like China is not due simply to increased wealth at the top, but decreased wealth at the bottom as well. It cannot be otherwise, for the wealth that is created at the top is extracted from the lives of the people at the bottom.

First the interests of the primary corporate investors are served, making a few already wealthy people here in the United States and other Western countries far wealthier. Second, because the jobs are moved from the United States to places like China, there is a significant increase in poverty in the remainder of the United States population, thus creating a huge income and wealth gulf in the United States. Thirdly, the general populations of China and many other countries are consumed into a quasi-slave labor force, which reduces these populations to the lowest denominator of the poverty of capitalism. Observe the following quote from Davin discussing the excess Chinese rural labor force and its officially "restricted" migration to urban areas. "The situation has some real advantages for the state. The fast growing economy had access to a cheap but highly flexible labour force. Not only could extra labour be recruited at short notice, the uncertain legal status of unofficial migrants meant that they could be rounded up and returned to their villages when there was a downturn in the economic activity" (Davin 1999: 42). This process is similar to the unofficial/official practices in place to employ and deport illegal Mexican's used to pick fruit and vegetables in Southwestern United States.

Fourthly, some people in the exploited countries become part of the wealthy classes by providing the intermediate industries that are needed in the producing countries: transport companies, certain component companies, and retail industries all thrive and produce a wealthy class within the exploited countries. They can also quickly grow and have their own production industries.

The result of this general process of economic globalization is an ever increasing gap between the wealthy and the remaining populations of the world. While a few new wealthy people are added to the global stratification system, proportionally far more people are added to the growing lower classes of the world, reaching across national boundaries and looking more alike over time. The media pictures of sweatshops and poverty are increasingly more difficult to differentiate from country to country. The two primary ingredients of wealth production are labor and resources. Maximizing profits depends on the extraction of both labor and resources, to the maximum extent possible, from as many people as possible at the lowest attainable cost. When I say "as many people as possible" I include the vast number of people who make up the labor pool reserve by having no income and no viable means of sustaining themselves and their families.

*Why globalize the capitalist economy?*

If the globalization of the economy would not have increased the economic gap between the rich and the rest of the population, there would not have been any motivation for the wealthy to make it happen. The confinement of production industries to the Western countries where the wealthy people reside was not producing the maximum results possible because the labor costs and environmental protection laws (however weak) served as obstacles to huge profit increases. The wealthy from Western nation-states could not demand as much direct deprivation from the workers in their own countries as they could in other non-industrialized nation-states. Also, environmental protection laws in Western nation-states, however weak, made it relatively more difficult and costly, than would be the case in other nation-states, to exploit available natural resources.

Greater profits come from a broader base of labor supply and resource extraction. More workers mean less pay for all workers. Less pay for all workers means more wealth for the wealthy and more poverty for everyone else. It is important to keep in mind that alternative economies, like subsistence farming, are not made up of people waiting around to become part of the global workforce. The people of these economies must be forced into the global workforce in order to assure the absolute maximization of profits for global capitalists.

Whose idea was it to globalize capitalism? Was it the non-wealthy segments of the population? Were there international conferences of representatives of all the working people of the world established to discuss the possibility of globalizing the economy around the principles of capitalism? Of course there were no such meetings. There were, however, meetings of the wealthy capitalist think tanks to strategize on ways to make the globalization of capitalism happen. There were also massive demonstrations in the United States and in other countries representing widespread opposition to the globalization of the capitalist economy. These demonstrations protested the passage of the laws, like NAFTA and GATT, which essentially relegated national constitutions to secondary status relative to corporate appointed international business committees established to oversee economic globalization via the World Trade Organization.

*Implications of class sub-cultural characteristics*

As we look at the different class characteristics identified above in this chapter, we are not just seeing coincidental group behavioral formations. Cultural and sub-cultural characteristics of groups of people are created within long standing social and environmental contexts. Peoples of various locations adopt behavior patterns and rituals consistent with the food, weather, vegetation, and natural protections or dangers of their particular geography and human/non-human neighbors. What is the context of social class sub-cultural characteristics? Is it any of the above mentioned socio-environmental factors? No, it does not seem to be.

The context of the evolution of social class sub-culture is the economic imperative of the wealthy capitalists. As we look at the characteristics of the various classes, we see that working and lower classes are designed to accept their fate—they internalize their life condition and learn to be satisfied with what they have been dealt. If anything, there is an expectation that things could get worse at any moment, and they often times do. This disposition of the lower classes is important in order to keep this large segment of the population ready for the worst demands of the economy. The working class had this disposition offset by the prevalence of labor unions during the middle part of the twentieth century, which is why the upper class felt they had to destroy the labor unions. Working class people were not only seen as taking too much of what the upper class claimed as their wealth, the working class was not sufficiently flexible to fill the various labor slots the upper class wanted to fill. When one considers the millions of good paying working class jobs that have been eliminated over a relatively short period of time, one can't help but wonder how the working class people allowed this to happen to the extent that it has. The process of breaking the unions and denigrating the working class has been well planned and methodical. Wealth driven think tanks and political groups have set the middle class against the working class with phrases like "we can't have the tail waging the dog" or "the unions have gone too far."

The middle classes, on the other hand, are the show pieces of the American Dream. Their job is to keep production moving at a faster rate in order to achieve that ever illusive upward mobility into the upper class, which rarely and only coincidentally, happens. The middle classes, especially the upper middle class, are shaped into the sub-cultural illusion of being better than the lower classes and always just at the brink of moving into the upper class. This disposition generates a great deal of middle class work on behalf of the upper class (by accountants, managers, architects, contractors, consultants, etc.) and contributes greatly to upper class wealth. The professional veneer that middle class people work under is a pretext for work without end. You go home when the work is done, and the work is never really done. So, when you do go home you take your work with you or spend the night worrying about it or possibly both. The upper middle class big home with the nice front yard which comes with huge monthly payments to the bank, the sizable new car payments, payments to the private schools for one's children, and the credit card payments for the vacation long since passed, all add up to a social reality out of control.

If the sub-culture of the middle class was built on living a relatively simple life without status driven consumerism and the perpetual race for a "better" life, the treadmill would turn too slowly and production for the upper class profits would not be acceptable to the upper class investors. Much of the control that middle class people believe they have is an illusion of control. As circumstances become more difficult for the working and lower classes, the middle classes are next in line for having their labor and wealth extracted: lower pay, longer hours for those with jobs, and minimal employment. Yet, the sub-cultural characteristics of the middle class keep the people of the middle class ever nimble and always ready to jump through another new hoop in order to hold their position within the class system.

## Economic Stratification

### *Wealth and income*

Available evidence indicates that the gap between rich and poor has been increasing over the last approximate 40 years at a rapid rate and continues to do so (Bassett 2010a, Domhoff 2010, Johnston 2007, Feagin et al. 2006, Lardner and Smith 2005, Wolff 2003, Mueller 1999). For example, the wealth of the richest 2 percent of United States families nearly doubled during the period from 1984 to 2005, while the poorest quartile of families became poorer (Science News 2007). The level of wealth inequality in the early part of the twenty-first century is almost double what it was in the 1970s (Wolff 2003). In 2003 the top 1 percent of the United States population owned approximately 58 percent of all United States based corporate wealth, which is a 50 percent increase from 1991. The bottom 20 percent of the population on the other hand saw a loss of 57 percent of the corporate wealth during that same time period, owning 0.6 percent of corporate wealth (Johnston 2006).

Income disparity over the same time period is comparable to wealth disparity. From 1967 to 2003 the portion of total income attained by the top 20 percent of the population increased from 43.8 percent to almost 50 percent, while the portion of total income attained by the bottom 20 percent dropped (Lardner and Smith 2005). Similar data have been reported by Domhoff (2010). The top 5 percent alone increased its portion of the national income from 17 percent in 1960 to 22 percent in 2002 (Feagin et al. 2006). A similar way of looking at that same issue is to note that "The income ratio of the top 5 percent of earners to the bottom 20 percent … increased from 6.3 in 1967 to 8.6 in 2003" (Lardner and Smith 2005: 31). Analyses of tax returns, which are conservative estimates for the wealthy, indicate a 148 percent increase in income for the top 1 percent of the United States population from 1973 to 2000. The lower 90 percent of the population saw a 7 percent decline in income during the same period (Lardner and Smith 2005). Indeed, the income of the top 1 percent of the United States population is greater than the income of the entire "bottom" 90 percent of the population (Pizzigati 2004). The gap between the top 1 percent of the United States population and the lowest 20 percent of the population has more than tripled over the last thirty years (Sherman and Stone 2010). Yet, income taxes have continuously decreased for the wealthy and increased for most other people (Zepezauer 2004, Bartlett and Steele 1994).

Looking at non-wealthy groups one finds the entire lower 80 percent of households within the United States control only about 16–20 percent of the country's wealth, and the bottom 18–20 percent of the population has essentially no wealth at all when assets are weighed against debt (Lardner and Smith 2005, Wolff 2003). During the twelve years from 1980 to 1992 the annual income of the top one percent of people filing taxes increased by 215 percent (unadjusted for inflation), which is three times the rate of inflation during that same time period. The incomes of the vast majority of everyone else in the population did not keep up with inflation during that 12-year period. The bottom 80 percent of the population saw their share of the nation's income drop by 10 percent from 1979 to 2003 while the top 1 percent saw their share of the total United States annual income increase by 20 percent during that same period (Domhoff 2010). Similar data have been reported by Bartlett and Steele 2006). The top 1 percent of the population has 33 percent of the wealth in the United States, but the group with the fastest growing income is the top 0.01 percent, many of whom are CEOs of large multinational corporations. CEO income has increased dramatically since 1970, going from 79 times the income of average production workers to 431 times in 2004 (Heiner 2010, Aslam 2005). The gap between CEO pay and plant worker pay has increased over 500 percent since 1990 (Eitzen and Leedham 2004). Some countries have laws preventing CEO salaries exceeding a certain amount over the average worker's pay. CEO salaries in some European countries are no greater than 20 to 30 times the salaries of the production workers in those companies (Eitzen and Leedham 2004).

One might argue that everyone is better off in the United States since the workers are so much better paid here than in places like Europe. That argument is not accurate. European countries such as Germany, Switzerland, Austria, and even the European Union as a whole, have higher average pay for production workers than does the United States. Commensurate with the demise of unions, the average weekly wages of workers in "constant dollars" in the United States were actually lower in 2005 than they were in 1972. In comparing the bottom 20, 40, 60, or 80 percent of the population with the top 20 percent, the United States has the greatest gap relative to the income distributions of the 16 richest countries in the world (Hurst 2010). This is further evidenced by the United States having the highest Gini Index score of those same 16 nations. The Gini Index is a standardized 0–1 value that reflects the amount of income inequality in a population. The United States is also lowest on other important indicators of equality and health, such as the percentage of children in poverty (Smeeding 2008).

### *Two hundred and sixty-eight thousand dollars an hour*

According to Forbes.com, the 2009 annual income for the top ten CEO's in the United States ranged from $61.3 million (Deere & Co. CEO) to $557 million (Oracle CEO) (DeCarlo and Zajac 2009). In many places in the United States today a person is quite fortunate to be paid $15 an hour, which comes to $31,200 a year, based on an eight hour day and a five day a week job. Many college graduates are making less than that amount. If one breaks down the Oracle CEO pay to the same eight hour a day, five day a week time-frame, the Oracle CEO 2008 compensation comes to $267,788 an hour, an amount that is greater than the combined *annual* salaries of three university full professors at many universities. The questions that a person making $15 an hour has a right to ask are: "How hard can a person work to earn that much more than I earn?" Is it really possible to work that hard? Or maybe it is speed that makes the difference. How fast might a person work to expect to be paid that much money per hour: "faster than a speeding bullet?" Perhaps the real issue is intelligence! How smart must a person be to justify being paid over 267 thousand dollars an hour? Maybe someone qualifying for that much money per hour has an unusually large brain that requires an oversized head or another separate body compartment. Pictures of these CEOs show no such unusual features.

While it might be humorous to imagine the basis for income differences, the causes of the disparities are important to understand. The questions just asked help us get past some of the false assumptions about income. If we think carefully we know that there are no human qualities that justify the current differences in income in the United States. These are questions seldom asked by the average person working a job in the United States. It is assumed that the standard reasons given in one's education and in the media throughout our lives are reasonable justification for the painfully comical difference in the incomes of people who are basically the same in all important respects.

The importance of the above statistics does not lie in the exact values. What is important about the provided information is that the striking gaps between levels of wealth and income have existed for a long time, and those gaps have dramatically increased rather than decreased over time. We do not need to update these figures every year or even every five years to understand the important issues related to inequality. Those issues are imbedded in the theories that inform us about the nature of social reality, the systemic problems emerging out of greed, and the oscillating nature of those problems as they are fed by carefully constructed institutions designed strictly for the self-interests of a few wealthy people.

## Global Stratification

The growing wealth gap is not restricted to the United States. Determining the number of poor people in the world is very difficult for many reasons (Reddy and Pogge 2005); but even the most conservative estimates show poverty at around 25 percent of the world's population (The World Bank 2010), an estimate considered to be quite low by others (Reddy and Pogge 2005). Policies involving The World Bank are considered by many to be main causes of world poverty (Cobb and Diaz 2009, Stiglitz 2008, Perkins 2004, Parenti 1995). Yet, The World Bank projects itself as the leading authority on world poverty and poverty reduction. Their methodologies for measuring poverty periodically change to demonstrate positive outcomes when such outcomes are not reflected in reality, which can be observed by carefully examining their information (The World Bank 2010) or by reviewing analyses of their methods (Reddy and Pogge 2005). At one time The World Bank projected poverty figures as high as 44 percent of the world population.

The complexity of determining global poverty levels and change in poverty levels over time can be observed in the example of China. Using The World Bank poverty line of $1.25/day, China is reported to have gone from 85 percent poverty in 1981 to 15.9 percent poverty in 2005 (Grameen Foundation 2010). What does this mean? What would a critical theorist tell us—someone who can peel away the various layers of reality? This is an important question because 90 percent of the people The World Bank claims moved above the poverty line since the 1980s are from China. Does the claim that the number of people in China making less than $1.25 per day changed from 85 percent of the population to 15.9 percent tell us that poverty has decreased in China?

The above question cannot be answered outside of the context of understanding globalization. As pointed out by Stiglitz (2008) and Hurst (2010) globalization has had serious detrimental effects on world populations with respect to inequality and poverty, including within the United States. As multinational corporations moved to other countries they made the non-wealthy segments of the United States poorer since those people had fewer employment opportunities. The countries to which the corporations moved had to make adjustments to accommodate the powerful corporations being assisted by the United States government (Cobb and Diaz 2009, Perkins 2004, Parenti 1995). Communal land was privatized or taxed so that the billions of peasants worldwide could no longer live a subsistence life. These strategies forced the peasants into the private international workforce. Few Westerners understand the difference between being a peasant and being poor. They are not the same thing and are not closely related outside the context of corporate labor-force recruitment. Peasants can live a healthy and happy life if left alone by outside forces. The disruption of peasant culture for the purpose of labor recruitment is not new, going back to the turn of the twentieth century when peasants were recruited from various places around the world, like Southern Europe, using various unethical strategies to force them to immigrate to the United States and other industrializing countries. Contemporary globalization is the same process, but inverted. Instead of bringing the peasants to the corporations, the corporations move to the peasant populations.

Using The World Bank poverty criterion of less than $1.25/day, all peasants are poor, because they live off the land and have no income to speak of. As soon as they are forced into the capitalist economy as part of the global corporate workforce and are given $1.25/day, they are purportedly no longer poor. This process does not eliminate poverty, but instead systematically creates it by forcing peasants into a life of both absolute and abject poverty. Cross-culturally, poverty cannot be defined simply by the absence of a monetary income. The minimal amount of pay received by those who migrate to the cities for work does not nearly offset the cost of urban living and the demands of urban culture. Abject poverty in the colonized world is even greater than it is in the United States and other similar Western countries (Hurst 2010). Globalization has increased inequality in most of the rest of the world as well as in the United States (Hurst 2010, Cobb and Diaz 2009, Stiglitz 2008), and China is not an exception (Thakur 2005).

Defenders of the current economic system argue that increased wealth for the wealthy does not hurt anyone because it does not make others poorer, but better off. That is, their wealth trickles down to create greater wealth for the poor of the world, a position most stanchly held by the Reagan Administration in the 1980s. There is no evidence to support this claim (Stiglitz 2008). The extreme wealth of a few is not only created from the work of many other humans, but also from the exploitation of other forms of life, the environment, and the non-renewable resources of the earth: resources that will not be available for future generations and that, when destroyed, disrupt the balance of the earth's delicate ecosystem. The social and biological structures of the earth are continuously being adjusted for the simultaneous creation of future wealth for a few and future poverty for many.

The goal of people focused on wealth accumulation is to assure maximum profits that largely occur by making sure as little wealth as possible is returned to the workers creating the wealth. These workers make up the vast majority of the world's population. The success of the wealthy in this regard is actually evidenced by the increased numbers of poor and starving people around the world. In other words, every effort is made to cut off, rather than promote, the trickle in a "trickle down" economic belief system. Trickle down economics is intended to be the friendly face of laissez-faire capitalism.

The economic crisis in the United States that began in 2008, was (and possibly continues to be) due largely to the failure of the federal government to regulate large corporations, especially large financial institutions. Large scale deregulation began during the 1980s and continued to the current state of what is essentially a complete laissez-faire economic system. As the federal government rushed to bail out the failing giant corporations so that the economy would not collapse entirely, one could not ask for more convincing and decisive evidence of the failure of laissez-faire economic policies. This failure was later corroborated by the conclusions in the majority report of the Financial Crisis Inquiry Commission which states (FCIC 2011: xvii):

> There was an explosion in risky subprime lending and securitization, an unsustainable rise in housing prices, widespread reports of egregious and predatory lending practices, dramatic increases in household mortgage debt, and exponential growth in financial firms' trading activities, unregulated derivatives, and short-term "repo" lending markets, among many other red flags. Yet there was pervasive permissiveness; little meaningful action was taken to quell the threats in a timely manner.

The public debates since the crisis began have not reflected the true magnitude of the economy's failure as reflected in the above quote, and following the commission's report, minority reports have been quickly issued to protect the failed system and the primary players within it. Every effort is being made to exonerate the greed-based laissez-faire economic model that is the core of the financial crisis and the many corresponding social problems that the United States and many other nation-states currently face.

Focus has turned, instead, to the national debt created by bailing out giant corporations and by military spending on behalf of corporations. The pro laissez-faire capitalists who caused the 2008 financial crisis, and who are responsible for the largest national debt in United States history, have been working hard and fast to protect the current economic system—the system that created their unprecedented and exorbitant wealth. Observation of this process has been a clear demonstration of the significance of wealth being able to control the mainstream media and the role those media play in the social construction of reality. Laissez-faire economics allows the wealthiest people in the world to become wealthier from the work of everyone else. Given the lack of socialization in the United States and other world dominant countries toward a "common good" ethos, why wouldn't wealthy people do everything they can to protect such an economic system?

The needed remedy to make sure that the laissez-faire economic model is not maintained is a re-socialization of the public, especially the wealthiest members of the public, to understand the problems related to greed and economic policies based on greed. Such a re-socialization process would have to be integrated into the schools and into the media in such a way that the vast majority of people in the United States would understand that an economic system based on greed is one that cannot succeed in the long run. Unfortunately the opposite socialization continues to occur in the schools and media, promoting greed-based competition and a winner-take-all mentality.

## Who Takes the Risk?

A popular explanation that people in the business world like to use for the exorbitantly high salaries of CEO's is that they take all the risks while plant workers just do a basic job. This is an important and unsubstantiated claim. What does it mean to take the risk for a company? Let us assume someone works 10 hours a day six days a week in a difficult job, and saves nearly every penny earned for ten years. This person then invests every hard earned dime into starting a small business that initially employs a small number of people. This behavior pattern justifiably merits the distinction of assuming significant risk. The probability of losing everything that was saved is very great since most startup businesses fail. Even if the business is successful, high risk will continue to exist for a long time to come—albeit actual risk for the owner decreases the more successful the company becomes. One might argue against this claim by saying that with success there is more to lose as time goes on. That, however, is part of the point being made. The more the owner has to loose, the more the owner has gained from others, and the more security the owner has as an individual—even if something happens that results in a major loss to the company. Risk, under these circumstances, should not be based on how much one has to lose but more so on how close one is to having nothing. A person that has successfully accumulated wealth is not likely to indefinitely invest all of the accumulated wealth back into their own company.

On the other hand, the longer plant workers stay with the company and invest their time and energy into making the profits for the company, the greater their risk becomes. Their risk actually increases with time while the risk of the successful company owner is decreasing with time. This is because the plant workers reach a point where they have invested a large segment of their lives into the company and are no longer marketable for other comparable jobs. Their low pay has most likely not allowed them to accumulate surplus wealth beyond modest savings that might get them through a few months at best. If they are non-union workers it is likely that they have little in the way of savings. The owner of the company has maximum control over the situation, while the average plant worker basically has none. If a reasonably successful company takes a sudden turn for the worst, the owner can liquidate assets and start over at something else. The workers on the other hand, who have made the products and have been the backbone of the company for many years, are simply out on the street. Other employers are not going to hire a person who is middle-aged when they can hire someone much younger for the lowest possible pay.

One can hardly blame company owners for liquidating if their companies are truly losing money, and there appears to be little hope of recovery. Unfortunately, most major successful large companies that have been closing between 1980 and 2006 have not been closing because they could not make profits. They have been closing because the CEO's saw the potential for making greater profits somewhere else. A CEO who becomes the head of a 75–100 year old multinational corporation assumes little risk today. If the company doesn't do as well as projected for a few years, the CEO is given a golden parachute and hired by another similar company. The unsuccessful CEO has probably been paid more in one or two years as than the average plant worker could make in a lifetime. Released CEOs exercise their stock options and most often move on to yet other companies for more money and better stock options. There is no real commitment to the companies for which they work—only their compensation package and the immediate task at hand. In recent years the task at hand has been almost exclusively cutting costs, which quickly translates into workforce reduction. People who have dedicated their lives to the company are unemployed so the wealthy investors, still making large profits, can make greater profits somewhere else.

From approximately 1980 to 1991, during the President Reagan and President G.H.W. Bush administrations, approximately 22 million United States workers were displaced by plant closings, primarily because of companies moving to other countries for low cost labor (Perrucci and Wysong 2008). When these layoffs occur so that CEO's and major stock holders can make greater fortunes, who should we say has incurred the greater risk: temporary CEOs charged with conducting layoffs, or the factory workers? It is the unprotected factory workers who are now without income in their middle years and have a house mortgage, children in school, and credit card bills to pay. Working class people know more about the realities of risk than do corporate CEOs. Yet, the socially constructed and carefully maintained reality is that "risk" in the business world is something only experienced by corporate CEOs and other company executives.

*Enron or end run?*

Enron was a large energy company that, among other things, brokered electrical power and other energy sources around the world. It is the company accused of deliberately creating a power shortage in California so as to extort higher rates from the Californians and pressure California into building more nuclear power facilities. This debacle created such immediate devastation and panic that a popular governor was removed by special election early in his second term, and a handpicked replacement was "elected" in his place (Phillips and Project Censored 2004a). Since the CEO's of Enron were tightly connected to powerful political figures, such as the two Bush presidents, it is difficult to know who all was involved in this created social disorganization and corresponding political coup. If you look at the methods used and the ensuing results, it is a stark reminder of what imperial nation-states have done to third world countries for many decades; that is, create widespread social disorganization and create conditions for aid that will make the region more controllable and thus more useful for supporting capitalist interests. Until this planned power shortage was executed, California had been a stronghold for the Democratic Party, and the frontline for many liberal social initiatives in the United States. With the greatest number of electoral college votes in the presidential elections, there was a sense among some powerful right wing capitalists that California was a problem that needed to be fixed. Indeed, for the purposes of serving wealthy interests, Enron made a large contribution toward bringing about that "fix."

When there is reference to the Enron scandal, however, the topic is typically not what Enron did to California on behalf of the wealthy, but what Enron did to its workers and the business world in general. The Enron scandal that broke in 2001 is a caricature of business as usual in the corporate world. The CEOs of this huge multi-billion dollar company boasted of the risks they took on behalf of the company, which amounted to occasionally buying other companies, but mostly finding clever ways of doing accounting so that the company always appeared to be making far more money than it was. One of their primary accounting schemes was labeled "mark to market" whereby anticipated long term future profits were considered part of the company's current value. Enron convinced the previously respectable Anderson Consulting firm to accept this accounting scheme, a decision which eventually almost destroyed the Anderson Consulting company. The accounting schemes for creating artificial company value kept the stock values increasing, which the CEOs used to make more "high risk" investment transactions. When the facade began to fall apart, the CEOs sold their stock holdings without informing anyone else and ran away with hundreds of millions of dollars, leaving the workers of the company with nothing—not even their retirement funds (Raver 2006).

The practices of Enron executives are not as wild and out of the ordinary as they may seem. Enron simply took standard corporation operating procedures and pushed them a little beyond the comfort zones of even the most hardened greed-based capitalists. The most serious source of discomfort was the carelessness with which the Enron CEOs exposed how western capitalism operates. The stock values of Enron were still continuing to rise when the company was genuinely in debt 30 billion dollars. The debt was actually hidden through fake companies explicitly created for that purpose. When average people allow their job related retirement funds to be invested into stocks (most people do not buy stocks otherwise) they believe they are buying little pieces of actual companies that are worth the reported stock value. Reported stock value, however, has little to do with what a person owns when buying stock, since stock value is little more than the business world's psychological disposition toward a company on a given day. Psychological dispositions in the market can be easily manipulated by the people who have the power and resources to control perceptions of reality.

## "Tax Reform"

A significant factor contributing to the ability to increase and retain wealth is taxation. This is why political administrations most committed to serving their wealthy constituents focus heavily on what is euphemistically referred to as "tax reform." Tax reform in modern times has most often meant tax relief for the rich and a greater tax burden on everyone else. Since 1955, the tax brackets of the higher income people have been changed to allow people with extremely high incomes to pay proportionately less of their income in taxes and people with low incomes to pay proportionately more. The most recent changes of this nature took place under the G.W. Bush presidency and specifically benefitted the top 2 percent of the population (Hurst 2010). With the wealthy (who control most of the resources and money) paying less in taxes, the rest of the population, which has comparatively little wealth, has to find ways of carrying the burden of maintaining the social and physical infrastructure of the United States. Exactly how this can be done is uncertain since current global economic practices dictate jobs moving to other countries, resulting in a significant loss of taxable income here in the United States.

Corporations have also enjoyed considerable tax reductions over the years. In the 1950s corporate taxes averaged about 28 percent of the federal tax base of the United States. By 2003 that percentage had dwindled to about 7.4 percent.

Many of the largest corporations based in the United States have years when they pay no taxes whatsoever, and even receive large tax rebates from previous years. The wealth from corporations paying less in taxes is transferred to the income of the individuals who are the major share holders of those companies, causing the individual incomes of the top 1 percent to increase dramatically. Hence, while the wealthy continue to pay smaller percentages of their income in taxes, their extremely elevated incomes due partly to corporate tax breaks result in the wealthy paying higher actual amounts of taxes. Paying higher amounts of taxes results in the lobbyists of wealthy people forcing the political system to lower their tax rates even more, and so it goes. It is an endless cycle of wealth from corporate tax breaks being transferred to wealthy individuals who then effectively lobby for tax breaks of their own. Complaints that wealthy people are paying more actual dollars in taxes than they used to pay need to be viewed within this context of continual plunder.

An important irony: while wealthy people continuously and effectively lobby for greater tax reductions for themselves and corporations, under the guise of wanting less government and greater individual freedom, they at the same time demand the use of very large amounts of United States tax-based resources to further enhance their own wealth. The best example of this behavior pattern is the use of various United States security agencies, including the CIA and complete military system, to disrupt and disarm other nation-states where corporations seek cheaper labor, additional natural resources, and new product markets (Cobb and Diaz 2009, Perkins 2004). This behavior pattern represents, not only the greatest expenditure of the United States government, but the greatest devastation (by far) to the earth's natural and human made environments (Sanders 2009). Sociologists are just now beginning to systematically analyze and understand the size and scope of the military's environmental footprint (Jorgenson and Clark 2009).

Wealthy people force lower federal taxes for themselves while demanding huge tax-based expenditures for military actions to help their corporations set up in other countries. The average United States citizen not only contributes their tax money to this process, but also contributes by participating in the military actions and/or accepting a lower paying job since many of the corporations have moved their jobs to the targeted countries. Some people might call this class warfare. If it is, there should not be any doubt as to who is winning.

## Classism and Capitalism: A Reciprocal Relationship

A hierarchical arrangement of people according to wealth and power most likely began to emerge with the earliest forms of resource surplus attainment and subsequent hoarding behaviors. As previously discussed, those who can get others to help them create their own surplus of resources must find a way to distinguish themselves from those who do not have a surplus of resources. This differentiation is important in order to get everyone to accept some people having a large resource surplus and some people not having any resource surplus at all. The rationalizations and corresponding characterizations of others as undeserving in whatever ways one is able to invent, based on whatever appearances or behavioral tendencies one can identify that are not also attributable to oneself, is what makes up the socially constructed concept of social class.

This process of class differentiation is greatly aided by the tautology imbedded in the circumstance. That others do not have a surplus is self evident—as is their identified different characteristics, whatever those characteristics might be. Hence, one condition must cause the other; that is, being short, tall, slow, fast, dark, pale, heavy, light, this family, or that family, and so on, must be the reason(s) for one not having a resource surplus. Such people are forced into to a different category, which we call a social class. Differential treatment of that class creates a different way of life which can then be a basis for future differential treatment … and so it goes in a cyclical fashion. The ensuing classism enhances the capitalists' efforts to attain greater surplus at still greater cost (in the form of greater labor expectations and greater deprivation) to the identified lower classes.

Upper class capitalists, on the other hand, must be ever prepared to defend, and even change if necessary, the characteristics that make some people less deserving than they are of the earth's resources. What is the purpose of: the periodic research showing how some groups have lower IQ's than others; the occasional welfare "reform" bills that are passed by Congress to make the poor more "responsible" and better workers; the worker retraining programs that come with the "free trade" legislation; tax "reform"; criminal law changes that result in more imprisonments; prison "reform" that converts prisoners to free labor for private corporations; and educational programs that blame poor schools and poor children for not getting high test scores? All of these initiatives, and many more, are designed to, not just take more from the poor to give more to the wealthy, but more importantly, to define the working and lower classes as the problem when circumstances are not exactly the way the upper class wants them to be. All of these programs project a definition of large numbers of people as unworthy of a reasonably comfortable standard of living.

## Abject Poverty Revisited

With the treadmill spinning at the modern rate of 50, 60, 70 or more hours of work per week and with many people below livable wage incomes, it is not surprising that many people fall off into the abyss of homelessness and the rawest forms of poverty—in the United States and around the world. Still, there are many others who just barely manage to hang on and keep from being completely impoverished. Sometimes referred to as the working poor, these are the people that keep the infrastructure of large urban areas operating in a seemingly fluid and carefree manner: the large hotels, restaurants, casinos, business buildings, streets, hospitals and so on: all kept clean and operating by the invisible hand of the working poor. I say invisible because segregation allows the middle and upper classes to go about their daily lives with minimal awareness of the working poor—that is, until a major disaster like hurricane Katrina occurs.

In 2005 Katrina hit the Gulf of Mexico and came up into New Orleans where it broke the levies and almost completely destroyed the city. The people living directly behind the levies were hit the hardest, and one should be able to guess who they were. They were the invisible poor of New Orleans: the people who kept the hotels clean for the tourists, carried their baggage, parked their cars, changed their linen, cleared their tables and washed their dishes. When the sky cleared and the damage was done, most of the middle and upper class people were gone, and the working poor, many without transportation and many with no place to go, were still there on the roof tops of their flood ravaged destroyed homes. There they were for the whole world to see as they begged for help on national television. Many others were already dead, and many died thereafter as the federal government took an unprecedented amount of time to respond to the disaster.

Aside from the characteristic of being poor, who were the people that were crying for help from the flooded streets of New Orleans on national television? What other characteristics did they have besides their abject poverty? The answer to this question brings us into the next chapter. In Chapter 7 we look at the interconnections between the various isms within the existing capitalist economy. Discrimination isn't just for the sake of beating up on certain groups of people for the fun of it, although it sometimes manifests itself in that way at the micro level. Discrimination directed at various groups keeps imperial capitalists supplied with plenty of working poor so profits can truly be maximized. Hence, discrimination, according to the various ism characteristics, is a way of funneling people into the lower classes, and classism is the safety firewall that keeps the victims of the other isms "where they belong" within the larger economic and social systems.

## Solutions?

As will become increasingly more apparent as this book progresses, there are no quick or short term fixes for eliminating the class structure and stratification. As mentioned at the end of Chapter 5, change that removes inequality is not viable without changing the way people see themselves and the world around them. Re-socialization programs are essential, and will be discussed more fully in Chapter 12. Once it is possible for all people to envision and accept social structures that promote greater equality, it will then be possible to create those social structures and maintain them. Until such change occurs, investigating and understanding the historical role of labor unions in mitigating class oppression is important. While no human institution is perfect, the positive value of unions has been nearly lost as part of a successful systematic program by the wealthy to discredit and eliminate unions. Helping workers organize reduces and partly stalls worker exploitation and class oppression.

## Chapter 7
# Gender, Race, Ethnicity, and the Isms

The process of creating artificial differences to control others for personal gain is greatly supplemented by seeking out groups of people with some actual differences. Women were most likely the first group of humans identified in this manner and for this purpose. Eventually groups of people from other geographical locations were sought out: people that looked different from their conquerors. Both women and dark skinned people were considered not human by some groups of White people/men during certain periods in history. False, decontextualized, and greatly distorted images, known as stereotypes, are used to maintain the lower status of differentiated groups over time. It is not known exactly when this process began in the world in general with humans, but we know that conquest and enslavement continue to this day. That is, people who are different than people from dominant groups (in the West typically being White men) in their appearances and ways of living, are denigrated and subsequently used as free or low cost labor so that dominant groups may live extravagant, high cost lives.

A common mistake that is made, however, is to assume that the relevant beginning of the isms lies with human prejudices toward other humans. This limited position is not only inaccurate in itself, but results in an analysis of the human exploitation process that is incomplete and, therefore, also inaccurate. Taking a human prejudice-based disposition toward the history of the isms contributes to the various forms of human discrimination being seen solely from the standpoint of White against Black, Black against Asian, Irish against Italian, Italian against Latino(a), male against female, able bodied against people with disabilities, young against old, straight against gay and so on. These oppositional standpoints are artificially created and direct attention away from the primary source of discrimination and oppression, which is greed directed toward labor and resource exploitation: hence, the ism tributaries flowing into the river of classism.

### Speciesism

One of the most important, and perhaps most often overlooked, realities of life is that living beings require sustenance that can only be attained from the consumption of other living beings, or matter that comes from other living beings. This is not a particularly profound statement in itself, but it is profound in its implications for understanding oppression. We tend to assume that our current state of dualistic thinking about which beings are valued and which are not valued has always been as it is today: human group against human group. As individuals growing up in a particular culture, humans do quickly internalize the divisions that are taught them from birth. But from where do those divisions come? How did the culture itself come to have these divisions imbedded into its many belief patterns and institutions? Where did the process of differentiation and use of "other" start?

This brings us to the topic of speciesism. Drawing on the conceptualization of William Graham Sumner and other sociologists that followed, we can consider the language being used to define which species of life should and should not be eaten and/or captured for various human uses as representing a form of in-group and out-group distinctions. *In-group/out-group behavior* is any action or tendency that separates beings with a particular set of characteristics from beings that do not have the exact same characteristics. Those beings considered to have the desired characteristics are members of the in-group, and all other beings are members of out-groups. In-group members are treated with general positive regard while out-group members are treated with suspicion and often as enemies to be controlled or destroyed (Davie 1963).

*Speciesism*, therefore, is the tendency for members of one species to view and/or treat members of another species as inferior in a specific or general way. Speciesism, like all isms, means that a self identified in-group (in this case a species) claims the right to make judgments about an out-group species, and the out-group species does not have the same opportunity or tendency. Since we do not really have enough information to know how other forms of life actually think about each other or us, the practice of speciesism is currently reserved for the human species. We do know that other forms of life eat other species, and sometimes do so in rather violent ways. Speciesism is a term developed by a rapidly growing movement to spare other forms of life from unnecessary harm and pain caused mostly by humans. This movement is currently known as the Animal Rights movement.

What is the earliest and most basic way in which human and non-human organisms have used other forms of life? Most fundamentally humans have used other forms of life as food and, thereby, as a means of sustaining themselves. How does one form of life decide that another form of life can or should be used for one's own purposes? With respect to food, there is, of course, a nutritional component which is worked out over time—most likely in a trial and error fashion, and originally with a relatively low level of objective consciousness about the meaning of the activity. As humans continued to evolve they most likely developed a greater ability to objectify themselves relative to the world around them, making decisions about how to relate to the objects (living and non-living) in their social and physical environments (Fromm 1941). By accentuating separateness humans could more easily justify the use of other objects to satisfy perceived personal needs.

*Ahimsa*

Over time some human groups, such as the Jains, Hindus, and Buddhists came to question the extent to which life forms are truly separate, seeing all of the earth's components as part of their own being and, hence, inseparable through time and space from their own welfare. Out of this way of looking at the world came the concept of ahimsa, which refers to an unwillingness to harm any living being. Many Native American peoples also developed an integrated view of the world, seeing all parts of the universe as pieces of their own life, both physically and spiritually.

*Western tendencies and life*

In most Western cultures there appears to be little regard for the sensitivity of other life forms, not to mention ahimsa. Other beings are not viewed as part of the same fabric of life as humans; nor is there a great deal of concern about the infliction of pain, irreverence, or disrespect (Alessio 2008, Berry 2004b, Francione 2002, Dunayer 2001, Nibert 2002, Singer 1975). We can go so far as to say that there is, among many Western peoples, direct or indirect satisfaction with the notion of killing other forms of life. The process of killing other forms of life may involve the infliction of prolonged pain and suffering upon those beings, typically with no notable remorse or regret. This kind of disposition toward other forms of life manifests itself most notably through: hunting for "sport," factory farming (which eating large amounts of meat supports), and frequent viewing of violent entertainment where death and destruction are commonplace. There are many ways in which non-human animals are treated as inferior to humans, and thus experience the worst that humans have to offer in terms of victimization, persecution, and oppression (Beirne 2009, Berry 2004a 2004b, Regan 2004, Greek and Greek 2000, 2002), with scant meaningful legal protection for non-human animals (Beirne 2009).

This kind of behavior and mental disposition can only come about if people are taught to think of themselves as completely separate beings from the other beings of the universe. This separateness most likely started with the need to take in sustenance and evolved into something far more encompassing. If we think of the fabric of life being made up of threads close to and like ourselves as well as threads further away and less like ourselves, we can think of differences between life forms without imposing hierarchical value upon them. What is closest to us in terms of appearance and DNA would be the threads that partially run through us, and as we move further away in the fabric we find greater differences from ourselves in appearances and composition. Differences do not have to translate into an assigned artificial magnitude or value, such as more or less pain, or more or less important. They simply are what they are: differences.

*Is speciesism necessary for humans to survive?*

Consumption does not require denigration of what we kill and eat. We know from the practices of some communities of people that the sources of their food may be considered sacred. For example, the buffalo are sacred for certain Native American tribes, and corn is sacred for others. Which approach makes more sense: revering what sustains us, or denigrating what we consume as inferior life forms? This is not a frivolous intellectual question. The answer has serious consequences for all forms of life, including humans. Denigrating other beings to justify eating them opens the door to denigrating other beings for other uses as well. If I think of something as inferior in order to feel good about eating it, why shouldn't I feel comfortable using it for other purposes? After all, "it is just a dumb animal anyway—right?" There is evidence that shows that humans who are abusive toward other humans are often people who have been abusive toward other forms of life as well (The Humane Society of the United States 2009, Hoffman 1998).

The uses of other life forms have been extended well beyond the necessity of sustenance. In addition to being used for food, other life forms are used for shelter materials, clothing, surplus food, labor, transportation, captive companionship, entertainment, research, and ultimately surplus wealth (Nibert 2002). How does one know where to draw the proverbial line between genuine needs for survival and greed-based preferences? The imperative of life and the corresponding need to survive do not require justification by use of any set of standards. People generally do not question a being's right to preserve its own life. How one chooses to survive, however, is subject to examination and debate as to its legality, morality, and efficacy. While survival minimally requires taking the lives (or potential lives in the case of fruitarians) of other beings, one need not view taking life for food as an expression of one's superiority. Indeed, taking the lives of other beings in order to survive is more realistically done out of one's own sense of vulnerability based on the need to live. That which saves us from death should not be considered inferior to us, but at the very least should be considered our equal.

*Preservation of the species*

Choosing to live, which is the tendency of most beings, requires not only consuming something now, but protecting sources of food in the future. To whatever extent there is a preservation of the species tendency among living beings, the "future" must include a long distance future. Preserving one's own species into the long term future is where most humans, particularly in Western nation-states, do not behave in accordance with what Native Americans refer to as natural law (LaDuke 1996, 1999). The more you destroy other forms and sources of life around you, the less likely is your own survival and the survival of generations that could follow. Natural law tells us that we can pretend that we are complying with certain standards that protect the environment and the fabric of life on the earth, but if we are not doing so genuinely, that is, clearly beyond the minimalist standards set up by politically motivated agencies like the Environmental Protection Agency, natural law will prevail. Human life will not be sustainable with polluted water, air, and soil; nor will it be sustainable without a certain balance among the existing beings that rely on one another for sustenance.

We are now in the midst of the sixth mass extinction of life on the planet Earth, which means that every year approximately 50,000 species of life are extinguished from the earth. This is the first mass extinction that will be caused by a particular species of the Earth: humans. "Fifty per cent of the Earth's species will have vanished inside the next 100 years; mankind [sic] is using almost half the energy available to sustain life on the planet, and this figure will only grow as our population leaps from 5.7 billion to 10 billion inside the next half-century. Such a dramatic and overwhelming mass extinction threatens the entire complex of life on Earth, including the species responsible for it: Homo sapiens" (Leakey and Lewin 1995: 1). The largest social structure of all is the Earth's delicate ecosystem, with all types of interaction and functional interdependence between the various life forms. Any denigration of life in any form is detrimental for the long term survival of humans.

It is most likely foolish to think that all species of life can or should last forever, including the human species. The important question related to this issue is how extinction should take place if the Earth is operating in a relatively balanced state. Under circumstances of relative balance, the extinction of species should take place gradually so that no single generation of any one species experiences the full brunt of the extinction process. Under circumstances of reasonable balance there is also the possibility of gradual adaptation to new environmental conditions so that species of life can gradually evolve into still other species of life, as has been speculated to be the case for millennia: hence, the theory of evolution. Current trends preclude gradual adaptation and result in painful experiences of environmental incompatibility, dislocation, and dysfunctional mutations. Additionally, some life forms are directly and deliberately created through genetic engineering without full consideration of all the possible consequences.

### *Role of pollution in species destruction*

Most serious species deformities are produced indirectly through various kinds of pollution. We read about cases of frogs being born with extra limbs, more than one head, and other deformities as a result of their habitat being polluted. Frogs are supposed to be the "canaries" of the natural environment. One might discount such findings related to beings like frogs as being a long ways from humans in the species fabric. Yet, we do not have to look at deformed frogs in order to understand where humans are taking the Earth. There are communities of humans where pollution levels are quite high: places like the Ukraine, where 7.25 percent of the territory was contaminated by the Chernobyl nuclear power plant disaster (Shargorodsky 2000) and where birth defects are unusually high. One need not, however, leave the United States for plenty of examples. There is the Knolls

Atomic Power Laboratory in New York, which has been found to be responsible for numerous health problems, the Three Mile Island Disaster where the radiation levels continue to impact health, and the famous "Death Mile" that was created by the people running General Electric Corporation knowingly releasing high levels of radiation into the environment.

Nearly every family in the area known as Death Mile, just downwind of the Hanford Plant, has a cancer victim. About 40 percent of children born in that area have problematic genetic conditions believed to be related to the radioactive contamination from the Hanford plant. Many of the conditions are quite serious and quite visible (Infact 1991). Wars, old and new, have had devastating effects on all forms of life. Effects from radiation and depleted uranium have been particularly harmful. There are many manifestations of environmental degradation caused by irresponsible, and sometimes illegal, corporate behavior as well (Heiner 2010) despite the existence of numerous international documents condemning such behavior (Greenwood et al. 2009).

*Lessons learned?* It is not speciesist to eat other forms of life that are most necessary to our own survival. Humans did not create the universal condition of life requiring life in order to survive. It is, however, speciesist to denigrate other forms of life, including what we eat. Choosing what we eat should not be based on a contrived hierarchical value attributed to other species by humans. Choosing what we eat should be based on what is healthiest for ourselves as individuals and as a species. The decision of what to eat should also be based on what is healthiest for the rest of the life on earth, especially given that we do have to eat something. A careful examination of the available credible evidence indicates that eating plants is far healthier for humans and potentially far less destructive to the total fabric of life than is eating animals. This claim was substantiated in a statement by the United Nations calling for a reduction in the consumption of meat and dairy products (Carus 2010). Unfortunately, even the use of plants as food for humans can result in destructive human behavior patterns if such use is carried out in a speciesist manner.

Speciesism is a serious systemic problem for humans. It results in the denigration of that which keeps us alive—other forms of life. Anything that is denigrated and treated as lower or of less value than oneself becomes viewed as an object to be used for one's own purposes, and those purposes have no limits. Hence, we see that denigrating other species in order to feel comfortable eating them gives humans permission to also use those species for furs, entertainment, labor, general clothing, building materials, research experimentation and so on, all of which are closely connected with business opportunities and profit maximization that lead toward excessive accumulation of material wealth (Nibert 2002). Denigrated life forms become objectified as expendable investment items. Under certain circumstances human groups are treated in this way. If speciesism is the foundation of the isms, it should not be surprising that it is similar in some important ways to the other isms (Spiegel 1997).

**Sexism: Let Me Count the Ways**

Treating women and girls as if they are inferior to men and boys based solely on their female identity is what is generally referred to as sexism. Sexism, like most isms, manifests itself in a variety of ways within social relations and social institutions.

*Sexism and language*

What difference does it make if grown women are called girls? We call grown men boys, don't we? These questions cannot be answered effectively without first dealing with the context in which sexism occurs. If we return to the discussion about "reverse discrimination" presented in Chapter 6 we see that discrimination is, by definition, asymmetrical. That is, more powerful groups discriminate against less powerful groups, and not the other way around. Men are not truly denigrated by being called boys unless they are Black men. Calling an adult woman a girl is one of many ways in which men diminish the status of women to indefinite childlike dependency, a state that is controllable by men. Of course, we recognize that the same holds true of calling Black men "boys" whether the caller is a White man or a White woman.

What is ironic about the use of the term "girl" to affirm the dependency of women on men is that sexism is really about the dependency of men on women. Men need women for sex, to clean their homes, to cook for them, to wash their cloths, to raise their children, and to do a multitude of undesirable jobs that serve as the foundation for the global capitalist economy, as well as any other male-controlled economy. Out of the smaller stature of women within individual households comes the social evolution of an entire group of people "known" since the beginning of recorded history to be inferior—that is, women inferior to men. As with species labeled inferior, the projected inferiority of women makes them fair game for denigration. Once something is denigrated it can be used for whatever the denigrator deems necessary. Here we begin to recognize the intersection of speciesism and sexism. Similar to seeing other species of life objectified as expendable investment items, so do we also see women objectified in a variety of ways, such as domestic laborers in their own and other peoples' families, and as slaves/low wage laborers for the global economy around the world.

When two men are verbally abusing one another and one of them calls the other a "woman," what does that mean? Now we have men calling grown women "girls" and men calling grown men "women." There are numerous names that men use to denigrate women, thereby revealing the status of women in a variety of social settings. If women are seen as weak and dependent, as well as having other undesirable characteristics, then one's male enemies can be served no greater insult than to be called a woman. Given the true intelligence of women, their resourcefulness, durability, and significant contributions to the social and physical world, men should view being called a "woman" as a compliment. Unfortunately, that is not what happens.

### Education

At the beginning of the twentieth century it was considered a sign of mental imbalance for women to pursue a college education, and few women did it. Today, in the early part of the twenty-first century, women are slightly over represented as undergraduate students across the United States. That is, relative to their respective population numbers, there are proportionately more women than men in undergraduate school. This progress tends to come up short when we look at where the men and women are located within the educational programs. While there has been progress in this area as well, it is still the case that women are over represented in the humanities and social sciences, while men are over represented in the physical sciences and in other majors that can lead to higher status higher paying jobs (GAO 2000, 2003b, Harding 2006). Science in general is an exclusive world largely reserved for, and controlled by, Western White men (Harding 1993).

A college education notwithstanding, most of the lower status lower paying jobs in the United States continue to be disproportionately occupied by women, and the majority of the higher status higher paying jobs continue to be occupied predominantly by men (GAO 2000, 2003b). When women are in the same jobs with the same education and experience they still tend to be underpaid by about twenty percent, a figure that has not changed since the mid 1980s (GAO 2003b).

### Workplace sexism: long-term and immediate indicators

The finding of unequal pay for equal work and qualifications is an important indicator of the level of current sexism in the United States. The income differences associated with different occupations, depending on whether they are filled predominantly by males or females, is an indicator of longer term sexism. That is, the social definition of what jobs are important and deserving of higher status and pay is something that takes place over a long period of time, and is something that becomes deeply imbedded into the psyches of all individuals via a well contained socialization process. Which position is more important on a daily basis and for the long term welfare of a community: a nurse or an engineer, an elementary school teacher or a college professor, a department administrator or an administrative assistant? The social value of most occupations can be debated relative to their real vs. socially recognized contributions to the common good. In many cases education requirements are elevated to enhance the exclusivity and prestige of a position more so than to sufficiently prepare a person for that position. Administrators come and go, but administrative assistants often have years of experience training those administrators into many important aspects of their job.

*Women's liberation: income and leadership*

Gender equity has not progressed as quickly as women hoped it would when the women's movement of the 1960s and 1970s occurred. There is some evidence that pay equity is actually declining, with full time earnings of women dropping from 77.8 percent of what men are paid to 77.1 percent (IWPR 2010). A similar drop in women's comparative pay was also reported earlier by Longley (2004).

Advancement in attaining leadership positions has also been disappointing. Of the top approximately 1000 corporations based in the United States, only about 2.5 percent of the top level CEO's are women, and of the Fortune 500 companies, 2.4 percent of CEOs are women (Gettings et al. 2007). These are among the most important positions in the world because they determine, through their corporations, what governments do and do not do worldwide. They either are themselves, or directly represent, the wealthiest and most powerful people in the world.

The second most powerful positions in the world are the government leadership positions that wealthy people/CEO's control. Of those positions worldwide, few are occupied by women. The Scandinavian countries and Cuba have the highest percentages with about 35–40 percent of their leadership positions being occupied by women. Most countries, however, have even fewer women in official government leadership roles, and the United States is no exception. Even at the more grass roots level of state legislatures women occupy only about 22.5 percent of the available positions. At the federal level it is much worse with women occupying 15.2 percent of the seats in the House of Representatives and only 14 percent of the Senate seats (NEW Leadership Nevada 2006).

In my own work as an advocate for women faculty members and in my research on gender inequality, I have found that the work of women does not receive the same amount of acknowledgement as the work of men, resulting in a tendency for women to start at lower salaries and be promoted more slowly than men (Alessio 1999, 2007).

*Family relations*

Women make up 46.8 percent of the United States labor force. Fifty-nine point two percent of women work outside the home and 74 percent of those women work full time (USDL 2009). Approximately 71 percent of women with children work outside the home and about 76 percent of those women work full-time (NWLC 2008). When both husband and wife work full-time outside of the home it would be reasonable to expect that they equally share the domestic responsibilities. That turns out not to be the case overall. There has been progress made, but the housework gap is still large, with women doing considerably more regardless of who works and who does not (Mixon 2008). As further evidence of the continuation of overt sexism in the United States, these findings, along with all the other findings cited above, reaffirm the importance of the isms to the maintenance of low cost labor at all levels of social organization.

By the mid-1970s we began to see two competing categories of men struggling to control the labor of women. On the one hand we have the traditional men who want women to take care of them and their homes as domestic family workers (consists of a majority of men at some level), and on the other hand we see the use of women by predominantly wealthy men (also some wealthy women) for low cost external labor and wealth production. In the former case, controlling women's labor and other activities has been accomplished in a variety of ways, including through direct violence (Stewart and Croudep 2010, Feagin et al. 2006, Ptacek 2000). In the latter case, women in the United States have fulfilled the same function as immigrant men—sometimes during alternating time periods and sometimes in competition with one another.

### *Controlling one's own body: abortion*

Sociologists, like politicians, tend to avoid the topic of abortion. It is a contentious and controversial concept that generates high levels of emotion. When and where does human life begin is often the question that drives this debate on the surface. Many people, pros and cons, would have us believe this is a simple matter, but it is very complicated, involving many religious, philosophical, spiritual, as well as biological issues. It is important, therefore, to keep in mind, from previous chapters, the manner in which social reality is created and the kinds of motivations that often drive those creations. Pro-choice does not mean anti-life, and pro-life (alternatively, anti-abortion) does not necessarily mean that one is supportive of protecting all life. Nor does pro-choice necessarily mean that one favors abortion. It simply means that one has a particular position on who should make the decision about whether an abortion should occur.

Not all pro-life people and not all pro-choice people are the same. Many pro-life people are serious about protecting all life under all circumstances. Some pro-choice advocates see pro-lifers as part of the patriarchy designed to control women. They cite as evidence the lack of concern among many pro-life people about stopping: wars, capital punishment, executions, genocide and so on. It is argued that a truly pro-life person would be equally focused on adequate health care for the babies who are born, which is not only a serious problem worldwide, but in the United States as well.

Realistically, there is only one person who can make the decision about whether she can bring a life into the world, and that is the woman who is carrying that life. There are many reasons why a woman may not be able to give birth (and it's not just rape cases). Under those circumstances she is going to have an abortion whether it is legal or not. Anti-abortionists refer to the large number of legal abortions that are conducted and blame the government for failing to criminalize abortion. In reality, we do not know that criminalizing abortion would dramatically change the number of abortions that occur. We know that there were many abortions before it was decriminalized but we do not know how many there were for certain because they had to be done secretly. Often times they were done without sanitary conditions and the woman died along with the fetus. Some women performed the abortions on themselves and were fortunate if they survived.

It is not likely that anyone desires an abortion, but when compelled to do so it is best if it can be done early and under sanitary conditions. With sophisticated pregnancy detection methods today it is possible to end a pregnancy within its first few days. IUD's that were used by women for decades (including many anti-abortion women) essentially worked as mechanisms for ending early pregnancies i.e., removing fertilized eggs.

*Patriarchy and abortion*

Some churches expend large amounts of resources to get governments to make abortion illegal. The religious people within those churches are probably very sincere about their concern for the life of a fetus. One might argue, however, that churches that are really concerned about the morality or sinfulness of the act of abortion should expend their resources educating parishioners and counseling women on how to make the best spiritual and ethical decisions for their own salvation. In other words, as a religious organization they would be more concerned about saving the soul of the person at hand than saving a potential physical life. If life is the most important issue then church leaders might be challenged to address the question of why they are not doing more to stop wars and improve health care. Some of the churches that expend considerable resources fighting abortion are the same institutions that have large amounts of money invested in corporations that produce weapons and corporations that promote wars for profits. Like most human constructed social institutions, the structure and function of the components of religious institutions are designed foremost for self maintenance.

Are the individuals who run the anti-abortion churches fully aware of the role they are playing within the institution's long standing effort to maintain itself as a social structure? The historical gap between the development of a position on an institutional issue, like abortion, and the current manifestation of support for that position, make latent functions difficult to realize, especially for emotionally involved people.

If men could get pregnant it is safe to assume that they would not want women, or female run institutions, telling them what they could or could not do with their own bodies. The challenge of modern nation-states, states, and communities, is to find ways of minimizing the likelihood that a woman would ever find herself in a position of needing an abortion. That challenge requires a completely different orientation to the issue of abortion than is currently found in the United States and in many other places around the world.

## Heterosexism

One of the most difficult isms to analyze is heterosexism: the belief that heterosexual relationships are normal and rightfully privileged, while gay and bisexual relationships are abnormal and, therefore, unworthy of rights equal to heterosexual relationships. I say heterosexism is difficult to analyze because, unlike with classism, speciesism, and sexism discussed above, it is not immediately apparent what the capitalist financial advantages are, from a labor standpoint, of maintaining an atmosphere of discrimination against gay people. Yet, we know gay and lesbian people were one of the earliest targets of the Nazis during Hitler's reign, and they are widely discriminated against and persecuted still today around the world. Gay, lesbian, bisexual, transgender (GLBT) people are harassed and denied their rights routinely. Many have been killed and because of their lack of acceptance and poor treatment, suicide rates are exceptionally high among GLBT youth (Johnson 2010, Gibson 2009). Some state legislatures have been crafting constitutional amendments to assure that gay and lesbian people will never be able to get legally married. Such amendments will have major social and financial implications for gay and lesbian people.

What is important to keep in mind is that any time a group is excluded from having the same rights as everyone else, members of that group are automatically contributing to lower labor costs for corporations. GLBT people have to be prepared to work in jobs beneath their training and educational level, and they have to be prepared to work for less income. In many places they will not be able to work at all unless they hide the fact that they are GLBT. Staying in the closet is less of an expectation than it used to be, but it is still the only way to be safe in a world quite hostile toward GLBT people. Many major institutions, such as the US military (until 2011) and the Catholic Church, forbid open GLBT relationships. What makes GLBT discrimination so complicated is that there appears to be more involved than the usual direct surplus labor demands of corporations. Yet, money is still involved.

### *Why churches don't support GLBT*

I should begin this section, as I could have the last section, with a disclaimer about churches and religion. An analysis of the position of churches on any one issue or combination of issues does not mean I am anti-religious or anti-churches. The goal of analyzing these social structures is not to denigrate them, but to better understand how they operate so as to make them more useful to the publics they serve. Churches are very large and powerful social structures and the debate about gay rights within the churches is important.

One can get a better idea of what the primary motivation behind the persecution of GLBT people may be if one asks the simple question, "what is the greatest actual difference between heterosexuals and GLBT people, and what is the actual impact of that difference on large powerful institutions like churches?" Is the greatest difference the way intimacy is expressed through sex? Most of the sexual activity of gays is no different than the sexual activity of many heterosexual people. Research studies have shown that the majority of heterosexual people participate in oral sex and many participate in anal sex (Buhi et al. 2010, Hans et al. 2010, Malacad and Hess 2010). Yet, we do not seek out and mistreat those heterosexuals that use various forms of sexuality. So what would be the motivation behind the persecution of gays? Another more pertinent question might be what is the connection between the desire to force gay and lesbian people to behave as if they are heterosexual and the desire to control women's fertility, as discussed above within the context of abortion?

As with antiabortion activities, heterosexist activities are led and perpetuated by religious organizations. If one examines carefully the teachings of the great prophets/messiahs of various religions, one has to question whether the most important reasons for churches opposing gay/lesbian relationships are actually religious. Even the bible quotations ostensibly pertaining to gays can be interpreted in several different ways and have contradictory quotes (White, M. 2010). What other reason could there be? Historically gay and lesbian people were associated with childlessness. The public perception most likely continues to be that gay and lesbian relationships do not produce children. Through the availability of insemination procedures to impregnate women and because of greater availability of adoption, that perception is no longer accurate. Perhaps because gays were historically without children and because that perception lingers, gay and lesbian relationships continue to be, from the standpoint of church leaders, an affront to the ability of the church to do "God's work," which includes multiplying and subduing the earth. Multiplying and subduing the earth is more than a religious calling. It is foremost a financial one. In the broader economy, more people translate into more money for production and retail industries. This is why public and even sociological discussions about the negative effects of overpopulation have been muted and have all but disappeared since the late 1970s. Every good Sociology Department used to have at least one Demographer. That is no longer the case.

While the manifest function of GLBT persecution and discrimination led by churches is fulfilling the word of God through the teachings of the Bible, the projected interpretations of the Bible are unsubstantiated and emotion based. What is very real (albeit a latent function) both in its existence and its consequences, is that the historical view of gay and lesbian people (less true today than in the past) is that they do not produce children. To the church the absence of children represents the loss of church membership, which in turn means lost revenues for the maintenance of the church. Maintenance of the broader economy is also an issue, but churches have a direct interest in maintaining heterosexism. It is quite likely that contemporary antigay ministers are completely unaware of the real reasons for their discriminatory behaviors toward GLBT people. Typically, there is a disconnect between the most important driving socio-economic forces that are in place and the irrational negative feelings people have toward people from other particular groups.

*Military and feminization*

Aside from the military being controlled by the competing interests of the most powerful elements in the social system, such as wealthy capitalists (who also play a role in the control of churches), there is another motivation for heterosexist behavior in the military. Many heterosexual men associate gay men with femininity, and femininity is associated with weakness. Under the "don't ask don't tell" (DADT) policy put in place under President Clinton, thousands of gays were discharged for not sufficiently hiding the fact that they were gay. That policy was eliminated through legislative action at the end of the second year of the Obama presidency. A number of forces converged to make this action possible, including the military's need for more soldiers to fight the oil wars in the Middle East. The need for more soldiers led to the inclusion of women into the military in the early stages of the volunteer army in the 1970s. Women, also associated with femininity/weakness, have been relegated primarily to support roles rather than direct combat. Lesbians have been discharged at notably higher rates than gay men under the DADT policy (Levine 2009). Women (heterosexuals and lesbians) have been sexualized in the military with many instances of sexual assault. In addition to concern about feminization, the military is concerned about its ability to control sexual behavior, which is complicated within a highly controlled physical and social environment.

## Ageism and Ableism

There are ways in which ableism and ageism directly intersect. One intersection occurs when people do become sufficiently old that they cannot physically take care of themselves in the same manner as younger able-bodied people can. Another important similarity that ableism and ageism share is that they cut across all other human categories. People from all ethnicities, races, genders, sexual orientations, and physical sizes and shapes are capable of becoming disabled in some way, and they are also capable of growing old. Both ageism and ableism are fully developed fields of study, like all of the ism areas. The work in these fields has been truly cross-disciplinary, with sociologists contributing an important part of this literature. Herein, I will only touch on the key issues.

*Ageism*

Ageism is the belief that people who are old are less valuable and less capable in comparison with people who are younger. The concept of ageism is sometimes extended to cover children as well, since adults make judgments about children that are similar to the judgments made about the elderly. Children are mistreated in ways similar to old people. Space prohibits a longer discussion of child abuse specifically. Issues related to the treatment of children and their rights can be accessed through the United Nations Convention on the Rights of the Child.

Like all isms, ageism has many stereotypes: older people cannot see/hear, older people cannot remember, older people are weak mentally and physically, older people cannot come up with new ideas, and when older people are sick they are often treated differently simply because they are "getting old." While all of these characteristics may occur in some older people, they do not occur in all older people. Just as importantly, they can occur in younger people and middle-aged people as well. The stereotypes of children are similar to those of older people, with the added dimension of children being treated as property. People start life with a devalued status based on age and commonly end life under these same conditions. Issues related to autonomy are key at both ends of the life cycles. People considered old who are also quite wealthy can sometimes mitigate their mistreatment by using their money to acquire the best possible care in their later years, if they can make these arrangements before members of their family or community have them declared incompetent.

Older people are frequently institutionalized before it is necessary and their resources and belongings taken by their adult progeny. There is a systematic process by which this created dependency occurs.

### *Ableism*

Sociological thought leading to a better understanding of the social conditions of people with disabilities began with the work of Irving Goffman in the 1960s. Goffman took the concept of stigma and shaped it as an effective sociological tool. People who have a characteristic that may be viewed as notably different, will find others tending to respond to them in accordance with that one particular characteristic. All other characteristics and corresponding qualities become, for the most part, secondary in importance when considering the person's identity. When this occurs, the different characteristic becomes a stigma, and the person bearing the characteristic becomes stigmatized. This process is similar to the process of labeling, but the difference is that stigmatization comes from an actual existing characteristic or quality of some sort. Labeling can be based on non-existent qualities.

Hence, stigmatization is the process by which an individual becomes recognized, not as a total individual, but specifically as a person with a particular socially undesirable characteristic, which could be a physical or known mental disability. Interactions are shaped by this recognition, continually reminding a person that they have this characteristic and that it is the most important indicator of who they are. It is easy to see how this process can not only apply to someone with a disability of some sort, but to people who appear to be older as well.

*Making people with disabilities "normal"*

One of the more controversial issues related to people with disabilities is whether efforts should be made to make people with disabilities look and behave like people not identified as having a disability. Some disability rights advocates maintain that they do not want to look and act like people considered "normal." They want the social and physical environment to be designed so as to not disadvantage them in any way: ramps/elevators instead of stairs, doors that are sufficiently wide, low door knobs that are not round and so on.

*Ableism, ageism, and labor*

Since the 1960s there have been a number of laws passed that support greater protection of rights for people with disabilities. Not everything in these laws is positive, however. The 1990 Americans with Disabilities Act gave permission to employers to pay people with disabilities below the minimum wage. Many people with disabilities are hired at below minimum wage in the services industries and given the least desirable jobs.

Perhaps one of the most important factors that applies similarly to people with disabilities and older people is that their reduced status and stigma within the communities in which they live often render them unemployed or underemployed. Older people are often pressured into retirement and then find themselves working in the service industries for minimum wage or less. This can happen because their retirement income is not adequate, or it can happen because they have nothing else to do with their time. In the latter condition, older people sometimes find themselves working for free just to have something to do.

Children, often treated as property, are sometimes forced into the labor pool prematurely. Despite the existence of child labor laws, there are many ways in which children are forced to work for the profits of others: sometimes by parents, sometimes as abducted children within the huge international slave trade, sometimes as the helpers of parents who are themselves trapped in sweatshops and labor entrapments of undocumented workers.

Children, older people, and people with disabilities have become important parts of the expanded labor pool in the United States and internationally. All of these devalued groups of people provide low cost labor for corporations. They are especially important to the place bound service industries in Westernized countries that cannot be moved or outsourced to other locations.

## Racism

It is quite likely that something approximating racism has taken place ever since different groups of people first discovered one another. Many of the great ancient cities and world wonders must have been built through a process of some form of enslavement, which requires differentiated groups of people. *Racism* is the ideology that considers a group's unchangeable characteristics to be symbolic representation of that declared racial group's inferiority, both in a general sense and with respect to other specific less visible and less concrete traits, such as psycho-social stability and intellectual acuity. The assignment of socially constructed negative characteristics to people with certain physical characteristics is done in a variety of ways. One way is to contrive and produce invalid evidence, such as IQ tests, and psychological tests. As previously discussed, such tests are tools created by high status groups to categorize and control socially defined lower status groups.

### *Segregation and prejudice*

*Segregation* is spatial and/or social separation of groups of people in accordance with their assigned status. All excluded groups of people experience some form of segregation at one time or another. The Civil Rights Acts of 1964 and 1965 ended legal racial segregation in the United States, but clearly did not end segregation as a practice in the United States. Anyone who does not believe that segregation still exists in the United States need only look at pictures of the 2005 hurricane disaster that occurred in New Orleans, Louisiana. While most of the upper and middle class White people were able to escape the hurricane, a large number of poor African Americans were located in a place closest to the flood walls and were unable to escape. Most were stranded without food and water for days on end. Notably insufficient relief was sent directly to the predominantly African American communities impacted by the disaster. Moreover, there appeared to be a deliberate stall on the part of the federal government in responding to the disaster. Segregation is coterminously a form, result, and cause of discrimination. An example of the latter is the accelerating impact of urban residential Black and Hispanic segregation on the foreclosure crisis that began in 2007 (Rugh and Massey 2010).

*Prejudice* is often mentioned within the context of discussing racism, but it applies to attitudes and dispositions toward all excluded disadvantaged groups. Xenophobia is a term that is similar to prejudice, but pertains typically to the fear, distrust, or hatred of foreigners—either in the United States or abroad. Like prejudice, xenophobia is maintained to support and perpetuate racism and discrimination, but it is not the root cause of racism and discrimination.

Relying on the concepts of prejudice and xenophobia to explain racism is like relying on inadequate education as an explanation for poverty. Like poverty, the root cause of racism is an insatiable human push for the highest possible profits using other people's labor. In the above example of the 2005 New Orleans hurricane the segregated African American community also illustrated the racially differentiated labor pool. The flood wall community contained the exploited service workers who maintained the infrastructure of the massive hotel, resort, and convention center industries of New Orleans.

### *Racism and the labor pool*

Racism has always been one of the most effective tools for assuring free or very low cost labor for wealthy capitalists. The most obvious form of racism for this purpose is slavery, especially the slavery that occurred during the early stages of the colonization and eventual establishment of the United States as an independent nation-state. The slavery that took place in the United States also happened in other parts of the world. Additionally, human slavery is still happening all around the world today, including here in the United States where undocumented workers are being held against their will for labor and other exploitative purposes. It is estimated that there are over 27 million people in slavery worldwide (Leach 2004).

Where outright slavery does not occur conditions are created so that people have to work incredibly long hours under substandard conditions for far less pay than they and their families need in order to adequately sustain themselves. This practice of maintaining near slavery conditions is one of the most devastating consequences of what is commonly referred to as the globalization of the economy. As previously discussed, the globalization of the economy is primarily a shift in corporate labor practices toward imposing industries on the people of other countries after disrupting the agricultural based economies of those countries. The desperate displaced people are then forced to become extraordinarily low cost labor for huge corporate profits.

### *Socially constructing race for labor*

Racializing selected groups for labor exploitation does not stop at slavery. It is a process that works its way into all aspects of human social life and all levels of the capitalist economic system. Racism has thus been one of the most effective means by which social class has been shaped and continually re-shaped over time. Sexism and racism, interconnected in very complex ways, have been the greatest producers of exploited labor and wealth for the imperial capitalists of the upper-upper class.

During the last quarter of the twentieth century, following successful unionization of the imported "inferior races" and the development of environmental protection laws, capitalist elites began to realize that the greatest possible profits for most corporations were no longer attainable by importing people to the United States for low cost labor. Corporate owners began to realize that far greater profits could be made by exporting their industries to the locations where the "inferior races" with "backward cultures" could be found. Under the label of globalizing the economy, production capitalists built industrial parks in parts of the world that, up until that point, were subsistence, gathering, and communal agricultural economies. Using the United States government and organizations like The

World Bank and the International Monetary Fund, conditions were established for corporations to move into other countries and take what they "need" through a process involving massive cultural and economic change. (Perkins 2004, Parenti 1995). Once the means by which people can sustain themselves is removed they are vulnerable to just about any conditions the colonizer wishes to impose upon them. Those countries that resist being "globalized" are severely punished with economic sanctions, weapons, and other punitive strategies (de la barra and dello buono 2009).

## Ethnicity

Discrimination based on ethnicity is similar to discrimination based on race. The primary difference is that ethnicity is most often associated with a particular group of people from a common social and cultural background. It also frequently identifies where people are from geographically. In other words, ethnicity has a fairly strong connection with biological, social, and specific geographical roots, while the notion of race does not necessarily. While a person's ethnicity is a more accurate description of who a person is, it is still the basis for widespread discrimination and oppression. Calling the Latinas/os and Hispanics ethnic groups, as is done by the census bureau, does not prevent people within those groups from experiencing discrimination. When Southern Italians were no longer referred to as a race and were then simply referred to as an ethnic group, the discrimination they were experiencing did not stop. There are numerous newer immigrant groups, such as the Somalis, Hmong, and Arab Muslims who are racialized ethnic groups.

## Does Racism Still Exist?

A poll conducted in 2009 shows notable differences between Whites and nonWhites in response to the above question. While 34 percent of Whites indicated that racism still exists, 50 percent of the nonWhites surveyed (Blacks and Hispanics) believe racism still exists. Fifty-two percent of the nonWhites, and only 8 percent of the Whites, believed they experienced discrimination by the police (Montopoli 2009). In some locations Black/White differences are far more serious than broader national tendencies. In Cincinnati, Ohio 80 percent of Blacks surveyed believe that Blacks are discriminated against in the workplace, while 90 percent of Whites are convinced Blacks are not unfairly treated (Peale 2001).

There is evidence that darker skin increases the likelihood people will experience discrimination, including the most recent immigrants (Hersch 2006). Sixty-nine percent of Black men and 74.8 percent of White men are in the civilian labor force (BLS 2010). This difference of nearly 6 percent is sometimes attributed by White people to a lack of motivation on the part of Black men. The problem is not restricted to the United States. Britain, an important part of the United States' cultural heritage, also continues to have serious discrimination problems (Parr and Addison 2010), and Blacks seem to be mistreated in many parts of the world (Butler Byrd and Jangu 2009).

Why would Blacks lack the motivation to work when the alternative is poverty and harassment for being poor? Notably fewer Black men than White men hold professional/administrative jobs in the United States, and far more Black men than White men hold service and unskilled labor jobs. Is relegation to lower status lower paying jobs a result of poor motivation? Why would someone choose to be excluded from the better paying jobs? They don't, as evidenced by successful race discrimination lawsuits, such as the one against the city of New York (Baker, A. 2010), and as evidenced by the work of leading scholars (Feagin 2008).

*Racism on every dimension of social life*

On just about any indicator that one can think of there are numerous data showing that discrimination toward Blacks still exists, not in a small way that will probably soon disappear, but in significant life threatening ways: access to health care, infant mortality, access to housing, employment opportunities, educational opportunities, pay, promotions, and so on. The list goes on. Even if there was an honest national effort to eliminate racism, the magnitude of racism in the United States would most likely require several decades for elimination to occur. One would think, for example, that by this time, more than forty years after the 1965 Voting Rights Act (revised several times since) that Blacks would no longer have problems fulfilling their right to vote. That is not the case. A 2005 study by law students at the University of Michigan was based on an examination of 323 voting discrimination legal cases over the last twenty-three years. They found 114 instances of illegal voting discrimination against racial and ethnic groups (Katz et al. 2005). This particular piece of datum is just based on what has been before the courts. One can only imagine what must be taking place that never sees the light of day. The issue of voter discrimination has become particularly noteworthy in the last two national general elections in the United States where large numbers of Blacks are believed to have been systematically prevented from voting in places like Florida and Ohio in order to assure the presidency of George W. Bush. This issue was discussed extensively in the mainstream media and in alternative presses for several weeks following each of those elections and there are still legal challenges ongoing.

*The 2008 presidential election*

An unexpected event took place during the 2008 United States presidential campaign and election: an African American, Barack Obama, was nominated and eventually elected to the presidency of the United States. There are a number of important issues related to this event.

*Barack Obama: the person* The first obvious issue is that an African American person was elected president while there continues to be widespread racism throughout the United States. It is of some relevance, however, that the person elected president, Barack Obama, is actually half African American and half White. There are two important sub-points of this issue. One is the fact that in the United States a person is identified as Black no matter how small the portion of their genetic makeup is actually from African or African American descent. With any notable fraction being African American, people are considered "less than" White, which means Black. In this case, Barack Obama is 50 percent African American and 50 percent White. While he has some distinctive African American physical features, the fact remains that he is just as much White as Black. Why are not people referring to him as the White president? Why is one half of him more significant than the other half? The emphasis on President Obama being Black and not White tells us that race truly does matter and that it matters a lot. Any part of a person that is Black publicly defines that person, and the public's consciousness adjusts accordingly.

The second important sub-point is that Barack Obama was raised by his White mother and grandmother. While they were not well off, his grandmother sacrificed to send Barack to good schools, and he eventually received his law degree from one of the most prestigious universities in the country, Harvard University. The influence of African American subculture on Barack Obama's behavioral characteristics is hardly noticeable on a daily basis. He does, however, have the ability to exhibit such characteristics when the situation calls for it, such as when campaigning in predominantly African American communities. It is in this respect that Barack Obama was far more acceptable to the White United States public than someone like Jessie Jackson, an African American who had run for president during an earlier election, or Julian Bond, who served in the Georgia legislature for many years. Both of these well known and highly articulate African Americans, and many other African Americans like them, have been distinctively committed to African American identity and civil rights for Blacks. Barack Obama has no comparable history, and while he has widespread support from the African American community, his demeanor and behavior patterns are quite different than those of most male leaders who are overtly pro African American, hence posing far less of a threat to White people. Notwithstanding, many White people are still quite threatened by him.

*The candidate pool* The condition of Barack Obama's election is one of great sociological interest. The four main candidates in the 2008 election were Hillary Clinton and Barack Obama on the Democratic side, and John McCain and Mitt Romney on the Republican side. Thus we have a woman, a Black man, an elderly man with physical disabilities, and a man from a persecuted religion. During the primary election between Hilary Clinton and Barack Obama we saw widespread sexism and racism; during the primary election between John McCain (72 years old with debilitating injuries) and Mitt Romney (a Mormon) we saw widespread ageism and religious persecution. During the general election between Barack Obama and John McCain we saw extensive racism and ageism/ableism throughout the country.

*The election atmosphere and afterward* In addition to complications created by the unusual characteristics of the pool of candidates, the political atmosphere at the time of the election included an outgoing Republican president responsible for many serious United States and global problems: unending unnecessary wars, massive United States debt, widespread unemployment, and a world-wide financial crisis. Indeed, President George W. Bush had public approval ratings comparable to the worst presidents in United States history.

It was under these circumstances that someone identified as African American was able to be elected to the presidency. None of this diminishes the exceptional qualifications of President Barack Obama, recognized as one of the most intelligent and best educated people ever to be elected president of the United States; nor does it diminish the brilliant campaign he ran and the cleverness of his fundraising. It is to say, however, that circumstances were more important to his election than the state of racism within the United States at the time of his election. Indeed, immediately following his election there were unprecedented threats on the newly elected President's life, there were serious acts of violence against Democratic headquarters with Barack Obama's picture being stoned, African Americans were assaulted, and the Klu Klux Klan activity surged with overt threats directly related to the election of Barack Obama.

In some important respects, the election of Barack Obama to the presidency is as much evidence of the continued existence of racism (as well as sexism, ageism, and religious persecution) in the United States as it is racism's decline.

## Native Americans and Latinos/as

Nearly everything that has been said about racism involving Blacks could also be said in relation to the treatment of Latinos/as and Native Americans. In fact, these groups are in even worse condition than Blacks on some of the most important indicators such as health care and educational attainment. One must always come back to the question of why these groups of people are under such continuous systemic and pervasive persecution. The answer is always the same: their mistreatment and corresponding devaluation serves an important function within the capitalist economic system. It keeps the cost of labor low so that wealthy capitalists can maximize their profits and become even wealthier. Who would clean the factories, airports, hotels, and hospitals? Who would pick up the garbage? Who would sew the garments in the sweatshops of New York City? Who would dig the ditches and clean the sewers? Who would work the furnaces in the foundries? Who would pick the fruit and vegetables? Of course all of this could be done if both costs and profits were shared by all in a reasonable fashion, but that is not the way the current economic system works.

*Gambling on their future*

Native Americans, since the invasion and conquest of their lands and peoples, have been extremely impoverished. However, they had a major breakthrough in the late twentieth century with the development of casinos on their reservations. Since reservations are considered sovereign nations, they were not restricted to the states' laws forbidding gambling. This has been a source of jealousy and resentment on the part of White populations and their government establishments. Governor Pawlenty of the state of Minnesota, for example, threatened to develop competing casinos if the Native Americans did not contribute part of their profits to the Minnesota tax base.

As a social category, Native Americans are still very poor, but the casino profits have allowed them to develop schools and scholarship programs for their children to begin to become competitive with White people in the United States. The casinos themselves have also provided jobs for the Native American people. Native Americans (some preferring "American Indian") have become major financial players in many states, with White dominated social institutions competing for substantial donor contributions from the more successful American Indian communities. There are many sociological issues related to this phenomenon, but one that stands out is the ever growing challenge Native Americans face in trying to preserve and revive their devastated cultures as they operate within the United States capitalist system of formal education and jobs.

## Undocumented Workers

In the early part of the twenty-first century, politicians in Washington DC have been debating the fate of over twelve million illegal immigrants in the United States. Legislation has been considered that will punish the "illegal aliens" and yet allow them to stay in the United States under certain conditions involving paying fines and learning American civics. The undocumented workers are mostly from Mexico and their presence in the United States is critical to the infrastructure of a number of businesses. Politicians find themselves in a difficult situation because they want to pretend they are tough and prone to enforcing the law, but strict law enforcement in this case would eliminate the cheap labor of many of their more wealthy election campaign contributors. If the undocumented workers were not in the United States the businesses that use them would have to pay higher wages to United States citizens, which would cut their profits considerably. As it stands now, millions of United States citizens remain unemployed. The issue is complicated further because the United States took most of the land where undocumented Mexican workers currently reside from Mexico during the Spanish-American war in the mid nineteenth century. As the "illegal immigrants" put it in their protest signs, "we didn't cross the border, the border crossed us."

New immigration legislation will most likely not end the steady stream of "illegal" immigrants coming into the United States, because it is the fact that the immigrants are here illegally that keeps them working for pay below the minimum wage and keeps them from making greater demands of fair treatment in the workplace.

### What about Asian People?

Data from Asian groups tend not to look the same as data from the Blacks, Latinos/as and Native Americans. This does not mean that there are not forms of discrimination against Asian people. There are many Asian groups from various countries, and each group has its own history relative to immigration into the United States. Some immigrant groups are refugees of United States military interventions into their countries. The Chinese that came to the United States during the late nineteenth century and early twentieth century were brought here to work the metal mines and lay the railroads. They came as part of the same labor pool as the Irish and the Italian immigrants. There has, however, been a more recent wave of Chinese immigrants since then.

Many of the Asian people that came to the United States during the cold war, and shortly thereafter, were from communist countries where capitalists were not welcome. Many Asians who came to the United States under those circumstances were from the more capitalist oriented segments of those populations—people with a business orientation and with fairly high levels of education relative to most people in those countries. Hence we see, for example, that many of the recent Chinese immigrants and their Chinese American children have much higher educational attainment levels than do many Whites in the United States. This is true of recent immigrants from other non-Asian countries as well. That point notwithstanding, all immigrant groups experience high levels of discrimination in a variety of important ways.

With the globalization of the Western capitalist economy, the Chinese living in China became one of the most important components of the glutted global labor pool. The devaluation of Chinese culture and Chinese people as human beings makes possible the conversion of rural Chinese subsistence farmers into factory workers and various other types of production workers within the global capitalist system. As a wealthy class emerges in China from the adaptation of their economy to global capitalism, stratification and poverty emerge as well. Whatever oppression the Chinese have experienced in the past, they are now destined to see massive poverty and hunger in their future. It is difficult for educated and reasonably well off people to remember that we have extensive poverty and hunger right here in the United States. Why wouldn't it exist to a far greater extent once China more fully adopts our economic system?

**Anti-Semitism**

Anti-Jewish behavior specifically is widespread throughout the world, and is perhaps most closely associated with the Nazi efforts to eliminate Jews (as well as other groups) during World War II. Jews tend to be the victims of prejudice by, and are frequently targeted by, segments of most other ethnic, religious, and racial groups. The reason for this phenomenon is largely unknown. There are many theories about it, but none that seem to adequately answer the question of "why?" Root causes of discrimination toward the other identified groups do not seem to apply to "anti-Semitism," at least not directly.

Perhaps a comparison with early Native Americans would be helpful. When the American Indians chose to die rather than work as slaves, they were deemed not useful, uncontrollable, and thus "in the way." People who are in the way of those who seek control of others are vulnerable to elimination—genocide. Perhaps the persecution of the Jews is more about the need for control than the need for labor directly. It is difficult to exploit the labor of anyone if there is a large enough group present that encourages resistance.

Jewish culture places a great deal of emphasis on literacy and independent thinking. When we look for highly self-actualized people we often find ourselves considering the lives of famous Jewish people, like Albert Einstein and Emma Goldman. People who are independent thinkers are difficult to control and thus are a significant threat to whoever is in control of the nation-state or any organization. The greater the desires for control by government/organizational leaders, the more Jewish people are perceived to be a threat. Eliminating Jewish people becomes a means by which the probability of control can be increased.

One should keep in mind that, while anti-Semitism has been used almost exclusively to describe anti-Jewish behaviors, it technically also pertains to other groups. Anti-Arab sentiments have been strong in many parts of the world, including in the United States and Israel. Isarel is in a continual state of war with Palestine over nation-state boundaries. Given Israel's strong military and financial support from the United States, Palestine has been greatly disadvantaged and thus all but destroyed in a multi-generational war that shows no sign of ending.

With the late twentieth century and early twenty-first-century invasions of Iraq and Afghanistan by the United States, and with the continuous war between Israel and Palestine, anti-Arab prejudices and discrimination have become stronger. The invasions of Arab countries and the corresponding prejudices are closely tied into the United States' and other Western countries' dependence on Arab oil. Imperialism on behalf of multinational oil companies to secure low cost oil plays an important role in the global social structure involving Arab nations and Arab people.

Finally, anti-Jewish behaviors specifically, as with more recently heightened anti-Muslim behaviors, are further complicated by having a religious basis. This raises the issue, not only of the complications related to the persecution of Jews and Muslims, but also the issue of religious persecution itself. There is not enough space to deal with the various occurrences and examples of religious persecution. It is, however, important to point out generally that the historical roots of religious persecution, which are deep and widespread, are well grounded in labor exploitation and land expropriation.

## Looksism

Most of the isms are validated through visual identifications. Whether it is gender, race, ethnicity, age, specific types of disability and so on, group membership is triggered by particular appearances, and those appearances have been assigned a negative or positive valence. Even social classes can sometimes be differentiated by appearances: different styles and designs of clothes, and different ways of carrying oneself. It is in this respect that looksism truly cuts across nearly all of the other isms. There is also an element of looksism that is independent of all of the other isms. As stated by Berry, "Bias against people based on their physical appearance can operate alone as a looks-based stigma or it can reinforce other "isms," such as racism, sexism, ageism, ableism, and classism" (2007: 9).

### *Sharpening the scalpel of discrimination*

The "looks-based stigma" is the component upon which this brief section will focus. First of all, it is important to sort out the process by which humans select their mates, which is a process that defies reasonable explanation. In many ways we have antics and behavior patterns that are not all that different than the mating practices of the bird of paradise. On the other hand, human attraction is distorted and confounded by the beauty and the beast sensationalism of media commercials and Hollywood fantasy. By the time a person is a fully grown adult it is difficult to know exactly what the basis for one's genuine attraction to another might be. Definitions of beauty change over time with changing commercial interests related to fashion and retail sales, and most ideal standards of beauty are literally unattainable. Beauty definitions also change across cultures and contexts. One of the more stable findings related to attraction within the United States is that men, more than women, seek beauty in a mate. Women, more than men, seek status and power when looking for a mate (Berry 2007). The notion that the pursuit of trophy partners, trophy children, and trophy animal pets, has a common basis in the quest for one's own status enhancement (Berry 2008) is somewhat disturbing, but also likely to be true among many people.

If one moves just a little beyond the huge amounts of money to be made directly from the beauty industries and the manipulations of beauty for the purposes of selling products, attaining power, and enhancing one's own status, one finds still another latent social function of looksism. When all the ism victims are aggregated into the low cost labor pool (peoples of color, women, people with disabilities, people from excluded ethnic groups, and GLBT people) has the amount of surplus labor been maximized: have profits been maximized? The answer is "no." While it is clear that many of the isms intersect with one another, none intersect more completely with so many of the isms as does looksism. All groups of people from every possible background have differentiated looks conveying different meanings relative to social acceptability, social status, and social power. If people from one of the excluded groups escape oppression ordinarily experienced based on their membership in that group, the finer features of their individual appearance within that group's broader characteristics will still serve to keep them available for low cost employment.

If it doesn't matter how smart you are when you are Black or a woman, it matters even less if you are Black, a woman, and considered unattractive; you must wait in the unemployment line with the rest of the excess labor pool. If your hard work and due diligence gets you the right degree for the current job market despite the fact that you are openly gay or lesbian, your "homely" appearance will add you to the ranks of the lesser qualified, and someone else will have "your" job.

Looksism squeezes still more out of the employable workforce to create an even larger pool of surplus labor, and thereby maintains the lowest possible cost workers to do the more difficult and dangerous production and service activities for corporations. Even some among the most privileged group of White young to middle aged men with a Northern European heritage can now make a contribution to the surplus labor pool. The closer a White man comes to the media-projected cultural ideal of handsome, the more likely it is that he will have the employment position he seeks. Tall traditionally handsome men who are not victims of any of the other isms typically have choices, even if they are marginally qualified within their respective occupations. Being born into money helps mitigate this problem for "unattractive" White men, as it does for all ism-based groups.

Looksism helps keep select high paying opportunities truly select and high paying—available only for the "best of the best." Hence, when we look at the CEOs of the fortune five hundred corporations it should not be a surprise to us that so many of them look alike. They are mostly White men who literally go from one CEO position to another attaining ever bigger and more lucrative salaries and compensation packages. Is it truly the case that the remaining 98 plus percent of the population could not do the job that they are doing? That is not a likely reality. While the highest most lucrative positions in the United States seldom seem to have enough "qualified" men to fill them, the rest of the population struggles to keep their heads above the sea of excluded group people who through one or more of the isms, and by the sheer might of their numbers, have found themselves contributors to the devaluation of labor and the maximization of profits for those few "highly qualified men" and their wealthy benefactors.

## Eliminating the Isms

While slightly different, all isms serve basically the same purposes: provide as many workers as possible for the lowest possible labor cost, and provide natural resources for the lowest possible cost. Moving forward in this book the reader will see still more evidence of racism as the criminal justice system is used as a means of keeping Blacks and other excluded groups devalued and contained. The containment in itself becomes an important part of maintaining a low cost labor supply, as prisons, most paid for by taxpayer money, are converted into private for-profit factories (Davis 1998, 2003).

Eliminating the isms requires elimination of the motivations that drive the isms. There have been, and continue to be, many re-socialization programs related to the elimination of the isms: employment diversity and affirmative action training programs, school and community awareness programs and so on. Those programs will not be sufficiently effective for their purpose until people are also socialized into an understanding of the socio-economic function of the isms for the production and maintenance of upper class wealth. Once that is accomplished macro social change programs can be effectively implemented, and sustainable equitable social structures can be planned and created.

# Chapter 8
# Inequality and the Social Construction of Reality

## The Careful Construction of Reality

Until the early 1970s the power of the media, especially the press and video media, was still not fully understood. Certainly politicians were already using the media in their campaigns, which required raising hundreds of thousands of dollars for advertising, but that was just an advanced version of handing out political flyers. There was a slight indication of what was to come in the video media industry in the first ever televised presidential candidate debates in 1959, when John Kennedy debated Richard Nixon. Kennedy came across as being photogenic and quick witted, while Nixon came across as awkward and stumbling. These debates were generally considered quite significant in the victory of John Kennedy. At that time, and for several years thereafter, politicians still did not have a complete grasp of what the media meant to politics, namely how important it was for shaping reality.

Nixon was eventually elected in 1968, and shortly after his re-election in 1972, the Washington Post began running stories that implicated Nixon in some illegal activities that occurred during the presidential campaign. The incident became known as the Watergate affair, since the crimes took place in the Watergate Hotel. People all over the country began reading about how high level officials in the government, and possibly the president himself, were caught engaging in illegal activities. Nationally televised hearings investigating the Watergate crimes took place and made the president and his closest advisors look very bad.

Just prior to Watergate the famous Pentagon Papers were leaked to the press, exposing numerous government supported illegal activities connected with the Vietnam War. The relatively open newspaper coverage of these events and the dramatic televised investigations of the Watergate crimes contributed greatly to the forced resignation of President Nixon. Nixon was an establishment friend of the large corporations and, for the most part, gave them what they wanted. It was, at the very least, an inconvenience for the corporation leaders to have to rebuild their support around someone else. The wealthy invest a lot of money in presidents and the press was now being recognized as a problem.

The lesson learned from Watergate by the powerful wealthy people is that the media is an effective tool which can hurt them if not controlled. Furthermore, controlling the media is a step toward controlling reality, and whoever controls reality controls the situation and the power vested within that situation. Hence, by the time the next round of high profile criminal hearings were being televised

(Iran-Contra), the media arena was different than in the 1970s. There was a great deal of struggle over what time of day the hearings would be aired, and who would be questioned during the available times. There was also a great deal of coaching that took place, so that everyone was highly aware that they were involved in a theatric performance to make their audience, the general public, see the world as they wanted it to be seen. Perhaps most effective in this regard was Lieutenant Colonel Oliver North, who became quite famous for his projected "in your face" macho save the country image. Young people were especially taken by him and many wore "Oliver North for President" t-shirts following the hearings.

*Social constructionism: Communists? Terrorists? And axis of evil?*

The Iran-Contra hearings that took place in the late 1980s and the associated crimes were turned into a campaign to promote the corporation driven United States government agenda of overthrowing governments of other countries: a campaign to promote imperial laissez-faire capitalism. The symbols that were used for that purpose were "communism," "imminent danger," and "patriotism." The participants in the criminal activities were presented to the public as bold patriots out to save the country from the imminent danger of communism. But one might rightfully ask how one can claim to be a patriot out saving the country while violating the very constitution that country is based upon? The unfortunate reality of this situation, that even the congressional investigative panel could not entertain, is that the Iran-Contra crimes were not about patriotism; nor were they about an imminent danger of communism.

Communism posed no threat to the people of the United States. Communism is an economic system just as capitalism is an economic system. The governments of communist countries were primarily interested in helping the oppressed masses of other countries who were trying to get rid of their Western controlled dictators. The Iran-Contra crimes were about corporate domination over other lands and other peoples for the purpose of making big corporate profits bigger and thus wealthy people wealthier at the expense of other countries and the millions of people living in those countries. Because communism was structured under the capitalist nation-state model, it could never operate effectively. That is not because communism is necessarily a flawed economic system, but because the nature of nation-states, whatever the economic system, is to oppress and control the people living within that nation-state. It is important to conceptually separate economic systems from political systems, even though they often times are deliberately intertwined in the construction of reality. Capitalism and Democracy are entangled in this manner.

*Capitalism is not democracy*

When corporate capitalists use the United States government by claiming to fight communist governments to spread democracy, they really are fighting communist economics in order to spread capitalism—often times at the *expense* of democracy both at home and abroad. The United States public tends to be confused about this issue because over time people in positions of power and wealth have used the media and educational systems to deliberately mesh capitalism and democracy together as being one and the same. Think of all the United States soldiers that have risked their lives or lost their lives thinking they were going to fight for democracy when in actuality they were going to fight for capitalism. The meshing and intertwining of economics and politics is intentional since one is far less likely to fight for, or have their son or daughter fight for, someone else's wealth than they would the freedom that democracy is supposed to represent. Keep in mind that some of the leaders that the United States government has overthrown have been popular democratically elected leaders.

Social reality is continually negotiated through the interaction process. Whoever has the last successful anticipation is the one who controls the situation and thus controls how reality will be defined. Perhaps one of the greatest ironies of all time is that the general citizenry of the United States pays billions of dollars in tax revenues to the United States government which is then in turn used to carefully and systematically deceive that same general citizenry. Most people in the United States have no idea that they are being deceived with their own money by their own government. The failure of the Congress to do anything of consequence to the many criminals involved in the Iran-Contra crimes was partly due to the media victory won by the involved government agents. While there were times when they looked pretty bad during the investigative hearings, overall they made their "patriots against evil communism" version of reality stick. The government officials involved in the crimes controlled the situation and eventually funding for the Contras was even reinstated.

*New symbols, same reality*

When we look past the Iran-Contra crimes of the 1980s to the George W. Bush presidency early in the twenty-first century, we see that crimes done secretly by the Reagan administration were done out in the open by the Bush administration. When clandestine National Security Agency and Central Intelligence Agency operatives failed, President Bush declared war on Iraq. Part of what allowed this to happen is the 2001 attacks on the World Trade Center and the Pentagon. As a result of these activities, the citizenry of the United States was poised for a major media-based control campaign. The attacks served that function in the same manner as the bombing of Pearl Harbor served the function of getting the United States citizenry psychologically prepared for World War II. Whether the United States government intended for the 9/11/2001 attacks to serve the same function as the Pearl Harbor bombings is uncertain, but not a moot point since there are many unanswered questions about the manner in which the attacks and world trade building implosions took place.

Prior to becoming part of the George W. Bush administration, on June 3, 1997, Dick Cheney (Vice President), Donald Rumsfeld (Secretary of Defense), Paul

Wolfowitz (Deputy Secretary of Defense), and other members of the eventual G.W. Bush administration, along with Jeb Bush (President Bush's brother and Governor of Florida), signed a Statement of Principles as part of their involvement with a pro-imperialist organization known as the Project for the New American Century (PNAC). These principles basically called for United States world domination by use of military power, suggesting the use of first strike strategies if deemed necessary (PNAC 2000). Middle Eastern countries like Iraq were identified as primary targets for intervention, and large increases in military spending were forcefully promoted. In September of 2000 (a year before the 9/11/01 World Trade Center attacks), a revised document, originally written by Paul Wolfowitz and based on the PNAC principles, was brought forward by PNAC to be ready for use in the expected upcoming Bush administration. Anticipating possible public resistance to post cold war military build up and deployment, the report states, "… the process of transformation, even if it brings revolutionary change, is likely to be a long one, absent some catastrophic and catalyzing event—like a new Pearl Harbor" (PNAC 2000: 51).

Hence, in the aftermath of the 9/11/01 catastrophic event the United States public was bombarded with new media-based control symbols. Instead of "communism" people were daily confronted with "terrorism." In place of the Soviet Union (evil empire), now broken apart, there was an "axis of evil" that included Asian and Middle Eastern nation-states: North Korea, Iraq, and Iran. This new symbolic communication, heard daily for literally years following the 9/11/01 attacks, escalated the constructed reality of fear so as to escalate the hidden reality of corporate United States greed based imperialism. Based on this cleverly constructed false reality the corporate United States government severely bombed and invaded Iraq under completely false pretenses (de la Vega 2005). With skillful and highly controlled use of the corporate owned media, the corporate United States government convinced the people of the United States that Iraq played a lead role in the 9/11/01 attacks and that Iraq was harboring huge stockpiles of biological and nuclear weapons that could be used against the people of the United States at any moment. Both of these serious claims were so systematically and thoroughly demonstrated to be false (Sirota and Harvey 2004, Shenon 2004) that even the mainstream corporate media felt obligated to eventually report that there were no weapons of mass destruction and no connection between Iraq and the 9/11/01 attacks (Schorn 2006).

## National "Defense" and Militarism

Once the team is on the field it is too late to turn back. In the public's "mind" everyone must foremost "support the troops." Hence, no matter what evidence comes forward it must be discredited, otherwise a person could experience intolerable cognitive dissonance. The imperative of victory, once the game has started becomes one and the same as the imperative of imperialism.

Defending the honor of the home school is the foundation upon which militarism is based. Militarism is the process of converting some people into soldiers, some people into the supporters of soldiers, and other people into enemies in the minds of the soldiers and in the minds of the supporters of the soldiers. All of this is done through the careful symbolic construction of reality that taps into the early socialization of men, and now increasingly, the early socialization of women as well.

The symbolic construction of reality requires consistent daily support of the mainstream media and a parallel system of curricular and co-curricular school activities. In addition to history classes, pro-military civics classes, and complex military-like athletics programs, the video game industry has added yet one more media dimension to United States militarism.

One of the greatest concerns of modern warfare has been that a high percentage of soldiers actually fail to fire their rifles once they enter combat, a discovery during World War II, when it may have been as low as 25 percent actually firing their rifles (Marshall 1978, Grossman 1995). Intensive firing programs have been instituted to correct this "problem" whereby soldiers are required to shoot more quickly without as much time to discern the legitimacy of the target. By the Vietnam War firing rates purportedly increased considerably, but were still not as high as some considered acceptable (Grant 2010). The high number of "non-hostile" soldier casualties in Afghanistan and Iraq, possibly as high as 19 percent (White, D. 2010), may well be a by-product of this accelerated training process, greatly aided by the high exposure of children to quick response repetitive killing video games. Some of these games are so realistic that the military uses them in their training programs. Children are being prepared to kill other humans in an enjoyable and exciting format (America's Army 2010). The volunteer army now consists of champions jumping out of Humvees digitally trained to kill (Moore 2004). To the sound of inspiring music from their headgear, they are ready to shoot anything that acts as a stimulus for the trained response. The military no longer has a significant problem getting soldiers to shoot. That problem has been reversed to create a more serious problem of soldiers killing innocent people. This is done in a variety of ways, resulting in estimates ranging from several hundred thousand to over a million Iraqi citizens killed. A leaked whistleblower video shows that killing civilians is sometimes indiscriminate and sport-like in the manner in which it is carried out (wikiLeaks 2010).

One might argue that it is best to train soldiers to respond to possible danger quickly so as to best be able to defend themselves. Such an argument, however, suggests that in a typical war there is actually some way of knowing, separate from whose "side" you are on, which life is more valuable: the life of the one who is shot or the life of the one doing the shooting. Furthermore, such an argument overlooks entirely the imperialist basis for war and the corresponding condition that soldiers on opposing sides actually have nothing against one another in reality. The soldiers who are shooting at one another are more like each other than the wealthy people for whom they fight.

*"How shall we escape?"*

In an essay by the above title, Leo Tolstoy, one of the most brilliant authors of the late nineteenth and early twentieth centuries, wrestles with the question of how humans can best get out of their dilemma of seemingly endless imperial exploitation through war (Tolstoy 1898). Imperial wars were a recognized problem then as well as now. Hence, the proverbial question of where shall we drive the wooden stake? His answer requires a re-socialization process whereby the average working people of the world will refuse to fight for the wealthy people. His position, formulated over 100 years ago, is that the answer lies in all people being sufficiently aware of the causes of war that they will refuse to participate. The alternative to this type of solution to such a large systemic international problem always comes back to power overcoming power through force. Under these circumstances, without an effective re-socialization process, the battle is never truly won. Wars continue and life is destroyed.

Cuba has enjoyed over 40 years of peace because the people of Cuba know that cooperation and enlightened education are the only means by which they can live without exploitation. The United States has used all of its secret service and spying capabilities to overthrow Cuba's current government. These efforts have been well documented and have consistently failed. While the Cuban government has been careful to subvert counter-revolutionary efforts by the United States government, and has sometimes, unfortunately, resorted to forceful measures, the primary reason for Cuba's ability to maintain its sovereignty as a non-capitalist nation-state is the education and awareness level of the Cuban people. They know that a life based on greed is an ill spent and destructive life.

*What happened in Vietnam?*

Is it possible that soldiers might one day refuse to fight because they realize the war they are in is not a worthy cause? It is not only possible, it actually happened during the Vietnam War. Eighty percent of the combat soldiers had a high school education or less, and most were working class youths. The officers were college educated and were being rotated in and out of Vietnam in a sped-up cycling process so that they could all be promoted at the expense of the combat soldier. The combat soldier's required tour of duty was twice as long as that of the officers. As the war dragged on with no actual recognizable purpose and no end in sight, the soldiers began to realize that the people they were told they were fighting for and the people they were supposed to be fighting against were basically the same people. They further realized that they themselves were not all that different from the people they were supposed to kill: working people who were farmers and who just wanted to make a living for themselves and their families (Winterfilm 2006).

In 1968 alone the army recorded 68 acts of unit and platoon levels of mutiny: soldiers as a group refusing to follow orders to fight (Geier 1999). By 1970 the number of incidents of mutiny had escalated substantially. Soldiers no longer followed orders and officers had to negotiate with them as to what they might be willing to do. Officers that insisted on having their orders followed were often the victims of fragging. Fragging was a process whereby officers were warned by their combat soldiers that they better back off from their inflexible course. If they didn't back off as warned they were killed by the soldiers. The army itself reported 126 fraggings in 1969, 271 in 1970, and 333 in 1971. They quit formally recording the numbers of fraggings after 1971, although there were another 1400 dead officers for whom the army could not account. All told, 20–25 percent of the officers killed during the Vietnam war were killed by their own men. By 1971, more than 25 percent of the armed forces were absent without leave (AWOL) (Geier 1999), and it is estimated that about 500,000 soldiers went AWOL during the entire war (Wikipedia 2010b).

The war resistance activities during the United States invasion of Vietnam took place within an atmosphere of a relatively free press. Reporters rode in the helicopters and jeeps with soldiers in Vietnam and reported everything that was happening on a daily basis. The false reality of spreading democracy was exposed and there was revolt among the soldiers and revolt in the streets of the United States. All of this reality media was helping to bring the illegal and unjust war to an eventual halt. The United States lost the war and tens of thousands of people were killed on both sides. This military loss aggravated the wealthy corporate owners who hoped to benefit from the war by expanding capitalism into Asia: new resources, new labor, and new markets.

*Soldiers revolt: not new* According to Leo Tolstoy (1899a) the following letter was sent to a commander in the Holland military. It was sent in response to the author of the letter being drafted to serve in the National Guard.

**Document 8.1 Letter of refusal to kill for the nation-state**

**The Beginning of the End**

During last year, in Holland, a young man named Van der Veer was called on to enter the National Guard. To the summons of the commander, Van der Veer answered in the following letter:

*"Thou shalt do no murder"*

*To M. Herman Sneiders, Commandant of the National Guard of the Midelburg district.*

*Dear Sir,—Last week I received a document ordering me to appear at the municipal office, to be, according to law, enlisted in the National Guard. As you probably noticed, I did not appear, and this letter is to inform you, plainly and without equivocation, that I do not intend to appear before the commission. I know well that I am taking a heavy responsibility, that you have the right to punish me, and that you will not fail to use this right. But that does not frighten me. The reasons which lead me to this passive resistance seem to me strong enough to outweigh the responsibility I take.*

*I, who, if you please, am not a Christian, understand better than most Christians the commandment which is put at the head of this letter, the commandment which is rooted in human nature, in the mind of man. When but a boy, I allowed myself to be taught the trade of soldier, the art of killing: but now I renounce it. I would not kill at the command of others, and thus have murder on my conscience without any personal cause or reason whatever.*

*Can you mention anything more degrading to a human being than carrying out such murder, such massacre? I am unable to kill, even to see an animal killed: therefore I became a vegetarian. And now I am to be ordered to shoot men who have done me no harm: for I take it that it is not to shoot at leaves and branches of trees that soldiers are taught to use guns.*

*But you will reply, perhaps, that the National Guard is besides, and especially, to keep civic order.*

*M. Commandant, if order really reigned in our society, if the social organism were really healthy – in other words, if there were in our social relations no crying abuses, if it were not established that one man shall die of hunger while another gratifies his every whim of luxury, then you would see me in the front ranks of the defenders of this orderly state. But I flatly decline to help in preserving the present so-called "social order." Why, M. Commandant, should we throw dust in each other's eyes? We both know quite well what the "preservation of order" means: upholding the rich against the poor toilers, who begin to perceive their rights. Do we not know the role which the National Guard played in the last strike at Rotterdam? For no reason, the Guard had to be on duty hours and hours to watch over the property of the commercial houses which were affected. Can you for a moment suppose that I should shoot down working people who are acting quite within their rights? You cannot be so blind. Why then complicate the question? Certainly, it is impossible for me to allow myself to be molded into an obedient National Guardsman as you want and must have.*

*For all these reasons, but especially because I hate murder by order, I refuse to serve as a National Guardsman, and ask you not to send me either uniform or arms, because I have a fixed resolve not to use them.—I greet you, M. Commandant, J.K. Van der Veer*

The above letter effectively exposes the hidden reality of war, a reality that, if known by all citizens, would make it very difficult for wars to be fought. Keep in mind that the letter was written well over 100 years ago from this writing. The information the letter contains is not complicated, and neither is it information that should surprise anyone, but it does. Once in combat, soldiers often learn the real purpose of the war from their direct experience—hence, the high number of desertions. Why then is it not known by all in the general public and acted upon accordingly? Control of information flow is critical to controlling reality, and the reality projected in the above letter does not serve the interests of those with the greatest power to control information.

*The volunteer army*

Once the Vietnam War was over in 1975 and the troops were either withdrawn or held as prisoners, President Nixon eliminated the draft and established an all volunteer army. At that time, given the devastating military loss of over 58,000 United States soldiers, many people laughed and joked about who would want to volunteer to be in the military.

In the 2003 war in Iraq, especially as national guard troops were being sent into battle, it became clear from interviews with soldiers that many of them joined the military because they lacked other viable ways of either making a living or paying for their education. They did not expect to ever have to serve in combat and many were not mentally prepared to do so. The Pentagon estimates that the number of soldiers deserting the Iraq war had reached 8,000 by the beginning of 2006, and it is estimated that about 40,000 United States soldiers have gone AWOL since 2000 (Wikipedia 2010b). The British army estimates that about 11,000 of their soldiers have gone AWOL during the Iraq war as of the beginning of 2008 (Quin 2008). There have been some high profile cases of United States soldiers escaping to Canada, which has, since the Vietnam War, technically closed its borders to United States conscientious objectors (Levey 2007).

Hence, the all volunteer army is not truly based on volunteering. If bad enough conditions are created in one situation, other bad situations can look pretty good. This is a classic form of negative reinforcement. One can avoid the pain of unemployment and/or underemployment by joining the military. New recruits are now also promised $60,000 to join, since the high probability of injury or death in Iraq and Afghanistan has become a major deterrent for joining the military. From 1998 through 2003, the Department of Defense increased its spending on recruitment advertising by 98 percent, from about $299 million to $592 million and has an overall recruitment budget of nearly $4 billion (GAO 2003a). The largest portion of that $4 billion is for recruiters, who target youth in their early teens by visiting their schools, participate in their activities, romanticize the military experience, and get early commitments without parental consent through the Delayed Entry Program (Ya Ya 2010). Much of the contact provided by recruiters in the schools is due to the National Defense Authorization Act of 2002 that requires schools to accommodate military recruiters just as they would college or employer recruiters, or face losing federal funds. Using sophisticated media and propaganda devices recruiters have become highly skilled at creating a very attractive false reality that promises to alleviate the pain of likely or existing unemployment.

What young people don't know when they commit to the military is that, "There are nearly 150,000 veterans in homeless shelters and on the streets in the

United States and more than 300,000 veterans experience homelessness over the course of a year. A growing number of veterans are also severely rent burdened, with 500,000 paying more than 50% of their income on rent" (Jericho Project 2007). In the Iraq War alone, officially 4,413 soldiers have been killed and 31,874 have been physically injured. Twenty percent of the injured have serious brain or spinal injuries (White, D. 2010). Some sources indicate the official estimate of the number of wounded is low and that the actual number is probably over 100,000 (Griffis 2010). Regardless of their characteristics going into combat, combat veterans are more likely than other veteran and non-veteran men to experience disabilities and be unemployed (MacLean 2010). The psychological problems of Iraqi veterans who are suffering from Post Traumatic Stress Disorder (PTSD) are so great that it is difficult to measure at this time. We do know that tens of thousands are being treated, thousands more need treatment but are not getting it, and there are at least 1,000 veteran suicide attempts a month (Keteyian 2008). Fifty percent of Vietnam veterans (about 1.7 million) have suffered from PTSD (eMedicineHealth 2010). These data are quite inconsistent with the exotic travel and long term opportunities promised by the military recruiters. There is no question about who is winning the struggle for control of the reality surrounding military service. It is the wealthy controllers of multinational corporations who buy legislators who then pour billions upon billions of dollars into the military to make foreign lands safe for corporate plunder and labor exploitation. If young people could be socialized into the true reality of the military experience there would not be much of a military presence, despite the deliberately denigrated domestic economy.

### *One hundred years later: why don't we know?*

Why are the people of the United States less informed now than the above quoted Van der Veer was over 100 years ago? Aren't people supposed to be getting smarter? Isn't civilization supposed to move ever forward to greater and greater heights of humanity? The same forces that are described in this letter, written over 100 years ago, are in place today. The difference is that wealthy powerful people have much greater control over information than they did in the past.

## Censorship: The Best Protection Money Can Buy

People with a lot of resources who want to protect their resources, took a two pronged approach toward maintaining a publicly accepted false reality. First, they made sure that the United States government would no longer allow journalists to freely cover wars. Journalists had to be restricted so as to only see and report what the corporation controlled government wanted the public to see and report. This strategy was first tested in President Reagan's invasion of Granada, followed by the media sensationalizing of the 1991 Gulf war under President George H.W.

Bush, and then followed again by the 2003 Gulf war under President George W. Bush. During the 2003 Gulf War, the media were housed in a special camp and only occasionally were allowed to leave that area.

The Arab media network Al Jazeera, however, was actually doing real coverage of the war and the difference between the two media presentations made it seem like different wars were being covered. So disconcerting was the Al Jazeera reporting of the war to the United States government that Secretary of State Powell was sent to Qatar, where Al Jazeera is based, to pressure their government to do something to stop Al Jazeera from so freely reporting what they were seeing. Ultimately, Al Jazeera reporters were attacked by the United States military and four of them were killed. The military had been notified of where the Al Jazeera press would be located. In one instance, the military claimed self-defense but an investigation revealed that there was no firing coming from the Al Jazeera location.

*Ownership facilitates censorship*

The second prong of the strategy of people wanting to protect their great wealth was to buy nearly all of the media, and that is what has been done. The regulatory process governing monopolies and governing how the public airwaves are used were quietly set aside during the 1980s, the decade of deregulation of just about everything that ought to be controlled. As incredible as it may seem, there are now a handful of corporate media giants that own most of the media in the United States, possibly as much as 90 percent. The six biggest United States based media corporations are: News Corporation, Time Warner, Viacom, Walt Disney Company, General Electric, and CBS (Freepress 2009). If you are reading a newspaper, watching television, watching a movie, or listening to a music CD, chances are excellent that it is a product of one of these parent companies. They have literally purchased nearly all of the newspapers, television/radio stations, and major recording studios in every part of the United States, as well as in many countries outside of the United States.

How does this impact the lives of average citizens? Most people in the United States are being prevented from knowing the truth about what is happening in the world by systematic censorship built into all of the mainstream media outlets (Phillips and Project Censored 2009). Not everything is controlled in the media every day, but the important stories that could make a difference for the people who own the media are either edited to satisfaction or censored altogether.

Project Censored publishes the top 25 censored stories every year. The top 25 are just a few among many. When one looks at the Project Censored selected stories one realizes that censorship in the mainstream media is very real. When documentary film creator and producer, Michael Moore, was ready to release his politically controversial *Fahrenheit 9/11*, the company with which he had a contract was prevented from showing the movie by Walt Disney Company. Disney owned Moore's production company. Eventually, Moore was able to prevail, but not without a considerable delay. There have been numerous firings and reprimands of famous newscasters and reporters for airing moderately critical views about former President George W. Bush or his policies. Some of the victims, like famous newscaster Dan Rather, are actually pretty conservative people who were simply trying to protect their integrity as journalists by reporting the truth about important occurrences, such as President George W. Bush having been AWOL when he was in the National Guard (Duff 2010).

## Where Does One Find Truth?

If the mainstream media cannot be trusted to provide the truth, who can be trusted to do so? It is important to remember that one never really knows if the truth has been found, but there are ways of logically arriving at where one should go to maximize the likelihood of encountering reasonably factual statements. There are four main sources of published/disseminated information that are based on a claim of keeping the public apprised of what is happening in the world.

*Mainstream media*

First, there is the popular mainstream media which consists of: daily newspapers, popular books, TV "news" programs, talk shows, and "public" TV and radio. In relatively recent years the emergence of "reality" shows has increased confusion about what is entertainment and what is information. In addition to the issue of whether "news" is really news, we have the added question of whether the numerous television programs glamorizing crime fighting are entertainment or factual information based on science (Muzzatti et al. 2006). Much public confusion exists over this issue with many thinking it is the latter. As a dean I encounter students inquiring about what they need to major in to attain a CSI (Crime Scene Investigation) type position as a forensic criminal investigator. These programs not only blur the lines between what is possible and not possible, they reinforce stereotypes of excluded groups and, like the "news" distort who the most prevalent and most serious criminals might be (Muzzatti et al. 2006).

From earlier discussions, it is already known that the popular media is of questionable value when it comes to providing accurate interpretations of the most important events. They are owned by a handful of people who need to make sure that their view of reality is the only view of reality. But there is another reason the popular media is not a very useful source of information. The primary goal of the people who own the media is to make money, not to identify and disseminate accurate information. Hence, in addition to practicing censorship of important stories they do not want the public to know about, the popular media tend to sensationalize the stories they do publish or present. It is possible to get a useful story once in a long while, but for the most part the mainstream popular media is glitter and high gloss disinformation and/or trivia. While seemingly harmless, the mainstream media frequently does harm to various segments of the population.

When Hurricane Katrina hit the Gulf Coast a new version of the culture of poverty emerged as a way of blaming the hurricane victims for their own predicament. It was argued that the poor people of New Orleans did not leave before the storm hit the area because they lived a life of government dependency. Their welfare based lifestyle somehow took away their ability to think and act for themselves so they hung around helplessly waiting for someone to rescue them. This argument was made in a sufficiently convincing manner by public commentators that it seemingly became an accepted public reality. What promoters of this notion failed to consider was the extent to which the poor people of New Orleans were actually capable of leaving. Many did not have their own transportation or money to travel otherwise. Relocation travelling expenses were also problematic: housing, eating out, and so on (Brezina 2008). Additionally, a post hurricane survey revealed that the poor people of New Orleans did not typically behave as helpless people. They looked for jobs and did what they could to be self sufficient (Brezina 2008). There was no real evidence of the malaise of government dependency that was a serious and misleading part of the mainstream media created reality. Yet, poor people in New Orleans, many of whom are African Americans, were once again stereotyped and maligned.

*"Public" broadcasting* Public television and public radio used to be pretty good sources of information because they were at one time primarily funded by donations from average citizens and government (public) funds. As time has gone on they have become increasingly funded by corporations, which now insist on what they call "balanced" reporting. What balanced reporting means is that if a radio station reports on something bad that a corporation does, they have to then find something good to report about that corporation, or give another report that suggests that what the corporation did that was bad, was not necessarily so bad that anyone should be concerned about it. It is a way of neutralizing all the critical information that reveals the hard steel beneath the flowers—the metaphor used earlier in this book. The final conclusion with which the public must always be left is that perhaps the bridge is really made out of flowers after all: General Electric does bring good things to life, Nike shoes make you fly like Michael Jordon, and General Motors trucks help keep America strong.

Some small local public radio stations still exist that do a good job of maintaining their informational independence from the parent Public Broadcasting System. They are difficult to find and frequently in jeopardy. For the most part, Public Media has become part of the mainstream media. Only about 2 percent of the funding for National Public Radio comes from government money.

*Government documents*

Next, there are government documents that can be considered: agency pamphlets, agency data sets, agency reports; speeches, and public statements by appointed heads of agencies. The important thing to remember about government documents is that the heads of government agencies are often times political appointees. Politicians typically appoint people that will carry out their political agenda for them through that agency. Hence, many times reports are biased in a particular political direction. Some reports that are not connected with highly visible political agendas may be fairly accurate and straightforward. Agency data sets can be quite useful. Government data, especially collected numerical data on how many times certain events occurred, is usually pretty accurate, depending to some extent on the nature of the collected data. Speeches and public statements by appointed heads of agencies are usually not useful. They can, however, be used as data to analyze how many times a particular political leader has publicly lied about something, or how many times a political figure has made contradictory statements. In general, government documents can be useful if the context of the document is given careful consideration.

*Professional sources*

A third option is sources associated with professional organizations: professional conferences, professional books and texts, and professional journals. Professional sources of information are produced by or through a professional academic field of study and research. The academic field of study is often times associated with applied fields under the same professional canopy. The goal of professional organizations is to produce and disseminate information using methods deemed acceptable based strictly on the expertise of people within the field.

Professional sources of information are typically preferable to the popular media and government documents, albeit sometimes professional publications are based on government documents. What is supposed to make professional sources better than the first two mentioned sources is that professional publications use what is called a blind review process. It can also be referred to as a masked review process. A masked review is one where the reviewer, who is an expert in the field of the submitted work, does not know who the author is. This process is supposed to eliminate bias and favoritism when a decision is being made to publish a submitted work. The masked review process works sometimes, but not always. For people who do a lot of writing and reading in a field of research it is not difficult to determine who wrote a particular piece, or possibly who the author's mentor might be. Additionally, professional publications are not without their own political ties. Funding for research projects often comes from government agencies, or worse yet, directly from a corporation or a foundation associated with a particular corporation. Information unfavorable to the current sponsoring government agency or unfavorable to products of a sponsoring corporation will almost certainly result in the loss of funding for future research projects. Researchers who depend on those kinds of sources for their funding often engage in self-censorship in order to assure that their funding will continue.

Another source of professional censorship is universities out of which the professional academic disciplines typically operate. Most universities depend on external funding from wealthy donors, corporations, non-profit foundations, or the government. For departments to survive in most places within academia they must not be out there irritating the University's donors. Such behavior could be costly to the University and thus the particular department. Hence, since the nineteen eighties most departments around the country, including Sociology Departments, have been careful to hire and tenure people that do not stray too far from the mold of what is conservatively acceptable. Newer faculty members have to be careful until they are tenured so as to not appear to be too far out of step with the status quo. Once faculty members have tenure they have a reasonable amount of academic freedom from which they can disseminate what they believe to be the most accurate information. Until then, they must be careful. When ultra conservative political administrations are in power, even tenured faculty members are targeted. University administrators, under pressure from corporate owned politicians or possibly corporations directly, will use various strategies against tenured faculty members in order to get rid of them.

*Alternative media*

The fourth general source of information is called the alternative media, or sometime it is called the alternative press: not for profit videos, not for profit books, not for profit journals, not for profit newsletters, conferences organized by not for profit organizations, and small independent presses that have a particular message as the basis for their existence.

The alternative media is so labeled because it gives the public an alternative to the systematic pro laissez-faire capitalism biases that are typical built into the mainstream and professional media sources. Alternative media cover a wide range of written publications, audio materials, and video materials produced by not-for-profit organizations that have an interest in solving some particular social problem in the world. There are literally hundreds of these not-for-profit organizations that receive their funding from other larger not-for-profit organizations, private donations directly, and membership fees and donations. Large philanthropic donations are usually from people who are interested in working on solving the same problem as the not-for-profit organization to which they donated their money. Typically, these issue based not-for-profit organizations are trying to bring about some particular social change and are open about what they are doing. They produce and disseminate information that they believe to be the most accurate given all the evidence that is available. They draw on various other sources of information and often conduct their own research. Their publications, tapes, and videos are typically made available at a low cost, and sometimes are provided free with membership into the organization.

An interesting example is People for the Ethical Treatment of Animals (PETA), which is an organization that will provide its members with free videos and various forms of written publications to help them disseminate PETA's information to others. PETA is a large and active not-for-profit social change organization. They send activists all over the United States to speak and organize protests on behalf of animals. Other alternative media organizations produce a particular journal or newsletter to provide a service to the public in regard to information about some particular issue. The issue often involves information that has been censored from the mainstream and professional media outlets. In some instances that is their only function.

*Magic and objectivity*

With the alternative media, information seekers typically know where they stand. They are not being misled that the information is somehow magically objectively purified without bias and without any hidden agenda. There is no such thing as an unbiased piece of research or pure objectivity. Unless a person is raised in a vacuum bubble of some sort they are going to have externally shaped views of social reality that will impact how they see and how they study the world around them. It is much more honest to identify one's biases for the information seeker and then proceed to compile as accurate information as one can within the parameters of those biases. PETA is an organization based on the belief that non-human animals are mistreated. They do not try to hide that belief. It is the purpose for their existence. From that belief they go on to provide a lot of convincing evidence that such is the case, and their evidence is extremely difficult to refute or deny. This is the manner in which most alternative media organizations proceed (Andrzejewski 2007).

The fact that a media form is alternative does not mean that it is providing flimsy undocumented information. Typically their work is better documented than the mainstream media, and comparable to the professional publications. The difference between the professional publications and the alternative media publications is that they draw on almost completely different sets of sources. If a scholar has a particular bias it is not difficult to find others with that same bias. For example, in preparing to write this book I read a chapter on militarism within a social problems anthology that represents some of the most important sociological information available from *professional* sources (Ritzer 2004). The author of the militarism chapter cites approximately 140 sources. I could find nothing in the entire nineteen pages of the chapter worth passing on to the readers of this book. I was so disappointed that I contacted the author of the article, and we had an interesting email exchange. He did eventually admit that ignoring imperialism and illegal United States invasions of other countries might be an important omission. This comment is not meant as a criticism against the author of the article in question or the book containing the article. It is to say, however, that truth can lay on a broad continuum of ideas, and finding support for those ideas, no matter what they are, is typically not that difficult. When it comes to the mainstream media and professional publications, however, what is left out is often far more important than the accuracy of what is included. As the reader may have noticed, this book uses documentation from a wide range of sources, but a large amount of the information comes from alternative media.

While it isn't always necessary, the evidence that is provided in the alternative media can often times be crosschecked with mainstream sources. For example, reference to the involvement of the United States government in the drug trade was occasionally seen in the less notable sections of some mainstream newspapers. It is not likely it would happen today. If people look hard enough they can find these references in past newspapers, but not easily. Quasi-hidden stories are provided so that the newspaper management could say they did not exclude the important information. Sometimes the mainstream media reports on controversial issues specifically to refute them. Again, one could probably find examples of this approach in relation to the United States government involvement in the drug trade.

### *Dark alliance: the legacy of Gary Webb*

Gary Webb was an award winning investigative reporter for the Mercury News in the 1980s and 1990s during the Reagan, Bush and Clinton Administrations. The Iran-Contra crimes mentioned earlier were not just illegal activities to fund an illegal war. They were also crimes that involved the illegal importation and distribution of drugs in order to make money to fund the Contras. The CIA and other arms of the government were involved, and had drug lords on the United States government payroll. Gary Webb exposed these illegal and highly immoral activities through a series of articles in the *Mercury News*. One of the biggest Nicaraguan cocaine dealers, located in the United States, admitted his involvement in smuggling drugs into the United States to help support the CIA's illegal war in Nicaragua (Webb 1999).

### *Controlling the press when it matters*

As a result of the pressure placed upon the Mercury News by the CIA and the corporate media, the paper retracted the stories and essentially fired Gary Webb, thereby destroying his career. The corporate media, including all of the big purported champions of the mainstream "free press," reconstructed the horrendous reality exposed by Gary Webb in order to mask the involvement of the CIA. In so doing, they further destroyed Webb's credibility and his record of excellence as an investigative reporter. In response to the claims against his work, Webb continued his research and put his findings into an extremely well researched and documented book (Webb 1999). Gary Webb was eventually vindicated, but not until his life, and the lives of many others, were ruined.

*Government admits administration's crimes*

The investigation of the Inspector General of the CIA confirmed Webb's findings (Parry 2004). "At Webb's death, however, it should be noted that his great gift to American history was that he, along with angry African-American citizens, forced the government to admit some of the worst crimes ever condoned by any American administration: the protection of drug smuggling into the United States as part of a covert war against a country, Nicaragua, that represented no real threat to Americans" (Perry 2004: 7).

Given the near complete lack of coverage of these serious crimes, how would the public know that in 1989 Oliver North, Richard Secord, John Poindexter and other high level officials working for the United States government were banned from ever returning to Costa Rica by then President Oscar Arias? Costa Rica is a country with which the United States supposedly has friendly relations. Would they ban high level United States government agents without just cause? As stated by Peter Phillips and Project Censored, "Corporate/mainstream media have become dependent upon the press releases and inside sources from government and major corporations for their 24-hour news content and are increasingly unwilling to broadcast or publish news that would threaten ongoing relationships with these official sources" (2004a: 218). In many instances it goes beyond being unwilling to simply being unable. As the corporate media directorates become increasingly interlocked with other corporate directorates, it is not always possible to know whether one is biting the hand that feeds oneself, or perhaps more accurately, biting one's own hand.

*Drug money and wealth*

What is perhaps more significant than the above, is that in 2005 the United States continued to launder over half of the world's drug money: somewhere in the neighborhood of 250 to 300 billion dollars a year. Once it is laundered its value increases several times over. This drug money laundering most likely continues as of this writing. Laundered drug money is apparently a major source of income for corporations and politicians. Some scholars believe illegal drug money has become a stable part of the United States economy. It is believed to be a major source of political campaign contributions and a significant subsidy to the value of corporate stocks. "The money from the drug transshipment trade flows out of Haiti to criminal intermediaries in the wholesale and retail trade, to the intelligence agencies, which protect the trade, and to the financial and banking institutions where the proceeds are laundered. Wall Street and European banks have a vested interest in installing 'democracy' in order to protect investment in Haiti's transshipment trade routes" (Phillips and Project Censored 2004b: 78).

The involvement of the United States government in the drug trade might not be so hard to ignore if there were not so many lives ruined from drugs and if US prisons were not filled with people who were involved with illegal drugs—many for growing a few plants in their basement or for carrying a couple joints. Illegal drugs are a major social concern related to the health and welfare of the United States and other peoples around the world. Why aren't the mainstream media informing the publics, especially in the United States, about this serious issue? The same people who profit from government involvement in illegal drugs control the media.

## The Corporate Media as the "Matrix"

One of the greatest media metaphors for relating to the current constructed reality supporting corporate greed and imperial destruction of the earth is the movie series called the Matrix. The scriptwriter cleverly depicts the future as a completely "false" reality made up entirely of a machine-controlled computer program called the matrix. Upon suspecting that something is wrong, a person can choose to take a red pill or a blue pill. The blue pill will relieve the suspicions and relax one deeper into the matrix. The red pill will plunge one into the "true" reality, which is a raw and difficult underground life of trying to expose and disrupt the "false" reality—a reality powered by human bodies that have been separated from their minds.

### *Purging the mainstream "information"*

The metaphor of the Matrix posses some interesting and quite relevant questions for people in the modern western world, and in particular the United States. Citizens of communities, as well as students of Sociology, might entertain the dilemma of which of the two pills they want: the red or the blue. Are people comfortable with a virtual disconnect between their bodies and their minds? Imagine circumstances where people's bodies experience various forms of corporation generated abuses (overwork or unemployment/ food toxins and environmental toxins/militarization of their children's lives/deprivation and starvation), and their minds at the same time believe life is as it should be—driven by the invisible hand of the free market. It is no longer metaphorical to consider how close we are to the just described circumstances. Among the working and lower middles classes especially, people in the United States feel fortunate if they can just open another beer and watch a football game until they have to go to work on their second or third job. They are unaware that they are working harder than anyone else in the industrialized world (Gelb 2007), and that they have very little actual control over their own lives.

### *Small solutions can be big steps*

What this chapter tells us is that the people of the United States and of the world in general need to democratically create and control their own economy and their own media and airwaves, or they will continue to let the media and, hence, the economy, control them. Until the media and economy are democratically structured and regulated, the best people can do is take the red pill—that is, utilize the alternative media for information and thereby purge their neurological systems of large misleading segments of their past education and the mainstream popular media.

While the United States is a long ways from a democratically controlled economy, there are illustrative microcosms of how such an economy might work. Isthmus Engineering and Manufacturing in Wisconsin and Alvarado Street Bakery in California are two examples of democratic worker-owned businesses that are operating very successfully (Moore 2009). There are many others that could be identified as well. While it is true that worker owned businesses do not in themselves offer a general solution to the problems of free-market capitalism (Proyect 2009), they represent an alternative to what is most problematic about capitalism: a few people greedily hoarding large amounts of wealth at the expense of the people who create the wealth and anyone else who might be perceived as being in the way of maximum profits. "Expense" as used above usually includes insufficient pay for workers, damage to the worker's health, and damage to the worker's environment.

Businesses that are democratically owned by the people who work in them represent an important component of anarcho-syndicalism, a version of anarchism that is based on the concept of workers collectively taking over their work environment and conditions. Anarcho-syndicalism is an alternative to free market capitalism, but it is not something that can be imposed on a group of people. It is something that, by its own definition, must evolve from a grass roots movement based on knowledge of what is best for the local communities it touches. Accurate information is critical, which is why democratically controlled media and a democratically controlled economy go hand in hand. The current most difficult challenge lies in educating a sufficiently large enough segment of the United States population toward an understanding of the importance of democratizing these institutions—given that mainstream media are severely corrupted and thus systematically misinforming the public.

# Chapter 9
# Criminology and Criminal Justice

## What is Crime and Where does it Come From?

Most definitions of crime contain a core component that identifies crime as the violation of the laws of a social unit, such as a nation-state (Siegel 2007). We tend to accept this notion uncritically, as if the laws of a nation-state or other social unit are divine, occur in a vacuum, or, at the very least, represent some majority sense of the most important prevailing norms of our human communities. Criminologists recognize that none of the above is true. Laws are the products of legislators and other government officials who often are controlled by special interest power and money (Siegel 2007, Coleman 2006). All groups within social units have their own interests and there are many interests that cut across groups. As one would expect, however, those who have the greatest number of effective lobbyists (those with wealth and power) will be the victors in the struggle for control of the law. What is best for the vast majority of the population will not matter.

### *For whom are laws created?*

The point made is that law is not divine, occurring in a vacuum, or shaped from the interests and norms of the general public. The idea that law somehow represents the interests of the general public is one of our nation's greatest myths. Law is based on what people who have the power to influence the law want in order to bring maximum rewards to themselves (Zepezauer 2004, Barlett and Steele 1992). Most of the time that tends to be what is in the best interests of about the one to ten percent most affluent people in the population. Contrary to what politicians (who support the interests of those few wealthy people) would have us believe, what is best for the rich is not typically what is best for the rest of the population. In fact, the interests of the rich are most often in direct conflict with the interests of the remaining population, as evidenced by the growing disparities between the two (Eitzen and Leedham 2004). For example, a third of the income of the top one percent of the population is based on capital gains. This is why the wealthy and wealth motivated politicians have for a long time been trying to get the capital gains tax removed, and finally succeeded in having it reduced from 28 percent prior to 1997 to ultimately 15 percent in 2003. *Ninety-three* percent of the US population has no capital gains annual income at all (Barlett and Steele 2004).

Laws and law enforcement strategies are created by the most powerful people to increase benefits to themselves and to control, and protect themselves from, the less powerful people. Controlling the general population is important because wealth creation requires labor, taxes from workers, and various other resources that the general population might claim. The process is almost never reversed. That is, laws are seldom enacted to protect the less powerful majority from the powerful minority. This is why socio-economic conditions continue to stagnate or worsen for most of the population and improve dramatically for the wealthy. Laws that have the expressed purpose of protecting the average citizen are often traceable to the interests of the wealthy. One of the earliest systematic demonstrations of this can be found in the previously mentioned classic study of the vagrancy laws (Chambliss 1964).

The most basic laws, such as those defining index crimes (sometimes loosely referred to as street crimes), are determined by and for the affluent, and typically enforced among the poor and not among the wealthy (Reiman 2001). While social scientists often claim street crime is more prevalent among the lower classes than the higher classes, there is insufficient evidence to support that claim (Reiman 2001).

*Who are the most serious criminals and what are their crimes?*

Most serious crimes are committed by powerful wealthy people, referred to by criminologist James W. Coleman as the criminal elite, and those crimes are clearly rooted in economic and social factors. Wealthy people are generally socialized to believe in the importance of continuously increased wealth accumulation, and are taught both in school and through their daily socialization that greed and the fulfillment of greed are expected means of attaining wealth. There are also many non-wealthy people who have the same socialization as the wealthy, but do not have the means to fulfill that socialization. One might correctly argue that the poor probably commit crimes for economic gain also, but they do so on a much smaller scale than do the wealthy who can use corporations, the government, and various other tools for their crimes. As stated by Chambliss (originally in 1975), "... crime becomes a rational response of some social classes to the realities of their lives. The state becomes an instrument of the ruling class, enforcing laws here but not there, according to the realities of political power and economic conditions" (2011: 265).

Index crime data typically are available on middle and lower class people only. The lack of systematic information about upper class involvement in index crime has resulted in criminologists referring to "crimes of the rich" and "crimes of the poor," which is another form of the simplistic dualism mentioned earlier. While there can be no doubt that there are crimes committed exclusively by the rich, there is no reason to believe the amount of their participation in index crimes is any less than the participation of people from the other classes. Indeed, their exclusiveness and privileged status allow one to comfortably argue that the rich enjoy considerably more latitude with respect to index crimes than do other people. It is quite likely that upper class people directly participate in rape, domestic violence, and aggravated assault with at least as much regularity as others. They are probably less likely to *directly* commit some other index crimes, such as non-domestic homicides, robbery, and arson, because they have the wealth and power to hire/force others to commit these crimes for them. The myth that wealthy people do not commit index crimes defies logic, countless individual personal testimonies, and any reasonable understanding of social reality. Unfortunately, it also defies current systematic data collection practices since wealthy people are typically excluded from the scrutiny of the police and law enforcement in general.

The case of Robert Durst, a family heir billionaire, represents an exceptional circumstance of a wealthy White person being tried for murder. He was suspected of the murder of his wife's best friend, and possibly his wife who had been missing for a time, so he was hiding from the authorities by posing as a mute woman. Living in a low rent apartment, he befriended a poor person, killed him, and then chopped him into pieces to hide the body. During his trial he claimed it was self defense. The prosecution claimed the defendant killed the poor person in order to steal his identity. In the 11/12/03 Minneapolis Star Tribune there is a picture of Durst nicely dressed and surrounded by his team of attorneys. The picture captures Durst's reaction when he was declared innocent by the jury.

Two weeks after Durst was declared innocent, the Minneapolis Star Tribune reported another story. A 350 pound Black man on drugs, Nathaniel Jones, was passed out on the front lawn of a fast food restaurant in Cincinnati, Ohio. Someone from the restaurant called the police who came to the scene, and in the process of trying to arrest the man the police ended up beating him with nightsticks until he died. It might be instructive to refer to yet another case: that of OJ Simpson, a wealthy famous Black man who was on trial for the murder of his ex-wife and her friend. It was one of the longest trials in the history of the criminal justice system—much longer than that of Robert Durst. Money finally won out over race and Simpson was found not guilty. A picture of Simpson at his trial would look similar to the described picture of Durst: well dressed and closely attended by his team of lawyers.

Notwithstanding the similarities between Durst and Simpson, few people in the American public doubted Simpson's guilt. As in the Durst case, there seemed to be a great deal of evidence against Simpson. However, the reason the Simpson trial took so long was most likely because he is Black. Perhaps that is also why it was so easy for the public to believe Simpson was guilty after he was declared not guilty by the courts. Most wealthy White people do not even go to trial for their crimes, and are seldom arrested—especially for index crimes. Durst is an exception. He might have never been tried for murder if he had not been arrested for shop lifting while wearing a disguise.

The above cases remind us that wealthy people are just as capable of committing index crimes as poor people. They also remind us that "justice" is not unbiased. It is a double privilege in the United States to be both White and wealthy and a double source of discrimination to be both poor and Black. Nathaniel Jones most likely would have been treated quite differently had he been either White or wealthy. It is highly doubtful that he would have been beaten to death. The humane way to treat a person who is passed out is to show concern and try to determine what is wrong and how one can help. Nathaniel Jones needed the attention of medical personnel—not police. If necessary he could have been allowed to stay where he was until the drugs wore off enough for him to become ambulatory and conversant. Unfortunately the restaurant personnel were probably concerned about losing business, and business concerns in a free market capitalist economic system are often considered more important than the value of life.

There are many laws that average citizens cannot even think about breaking, simply because they will never be in the positions that enable breaking them. Being in such positions is an important part of the privilege of being wealthy. Crimes related to these privileged positions are the most damaging to our communities in every important respect (Coleman 2006). Yet, it is the poor who go to prison and the rich simply keep getting richer (Stern 2006, Reiman 2001).

*Do people who control the law also break the law?*

One of the greatest ironies of the above discussed process of the development and enforcement of the laws is that the people who control the laws are also the most serious violators of them. Average citizens don't develop anti-trust laws and laws against monopolies. Average citizens don't develop laws regulating when wars can and cannot be legally fought. In fact, average citizens have had little to do with the development and enforcement strategies of any of the so-called regulatory laws. Most of these laws were developed to protect businesses from each other, protect segments of government from each other, or simply give government the appearance of legitimacy while it is protecting the interests of wealthy individuals and multinational corporations. The few regulatory laws that do result from public pressure are often deliberately designed so as to be almost impossible to enforce—what some people call hollow laws (Greider 1992).

In spite of the tremendous control the corporate elites have over the creation of regulatory laws, they are violated routinely in the board rooms of major corporations and in government agencies. Included in corporate decision-making is not just whether to break the law, but what it will cost the company if, in one of those rare instances, the company gets caught and is prosecuted. Corporate CEOs and board members are almost always correct in their calculations that it will cost far less to commit the crime than to obey the law.

Violations of environmental and high stakes regulatory laws, which most citizens do not have within their power to commit, cost average citizens billions of dollars. Thousands of lives are taken every year in the United States alone by CEO's making illegal decisions about product safety, working conditions, and environmental hazards (Coleman 2006). There are more deaths in the United States due to legally proven deliberate corporate negligence than there are due to all other types of individual murders combined (Reiman 2001). One can only imagine how many corporate negligence deaths there are that are never prosecuted.

People who control the law also violate the law because the greatest profits are always beyond what is legal. If the CEO's of a major corporation refuse to push the legal limits of their decision-making they lose the competitive edge that other CEO's will certainly pursue by going beyond the law. It doesn't matter where the line of the law falls, the profits are always significantly greater on the other side of that line. We must also constantly remind ourselves that corporate crime is not crime committed by a building or an office somewhere. Corporate crime is committed by people: CEO's and corporate board members making decisions under the shield of the corporation being treated legally as a person. Treating corporations as if they are persons protects the wealthy people who run the corporations from being held accountable for the harm they do (Boyer 2003).

*A focus on street crime*

When we see references to crime in the mainstream media or in the speeches of politicians, how often are they referring to the crimes of corporations or wealthy decision-makers? The 1994 federal crime bill represents a clear answer to that question. That bill was enacted exclusively to put greater controls on the already disenfranchised and marginalized segments of the population. Two purposes are served by putting greater controls on the already disenfranchised. The first is that it further protects the rich from the desperation of the poor (Whitman 1992). The second is that it distracts the public from the most serious crimes that are being committed by government officials and corporate leaders. Greater controls confuse the public into thinking that their government is protecting them when, in fact, their government is protecting the interests of the powerful people who control it (Coleman 2006). We see the dramatization of street crime, as the only crime, acted out in popular television programs that show police officers actually arresting people on the streets (Eitzen and Zinn 2006).

Politicians and the mainstream corporate media most often refer to data from the Uniform Crime Report (UCR), long established as a systematically biased source of data. One of the greatest shortcomings of the UCR is that it is based on police reports. Hence, the more police we have, and the more pressured police are to file reports, the higher the crime rate will be as indicated by the UCR (Dyer 2000). On the other hand, when police are pressured to reduce the crime rates in their precincts they tend to report fewer crimes. When New York City "computerized" its policing procedures using a program called COMPSTAT to provide immediate crime statistics for any precinct in the city, police commanders were charged with the responsibility of bringing crime rates down to specified levels within specified periods of time or be fired. After many lost their jobs some commanders started to advise their officers to not report crimes unless there was no possible way of avoiding it. Others downgraded the crimes in their precinct to keep them off the record (Rashbaum 2010).

During the early years of the twenty-first century, and especially in the years just prior to and during the global economic crisis of 2008, there has been a flurry of CEO arrests and even some prosecutions. Such arrests and prosecutions are a result of laws and public trust being so flagrantly violated that ignoring the violations posed the risk of exposing the underlying realities of corporation greed and malfeasance that make up the "normal" operating procedures of many large corporations, government regulatory agencies and some branches of law enforcement itself.

## The Myth of Eliminating Crime

Looking at victimization data, rather than the Uniform Crime Report Data, (produced by the United States Department of Justice) tells us that index crime has been pretty stable over a long period of time. For example, the National Crime Survey (NCS) results show the number of index violent crimes per 1000 persons in 1975 was 32.8, 33.3 in 1980, 30.0 in 1985, and 29.0 in 1990 (Siegel 1992). When I first wrote about this topic in 1995 (Alessio 1996), the data available at that time were holding the same pattern as just provided. I stated that it was not likely that there would be major shifts from the modest fluctuations that had occurred over such a long period of time.

Yet, as more data eventually became available 1994 marked the beginning of a dramatic ten year drop in crime rates as indicated by data in both the UCR and NCS (later referred to as the National Crime Victimization Survey—NCVS). According to Durkheim (1938) a stable amount of deviation from social norms over an extended period of time is considered normal, with sharp increases and decreases considered signs of either social discontent or social repression respectively.

There is evidence suggesting that what Durkheim wrote about may be relevant to what has been happening recently in the United States. By 2001 the criminal justice system cost United States tax payers approximately 167 billion dollars annually. That figure reflects a 452 percent state increase and a 492 percent federal increase in spending over a 20-year period, with much of that increase taking place in the last ten years (Bureau of Justice Statistics 2006). It is probably much higher than that now. A significant portion of that cost involved paying for the 1994 federal crime bill that, among other things, put 100,000 more police officers on the streets. These data do not take into consideration the cost of building new prisons or jails, which is considerable, and there is no evidence that prisons reduce crime. They may actually be contributing to more crime (Dyer 2000).

### *Human toll of trying to reduce crime coercively*

The human toll of accelerated law enforcement with respect to street crime is immeasurable. As of 2004 there were over 2.1 million people in prison or jail in the United States (Bureau of Justice Statistics 2006), and almost 2.3 million by midyear 2009 (West 2010). Every 100,000 people within the United States has 724 incarcerated (Mauer 2006). Among Black men the figure is 3,218 per 100,000 for state and federal prisons alone (much higher including jails (see chapter 6)). The prison rate is also notably high for Hispanic men: 1,220 per 100,000 (Bureau of Justice Statistics 2006). Currently about 1.5 million children have a parent in jail or prison in the United States, and over 7 percent of African American children have a parent in jail or prison. The number of people incarcerated in 1994 was about 69 percent of the number incarcerated by 2004. Much of this increase in incarceration is a result of the "three strikes and you are out" program that sends people to prison on their third criminal offense no matter how minor the crime—current or previous. This and other draconian sentencing strategies have built a huge prison population for cheap labor, with many of the prisons privatizing their workforce for corporations. Low cost (nearly free) prison labor has been identified as one of the hottest and fastest growing sources of profit for big corporations in the United States (Pelaez 2008, Davis 1998, 2003).

One does not have to stretch the imagination very far to recognize the tremendous harm such conditions bring to the lives of family members left behind: the difficulty in rearing children alone, the stigma associated with being the child of a prisoner, the strained interpersonal relationships, and so on (Mauer 2006). Whether or not the intensified law enforcement efforts have made a difference in the crime rate, they have certainly increased the number of prisoners in the United States and destroyed many lives in addition to those of the prisoners themselves. Re-entry into a non prison life, whether one is guilty or not, is extremely difficult, especially without social capital once on the outside (Hattery and Smith 2010).

The collateral damage that is done to innocent people in the process of intensifying enforcement is great. There are many documented incidents of police harassing people with broken tail lights or other minor traffic infractions. Sometimes their cars are impounded and they are left without transportation (Nieves 2006). Drivers then have to pay a heavy fine to get their car back. This approach to law enforcement is called the "broken window" philosophy. The idea behind this approach is that low tolerance for the slightest social violations will automatically result in a reduction of the more serious violations. In Oakland, California the program associated with this approach to policing is called "Operation Impact" (Nieves 2006). In these types of programs the police claim they are preventing more serious crimes by dealing with minor offenses or what they believe are predispositions to crimes. These approaches often involve profiling people, especially in poorer neighborhoods, which results in more people of color and more poor people being harassed and criminalized.

Programs like Operation Impact also have other unfortunate residual effects. Police sometimes develop a cowboy mentality with an "anything goes" disposition toward the public. They feel invincible and empowered to do whatever they choose to do at the moment. This attitude toward policing has resulted in thousands of police brutality charges being filed every year (Macionis 2005). Heightened policing intensity, encouraged by misinformed politicians who believe the police should be able to stop crime, also promotes a mentality and disposition of being at war, and the enemy often becomes the unsuspecting citizen who happens to be in the wrong place at the wrong time (McNamara 1997). Not only are innocent people injured or killed, but thousands of innocent people are arrested, convicted, and sentenced—sometimes to death. Between 1973 and 2003 over 130 innocent people were released from death row. That is death row, where one would expect "beyond a reasonable doubt" to be paramount. How many other innocent death row people have been executed and how many thousands of innocent people have spent the better part of their lives in prison as a result of wrongful convictions (Amnesty International USA 2010, Charleston Gazette 2006, Bedau 1998)? As DNA testing becomes more widely used in criminal cases a sketch of the answers to these questions begins to emerge. Texas has had 41 DNA based prisoner releases alone since 2001, with the most recent (January 2011) being a man found innocent after spending 30 years in prison (Carlton 2011).

### *Police corruption*

In addition to police brutality, a 1998 General Accounting Office report cites major police corruption cases in 11 of the largest United States cities. While drugs are often the center of their criminal activities, police also become involved in other crimes through the course of protecting their illegal drug endeavors, including murder and frame-ups of innocent people (Drug Policy Alliance 2010, Maggi 2010). Some researchers believe police corruption is a result of the realization that legitimate policing will not and cannot reduce crime. There is a demoralization factor and also a temptation factor which result in police setting up their own drug trade or protection racket (Drug Policy Alliance 2010, Webb 1999). These illegal police activities are another major source of financial, as well as human, costs associated with the "war on crime" mentality produced by over-zealous politicians trying to eliminate crime via sheer police force. Corruption and street crime committed by the police themselves, especially in places like Cincinnati, Los Angeles, Chicago, and New York City frequently find their way into the media. This is nothing new. Most major police forces (such as in Chicago) have long standing histories of corruption and internally organized street crime. Who is responsible for this kind of behavior from people who are paid to serve and protect the public?

As stated by a San Jose ex-police chief,

> During my years as police chief, I found that police misconduct often had its roots in subtle indications by supervisors to officers that the sort of 'extralegal' tactics common to quality-of-life policing were acceptable … In the end it is not tough cops who prevent crime; it is citizens' respect for the law … We need to impress upon cops, in New York and everywhere else, that a free society is directed by its citizens. (McNamara 2006: 2)

*Do the police reduce crime?*

The statement just quoted by a San Jose ex-police chief tells us a great deal about the nature of crime and the role of the police. There have been efforts in recent years to create a reality that more police results in less crime. Traditional ways of measuring crime have been dramatically altered to facilitate the construction of this reality. A careful review of available information reveals serious inaccuracies and inconsistencies resulting from the most recent alterations made in the data collection and analysis processes. The current evidence with which we are operating is relatively useless for the purpose of understanding crime and punishment in the United States. Relying on long term patterns in existence for about 60 years remains the best option in analyzing index crime trends.

No one can deny that the presence of the police in a particular location at a particular time might thwart the occurrence of a crime. However, police should not be everywhere in a self governing community. It is conservatively estimated that there are about 40 million index crimes committed in the United States each year. Some criminologists estimate the number of crimes per year could be as high as 100 million. A nation-state that attempts to control that much crime with police would by necessity become a de facto police state.

Have the police actually reduced the amount of crime occurring in the United States? It is not very likely. It is important to note that the people who continually call for the elimination of crime are often the same people who want more laws. Thousands of new laws are created every year all over the United States. While inadequate socialization is the basis for violence and other unacceptable behaviors, laws are the basis for crime. Without laws there would be no crime. Laws proposed to control average citizens target certain groups of people who are already behaving in a way contrary to the proposed law. If that were not true there would be no perceived need for the new law. To talk about eliminating crime via the creation of more laws is nonsensical. More laws give the police and other enforcement agencies more to do, but they do not help eliminate behaviors that come to be identified as crime via the creation of laws. Police can arrest someone they believe committed a crime, but most often they cannot prevent the "criminal" behavior from occurring in the first place.

The United States has become a nation-state based on the assumption that laws change behaviors at a communal aggregate level. That assumption is false in most important instances of human social life, and especially with respect to everyday life circumstances. Desirable behavior is created through socialization processes that make people want to become positive contributing members of their communities, and not through fear of being caught and punished, or what criminologists refer to as deterrence. There is little credible evidence supporting deterrence as a general principle of controlling (not to mention organizing) human behavior among adult populations. Sociologists have studied socialization processes for many years (Grusec and Hastings 2007) and application of their information could help make communities safe and positive places to live.

*Drugs and prison labor*

A large amount of the prison population comes from the incarceration of drug offenders (Mumola and Karberg 2007). About 25 percent of all people incarcerated by the criminal justice system are doing time for drug related incidents (JPI 2008), and the percentage is more than twice that (55 percent) in the federal prisons alone (DrugWarFacts 2005). The number of people imprisoned for drug offenses is now about the same number representing all inmates for all crime in 1980 (Center on Juvenile & Criminal Justice 2009), and the number of people in state prisons alone for drug related charges has increased 550 percent over 20 years (JPI 2009). African Americans are the most heavily targeted population for drug offenses in terms of government supported distribution of drugs (Webb 1999) and in terms of arrests and imprisonment (NAACP 2010). Of the people in jail for drug related crimes, about 43 percent are incarcerated for possession alone (DrugWarFacts 2005). That figure is even higher in certain states like California and New York (Center on Juvenile & Criminal Justice 2009).

In some countries, like Holland, drug abuse/addiction is considered a health problem and treated as such (LEAP 2010b, JPI 2009). Had Nathaniel Jones (the drugged individual beaten to death by the police) been living in Amsterdam he most likely would still be alive, and might even be living a relatively "normal" life. The only people incarcerated for drug related activities in Holland are the large scale drug dealers. Most drug related activities are not criminalized or are considered minor offenses. By medically treating people with drug related problems rather than forcing them into a life of crime, the demand for drugs is reduced and so is the large scale drug profiteering (LEAP 2010b, JPI 2009). Within a criminalized system like that of the United States, drug abuse behavior often continues after a person is imprisoned. For prisoners to have a chance to survive re-entry, it is essential that they have effective drug treatment while in prison (Hattery and Smith 2009) as well as afterward.

The question the Dutch ask is not, "how can we catch and punish people involved in drugs?" They ask instead, "How can we help people who need our help?" The result is that Holland has the lowest number of drug related deaths of the well known European countries (Sernau 2009, Eitzen and Leedham 2004). Countries that take the hardest criminalization stance on drugs, like the United States and Britain, have created high stakes investments in illegal drug markets that are now major components of the British and United States economies. The amount of money invested in the criminal justice system for drug purposes alone involves many billions of dollars each year. The laundering of the drug money has dovetailed with the legal segments of the United States economy in ways that have created what some might consider an economic "dependency" on drugs (Phillips and Project Censored 2004b).

Those countries that focus on helping addicts are reducing the cost of the drug trade to everyone, and in every meaningful way. Those countries that focus on punishing addicts increase social problems related to the drug trade, increase the drug trade itself, and increase the costs to everyone except the high stakes drug operators (LEAP 2010a, 2010b) and the banks that handle the laundered drug money (Phillips and Project Censored 2004b).

Large profits are now being made from the low cost labor being extracted from drug users who end up in prison. That, along with large profits made in the banking industry from drug money laundering, make change in drug polices in the near future difficult to imagine. CEO's are addicted to ever increasing profits resulting in ever higher salaries and stock options. A wealth dependency has been established, based partly on the drug trade, and that dependency is growing stronger with every drug related conviction.

Since President Calderon of Mexico declared war on drugs, the violence in Mexico has multiplied (Beaubien 2010), and continues to increase dramatically (Bowden 2010). Before Calderon's election the drug trade was semi-controlled by corrupt presidents who made deals with the powerful drug dealers. When those informal corrupt arrangements stopped, the drug dealers declared a counter-war on Mexico. President Calderon, who said he would never consider legalizing drugs, is now calling for hearings to discuss the possibility of drug decriminalization.

## Is the Criminal Justice System Working, and for Whom?

Typically politicians promote the idea that crime is rapidly increasing in order to scare people into voting for them and to get people to support stronger measures of public social control. It is difficult, however, to pass a major crime bill without being able to claim that it is working. Hence, the current phase of socially constructed crime reduction will most likely pass. If the hype about terrorism loses some of its social control impact, we may see politicians, once again, resorting to scaring the public with contrived propaganda about "run away crime rates." Scaring the public into believing that crime is rapidly increasing is a long standing practice in the United States. It is a tactic to justify and get public support for building more jails and prisons, so as to continue the incarceration of the poor and other excluded groups. It also provides a means by which greater social control can be exercised against the citizenry overall.

"Run-away crime rates" is another myth that serves as a handy tool for government officials and the wealthy who control the government officials. Fear is an important social control mechanism. Starting in the year 2001, following the destruction of the World Trade Center and part of the Pentagon, the fear of crime was supplemented by the fear of terrorists. The fear of terrorists was also a replacement for the fear of communists that prevailed immediately following World War II until around 1990, which marked the end of the Soviet Union.

With all of the manipulation of criminal statistics and the fabricated media propaganda about crime prevalence and corresponding crime rates, it is difficult to know what to think about the effectiveness of the criminal justice system. Is its stated function of serving and protecting the people of the United States being fulfilled? Are the billions of dollars funneled into the criminal justice system making us truly safer? Are most criminal activities being brought to justice in some way that makes everyone safer? Given the expense of maintaining the criminal justice system and the extent to which it intrudes into our daily lives, these are reasonable questions for one to ask.

*How many crimes are solved?*

When we look at index crimes, which are committed by all segments of the population and which can be directed toward anyone (although they are more likely to be directed toward people who do not have their own security system and guards), we find that only about 40 percent of all crimes are reported to the police. Of those, about 20 percent result in an arrest, which brings us immediately to having our hands on only about 8 percent of the index crimes committed—less than 8 percent for the less serious crimes and higher for the more serious crimes (Siegel 2007). While the arrest rate for murder is believed to be higher than for the other serous crimes, we have no victimization data on murder and, therefore, have no way of knowing how accurate the Uniform Crime Report data are. Matters get worse when it comes to convictions. Of those remaining eight percent, less than half of the most serious crimes and less than a third of most other crimes will result in a conviction (Siegel 1992). This means that in spite of all the lawyers, judges, courts, and police in the United States, less than 4 percent of all index crimes are actually solved. If the figure was 20 percent instead of 4 percent would we consider ourselves successful? We probably wouldn't consider ourselves successful if the figure was 60 percent.

Furthermore, not all convictions result in a punishment that fits the crime. For example, the violent, dehumanizing, terrorizing act of rape does not result in a prison sentence in 33 percent of the cases where convictions are actually won (Siegel 1992). Those rapists who do go to prison are, in many areas of the country, serving among the shortest terms, and being let out on parole to continue their heinous acts of violence. There are people serving longer sentences for growing a few marijuana plants in their basement than some of the people who are convicted of rape. The notion that we, the general public, are protected foremost by the incredibly large and expensive criminal justice system is an important myth that needs to be exposed.

*From where comes social order?*

What, then, does protect the general public from internal harm? People are so busy giving credit to the police and courts for their security, it never occurs to them to give credit to themselves. Again, I would refer you to the quote by the San Jose ex-police chief who said, "… it is not tough cops who prevent crime; it is citizens' respect for the law …" (McNamara 2006: 2). Most order within nation-states and communities that is truly consistent with the cultural values, beliefs, and customs of those people comes from the people themselves. Through the socialization of each generation, people become the carriers of how they are supposed to behave and why. The vast majority of people, who are adequately socialized, carry their culture and corresponding control mechanisms within themselves. Average citizens are responsible for existing social order on a daily basis, and not the police. One might disagree with McNamara on one point: it is not "respect for the law" that creates social order so much as it is respect for one another and the customs and practices that guide that respect.

Those who do not carry the cultural values and beliefs represent a minority. Wealthy people can also be included in this minority, and in their case they have the resources, motivation, and opportunity to do the greatest amount of harm to the greatest number of people. On the average, people raised in wealthy families have a socialization that is substantially different from the rest of the population. Their motivation for wealth and the lifestyle their wealth affords them, conflict with stated democratic values whereby all citizens are guaranteed an equal voice in the government, and the laws are to be applied equally to all citizens. Common within the socialization of some among the very wealthy are the beliefs that some people deserve to have more rights than others (privileges), and that the goal of maximizing profits takes precedence over the more fundamental values of a democratic community or nation-state.

For people with a great deal of wealth to accept the great difference between what they have and what the rest of the population has, there most likely has to be an acceptance of the idea that they deserve their wealth for some reason or reasons. These "reasons" must demonstrate that wealthy people are better in some important ways than others. A belief in being better than others also opens the door to a belief in the privilege of violating the social norms of the larger nation-state or community, which includes violating the laws. This statement should not be interpreted to mean that wealthy people are all bad. In Sociology, whether we are logically thinking through an argument or analyzing data, we think in terms of patterns and tendencies, not in terms of absolutes and not in terms of good or bad. Social life is extremely complicated.

As discussed in Chapter 6, most people have far more in common with the very poor than they do the very rich. While few want to identify with the poor, most people have far less chance of actually being wealthy than of being one of the many victims of the growing inequality in the United States—that is, underemployed, unemployed, homeless, war casualty, and imprisoned. Most non-wealthy people do not assume they have a right to live a privileged life outside of social norms and expectations. They contribute to social order daily with their routine conforming behaviors derived from their common socialization. Yet, non-wealthy people in the United States and most other countries have a much higher risk of being targeted by the Criminal Justice System than do wealthy people. The unequal treatment of wealthy and non-wealthy people is working well for the wealthy as evidenced by wealthy people becoming wealthier, and the rest of the population becoming poorer in a variety of ways.

*Socialization and social class*

It is often said that poor people are poor and turn to a life of crime because they were not raised properly—that is, they were not properly socialized. People from excluded and marginalized groups do strive to teach their children core cultural values found in most human communities: be honest, be fair, work hard, get an education, get a job, help others, be a good citizen, and so on. If these values are not upheld among marginalized groups and in the general population, it is most likely because social inequalities are prohibitive. The crimes of the criminal elites are the root cause of most other types of crime, especially crimes of the lower classes—directly or indirectly. Many wealthy people demand that public programs (such as health care, child care, welfare, government jobs, and education) be cut so that their taxes can be lowered and more of the tax base can be shifted to programs that support their profits, such as imperial wars and corporate subsidies. The diversion of tax revenues away from support for the non-wealthy to support for the wealthy is the most important indirect link between the crimes of the wealthy and the crimes of the non-wealthy. Without public support systems, the deprivations of the general public will not be mitigated in any way. Problems created by deprivation and mistreatment force acts of desperation that are typically manifested as forms of index crime. One of the last acts of the 2010 United States Congress was to approve continuation of tax cuts, including for the wealthy, which will mean the loss of billions of dollars for jobs related to infrastructure rebuilding and social services that would help the non-wealthy. Contrary to the long standing "reality" created by the wealthy, there is no evidence that tax breaks for the wealthy create jobs (Bassett 2010b), and polls show that public perception has recently broken through that false reality (Condon 2010).

The hardships experienced by the working and lower classes today should make one wonder why people from the lower classes are not engaging in more crimes of desperation as they struggle to take care of their families and keep up with what is expected of them and their children in the modern world. The reason working and lower class people do not commit more crimes is that most working class and lower class people were brought up (socialized) to respect others and to live by the rules of their families and communities. While this may also be true of some wealthy people, it is not true of the many wealthy people who have greed as the primary motivation for much of what they do in life. Upon reading this statement about wealthy people, the reader is likely to recoil with discomfort, accusing the author of engaging in a reckless form of bashing. Yet, these kinds of statements are frequently said about the poor and few people question them. It is commonly projected by wealthy people and many non-wealthy people that the poor don't know how to take care of their children, the poor are not properly motivated, the poor are lazy, the poor were not properly socialized, the poor have low IQ's, and so on. It is sometimes argued that taking children away from the poor will prevent the children from becoming criminals because they will not be socialized into a life of crime. For the poor, socialization is far less the problem than the absence of positive opportunities.

*Rich bashing* The intent behind discussing the under-socialization of the wealthy class is not to bash rich people, but to debunk the myths about the primary sources of crime and social problems in general. One should not think that wealthy people are inherently evil any more than one should think poor people are inherently lazy or dumb. It is important, however, to recognize that the culture of wealth, a culture built on greed and the justification of greed, is a culture steeped in the most insidious and far reaching criminal activities. Such was the case in the earlier centuries of kings and queens and it is no different today. Moreover, it is not just the criminal activities of the wealthy that force some of the non-wealthy into committing crimes, but many of their legal activities as well. The ability of the wealthy to successfully violate the law is only surpassed by their ability to control the law. Much of the "legal" behavior of the wealthy that should be illegal because of its hoarding, violent, and environmentally destructive nature, is just as harmful and destructive to the rest of the population and the world in general as is their criminal behavior.

Rather than finding ways of making the socialization process work for all people in an equitable manner, the federal and state legislatures continue to put billions of dollars into a criminal justice system that does not work for anyone but those who have the wealth and power to control it for their own purposes. For the rest of the population it is a tremendous tax burden, and even more importantly, an infringement upon collective and individual freedoms. Brutally and externally controlling the disenfranchised of the world forces more actions that illegally/immorally infringe upon the rights of innocent people. This is happening routinely today as the federal government detains innocent people without legal representation and without those people being charged with a crime. Habeas corpus, a long standing cornerstone of many Western legal systems, has been all but abolished in the United States following passage of the Military Commission Act of 2006. Infringement on human rights also occurs as illegal wiretaps are conducted on average citizens for general surveillance purposes, and as massive data sets are constructed to enable the federal government to instantly find people. Full body scanners at airports and the alternative security pat-down are the kinds of activities once reserved for criminal suspects. Now, all United States citizens, as well as non-citizens, are treated as criminal suspects. All of these human rights violations are conveniently done under the guise of fighting terrorism without any acknowledgement that these government actions against all people are, in and of themselves, forms of terrorism.

It is important to note that in other countries where "terrorists" operate there is typically a long history of imperial oppression by wealthy corporate owners via the use of the United States government. This is not a simple matter, but the underlying truth surrounding these horrific escalating circumstances has yet to be fully heard and understood by Americans and many other Western publics.

*Protecting the innocent or protecting wealth*

As stated earlier, it is likely that about 4 percent of index crime is brought to justice in the United States. The fact that so few crimes are ever brought to justice should be sufficient evidence that the police and legal system in general do not employ an accurate method for determining innocence and guilt. Hence, the notion that our system deliberately errs on the side of the guilty to protect the innocent is still one more myth that must be questioned. If it isn't the criminals that will necessarily experience consequences, as the evidence suggests, who will it be? Since index crimes are committed by all segments of the population, it should be possible to find a good cross-section of the population in our prisons ..right? That isn't what prisons look like. Black people are 7–9 times more likely to be imprisoned than White people and make up about 58 percent of the United States prison population (Parenti 2010, Whitman 1992). It is estimated that fifty percent of all Black men will be arrested some time in their life (Reiman 2001). Blacks in the United States are: 13 percent of drug users, but about 50 percent of all drug related prisoners; three times as likely to be in jail/prison as in college; and currently imprisoned at six times the rate of South Africans during apartheid (LEAP 2010a). Other peoples of color, particularly Native Americans, share similar "criminal" statistics. The category with the fastest growing rate of imprisonment is women. This change could be related to the greater dexterity of women for certain kinds of labor.

In the early 1990s an African American man, Rodney King, was severely beaten by police following a high speed chase. King had run a stop light. On the basis of that action a high speed chase was conducted that endangered many other citizens. High speed chases often result in the loss of innocent lives when people just happen to be in the wrong place when the chase comes through. In April of 1992 the four police officers who beat Rodney King were found innocent in court of wrong doing. Los Angles erupted into a major revolt, with buildings burning and innocent people being killed as a result of the anger and frustration of a people, Black people, being time and again abused and mistreated by the criminal justice system. The reader should keep in mind the tremendous racial inequities within the criminal justice system (LEAP 2010a).

During the LA revolt lives were lost and millions of dollars worth of damage was done. Is this the way poor and working class Black people prefer to behave, especially in their own neighborhoods? Is it the way any group of truly free people would want to behave? When people reach the point of committing random acts of violence and destroying their own neighborhoods, one must recognize that the actions committed are expressions of deep and serious pain. How aware are the police of their own role as protectors of wealth and controllers of the poor and otherwise disenfranchised? These are important questions that must be addressed when we think about what the real sources of social order are in our lives, and the actual role of the criminal justice system.

**Why the Wealthy are Concerned**

Because the oppression of people of color has been so great, they are the greatest threat to the wealthy. Their circumstances have forced them to realize the true nature and purpose of law in nation-states that are controlled predominantly by wealthy Whites, which is to protect the wealthy. Once faced with that realization, their contempt and anger is made known in a variety of ways. The revolt that took place in Los Angeles over the beating of Rodney King is a good example of the volatile nature of conditions where large segments of the population are being exploited and/or neglected. While there are also large segments of the White population neglected, conditions have been much worse among Blacks, and they continue. African American protests broke out again in Oakland, California just weeks from this writing when a White police officer shot an unarmed African American man. The incident was videotaped showing the officer shoot the Black man in the back while he was being held down, and yet the jury, with no African American jurors, rendered the lightest guilty sentence possible: involuntary manslaughter.

Those in positions of power know their ability to control Blacks through the schools and various other propaganda devices is rapidly diminishing. Rather than initiating policies and programs that would improve conditions for the growing numbers of marginalized people, which would require some immediate financial costs, the imperative of immediate maximization of profits demands that prison be the sole response to all who fail to accept their place within an increasingly more stratified social structure (Parenti 2010). Prisons have been built over the years at an unprecedented rate in order to step up the containment of disenfranchised people (LEAP 2010, Davis 1998, 2003, Currie 1994)—as well as create large scale forced labor conditions for corporations. During the 1990s the state of Texas alone built 77 new prisons (LEAP 2010a). Prisoners are becoming more aware of and organized around their exploitation as citizens and prisoners. In the United States organized resistance within and across prisons is emerging and will most likely continue to grow unless there is a dramatic decline in the use of prisons within the near future. Budgetary crises are now forcing prison reductions in some states.

While the criminal justice system is relatively ineffectual when it comes to preventing crime, it has been quite effective (with the help of mainstream media) in thwarting public protests and community organizing. In some situations, such as racial and labor revolts, the military is brought in to protect the privileges of the wealthy over the rest of the population. These actions are defended by telling the public that it is they who are being protected, and typically the public feels good about seeing these "trouble makers" and "hoodlums" being beaten and arrested. As the public watches this on TV they do not realize that they are watching themselves being beaten and arrested. It is more likely that they would be one of the people beaten (or their son or their daughter) than one of the people for whom the beatings are actually taking place. As we watch public protestors being beaten and arrested how many of us are aware that standard operating procedure among law enforcement agencies is to have provocateurs planted in the crowd to provoke violence and thereby justify violence on the part of the police. If you see a window broken during an otherwise peaceful demonstration, you can be almost certain the rock was thrown by a provocateur who will be described by the police as a member of an anarchist organization. Provocateur activities have been perpetrated by criminal justice forces continuously in the United States for many years (Wikipedia 2010c), and occur in other countries as well (Doctorow 2010, Nurmakov 2010).

Sociologically these are interesting situations. The protestors are attempting to use the media to raise public and government awareness about a particular social issue related to the misuse of power, such as a corporation driven war. In other words, protestors are about constructing (which they would argue is simply revealing) a social reality that will sway public and official perceptions in a particular direction. Symbolic Interactionism tells us that this cannot be done without controlling the situation—that is, having the last anticipation and, hence, the last action that moves perceptions in the desired direction. In anticipation of this outcome those in power are likewise challenged to control the situation so as to turn the protest into their own constructed reality. This is where the provocateur comes into play: a rock through a window and the protest is no longer about the socio-political issues at hand, but the violence of the protestors and the justification of the police in suppressing the protestors. Furthermore, since those in power are controlling the situation and constructing their desired reality, why not get more mileage out of the effort by labeling the protestors as anarchists? This activity denigrates the protestors because of the already socially constructed negative image of anarchists, and further reinforces the negative image of anarchism by associating it with the violence initiated by the police themselves.

### *What happens to wealthy criminals?*

The fear of street crime is continually being instilled in United States citizens by corporate media. The goal of this daily message on the evening news is to instill enough fear in the public to render support for more police and more prisons. Within this process the most serious criminals tend to be overlooked. We loosely refer to them as white-collar criminals (term coined by Edwin H. Sutherland), but that label is too general and too vague since many white-collar positions in our society contribute little to the most serious and most costly crimes.

Corporate CEO's involved in serious crime should be distinguished from the middle class types of white-collar crime, which by comparison are on a much smaller scale. The most serious crimes in the United States are committed by highly affluent people, sometimes with the assistance of components of our federal and state governments. These are the true criminal elites (Coleman 2006). Crimes of the criminal elites are far more serious, relative to financial costs and physical harm to people, than all the index crimes combined (Coleman 2006). A number of single corporate crime events, like the Savings and Loans crimes of the late 1980s, or the Enron crimes of the early twenty-first century, will each cost United States citizens several decades worth of total index crimes.

Despite their vast control over much of the law, criminal elites frequently and openly violate the laws of the United States, individual states, and local communities (Coleman 2006). Moreover, they are able to get the government to force/trick the American people into participating in many of these illegal activities. Such participation is perhaps best represented in the various United States invasions of undeveloped or developing countries where average United States citizens are called upon by their government, under the guise of protecting democracy, to help protect the interests of multinational corporations. When this happens, citizens, perhaps without realizing it, participate in violations of international laws which the United States, as part of the United Nations, is bound to uphold. In addition to the resultant millions of deaths, ordinary United States citizens, acting as soldiers, violate the human rights of the citizens of the invaded countries—sometimes replacing democratically elected leaders with dictators (Clark 2010, Jensen 2010, Perkins 2004, Parenti 1995, Moyer 1987). Since these invasions often constitute acts of war and most are not declared by Congress, United States citizens are also being forced to participate in violating the Constitution of the United States, which is supposed to be the cornerstone of the United States legal system (Clark 2010).

*Criminal elites and corporations*

Wealthy elite criminals, including the participating government officials, represent a failed socialization process, since their behaviors are so disparate from the values of fairness and justice—values we tout as the basis for the United States constitution and legal system. Unlike the poor, who are disenfranchised and/or marginalized, the criminal elites have the power to shape the reality around them at little cost to themselves. Consider the following examples:

- the CEOs of Ford Company who created the combustible Pinto and who in the 1990s forced workers in Mexico back to work at gunpoint;
- the CEOs of General Motors who deliberately destroyed our mass transit system;
- the CEOs of General Electric who conspired with the Nazis during WWII and who have dumped more hazardous waste than any other CEO's;
- the CEOs of the oil companies who have conspired to fix oil prices, and who, along with many other companies, have pressured our government to invade numerous third world countries, killing millions of innocent people;
- The CEOs of British Petroleum, who decided to save money by using inexpensive parts; resulting in the largest oil spill in history and immeasurable amounts of damage to the environment;
- the CEOs of the many companies who participated in the Iran-Contra affair that involved direct violations of Congressional order, the illegal selling of arms to the enemy, and the use of U.S. planes to ship illegal drugs;

- the CEOs of the Savings and Loans who stole billions of dollars from the citizens of the United States;
- the CEOs of the many pharmaceutical companies that have ruined or destroyed thousands of lives by forcing the falsification of research findings;
- the CEOs of Enron who convinced their workers to buy more Enron stock at the same time they were selling their stock because they knew the bogus company they had created was about to collapse;
- The CEOs of Goldman Sachs (currently under investigation) and other major banking and investment corporations that deliberately created fraudulent products, which they then bet against for personal profit, putting the corporation and all touched by it (millions) at risk of complete financial collapse, and causing the most severe economic recession since the great depression of 1929;
- The CEOs of Goldman Sachs, AIG and other similar major banking and investment corporations that, upon receiving a financial bailout from the federal government, misused their bailout funds for their own huge bonuses and exotic vacation trips/parties;
- and, the CEO's of Halliburton and other similar corporations who used the federal government to invade Iraq under completely false pretenses; resulting in the loss and displacement of hundreds of thousands (possibly millions) of innocent lives.

The above list is by no means intended to be exhaustive. It is the metaphorical tip of an iceberg that shows no signs of melting soon. The decision-making CEOs of all of these companies, and many more just like them, are guilty of the most serious and harmful crimes committed within the United States. Yet, the CEOs themselves are seldom viewed as criminals, and indeed, few have ever paid anything for their crimes, even when the corporations they run are convicted of serious criminal acts. One of the greatest myths of all about crime is that street crime and street criminals are our greatest threat and our greatest enemies. All of the street crimes put together cannot measure up to even a fraction of the wealthy elite crime that we know about. Furthermore, we have good reason to believe that we only know about a small fraction of such crime since comparatively few of our resources are spent investigating such criminal activity. Most of these criminal cases have to fall on authorities like a ton of bricks before they are recognized as criminal cases. Even then there is a tendency to rationalize the criminal activity into something less than crime … "a bad business decision," "only doing their job" and so on. A recent case in point is the Enron Collapse that resulted in thousands of people losing their investments and pensions, while the CEOs Kenneth Lay and Jeffery Skilling sold their shares and amassed huge fortunes. Lay curiously died just before his trial and Skilling was found guilty of several crimes and sent to prison. Skilling's case was reviewed in late 2010 by the Supreme Court and all but declared a mistrial (Flood 2010). The lower court is forced to reconsider the case and it is likely that

Skilling's team of lawyers will have Skilling exonerated and set free despite the millions of dollars in damages he did to tens of thousands of people.

Those who are aware of the serious problems that corporations present today will frequently speak about "corporations doing this" or "corporations doing that." It is easy to forget that "corporations" don't do anything. Only people can make decisions, whether it is from within the context of a family or a multinational business. People, not buildings or institutions, commit acts of greed and violence against other people, other forms of life, and the environment.

Even with the limited information available, it is possible to construct a long and impressive list of corporations found guilty of very serious crimes that negatively impact millions of people. Some of these corporations have been fined millions of dollars, and many more than once in recent years. In the vast majority of these cases not one person, not one CEO or Board Member, goes to prison for the crimes committed by "the corporation." Yet, someone growing a few marijuana plants in their basement could end up in prison for several years. Who is being protected from whom by the criminal justice system?

## Conclusion

Today, when people raise the issues presented in this chapter, they are accused by the corporate media, politicians, and other agents of wealth, of trying to start "class warfare." This is the latest myth related to crime, and its purpose is to hide the fact that, in many ways, class warfare already exists. As conflict theorists would predict, those with control of the greatest amount of resources are winning and tens of thousands of incarcerated people are prisoners of that war. As stated by one of the wealthiest people in the United States, Warren Buffet, "There's class warfare, all right … but it's my class, the rich class, that's making war, and we're winning" (Stein 2006: 1).

Both Conflict Theory and Structural Functionalism have much to offer in understanding crimes of the criminal elites. Conflict Theory tells us that class struggle for control of resources is to be expected in a free market capitalist system. Structural Functionalism tells us that within the social structure of global capitalism, crime, laws, law enforcement agencies, and large scale inequality each have an important function in the maintenance of wealth for the most successful capitalists. Symbolic Interactionism, as well, makes a major contribution toward helping us understand how dysfunctional social structures, like free market laissez-faire capitalism, are protected from public scrutiny.

### *Where from here?*

Does the analysis of crime and the criminal justice system in this chapter mean that the people making decisions impacting on the above identified processes are somehow evil malicious people out to destroy the lives of others? This chapter is not intended to convey that idea. People that commit crimes, whether they are criminal elites or street criminals, have complicated motives for their behaviors. Over time they rationalize that what they are doing is "normal" within some socially defensible framework, whether it is the framework of success as defined by a particular economic system, or the framework of deprivation driven by that same system. The more wealth people have, the more latitude and ability they have to correct the dysfunctional system that created their wealth. This is not an easy responsibility for wealthy people to accept even if they do realize the damage their wealth accumulation does in the world. A few wealthy people have successfully made that journey.

Crime in all of its various forms will not change until the variables causing inequality change. For the wealthy, crime is a means by which inequality is increased. For most everyone else, crime is an attempt to reduce inequality. There are exceptions relative to violence and interpersonal control. A man abusing his "intimate" partner uses violence to increase inequality between himself and his partner, but most crime is related to class warfare. Working toward eliminating inequality nationally and internationally by re-socializing people toward a different economic system makes other positive changes possible as well: de-criminalizing drug use, eliminating prisons as we know them, and converting combatant police officers back to peace officers who are truly public servants. Attempting to stop violence with violence simply does not work. It creates more violence. This is very difficult for people in the United States to believe, given that we are heavily socialized into a very violent culture, but the longitudinal and cross-cultural evidence is undeniable. Gentle and peaceful people do not always survive, but neither do violent people.

# Chapter 10
# Corporations, Nation-States, and Economic Globalization: Impact on Inequality

**What is a Corporation?**

Corporations were used prior to the creation of the United States of America. The English monarch created corporations to carry out specific tasks that he wanted to be done, either within England or somewhere in England's colonies. If you look up the definition of a corporation you will find a brief statement that essentially fits that description. That is, a corporation is a legal entity consisting of positions and resources that is chartered by a government to carry out some particular function. There will also likely be some reference to corporations having the legal status of a person (AllBusiness 2010).

In the United States it is the individual states themselves that charter most corporations. Most of the original thirteen colonies of the United States were actually corporations designed by the British monarch to extract the resources from the invaded territories. There were also corporations in addition to the colonies, perhaps the most famous being the British East India Tea Company. What most people probably do not realize is that the Boston Tea Party, which is typically billed as a rebellion against the King of England, was actually a result of competition between the British East India Tea Company and the colony merchants. The British East India Tea Company pressured the King to raise the taxes on the goods sold by merchants in the colonies so that the merchants in the colonies could no longer compete with the East India Tea Company (Boyer 2003).

The above information regarding corporations is important for a couple of reasons. First, it shows that corporations were created for specific purposes and were, for the most part, under the control of their creator, which was typically some government body. Second, it shows the potential for corruption between corporations and government, with corporations exerting pressure back onto the government unit that created them. There was no pretense of democracy during the time when English kings had complete power over England and its colonies. Nevertheless, an already corrupt circumstance can become more corrupt, as was the case when the King of England yielded to the pressure of the East India Tea Company. For the most part, however, corporations in the United States were highly controlled entities until the years immediately following the civil war. Charters granted to corporations were limited in terms of how long they could exist and their powers were specifically regulated. Among the many restrictions corporations had to abide by were that they could not own stock in other corporations, keep private records, or make political contributions to politicians or political units (Boyer 2003).

*Increasing wealth through greater control of the state*

The above three identified restrictions alone are significant relative to contemporary Sociology—both in the United States and around the world. Had the people of the United States maintained the restrictions and enforced them, corporations would be less effective tools of wealth for large scale corruption. During and immediately following the Civil War corporations began to take on a life of their own, practicing an independence that they legally did not have. Through their new found independence they were able to leverage increased power from the state, which mushroomed into the corrupt multinational corporations that control most of the world today.

It is important to emphasize, however, that the corporation was not the beginning of state control by the wealthy. The nation-state itself was created over a long period of time to accommodate the interests of the wealthy. It might be more accurate to say that the corporation emerged as an alternative route for the wealthy once royal positions (kings, queens, and noblemen) were no longer needed. Marjorie Kelly alludes to this point in her work *The Divine Right of Capital* (2003). Divine territorial royalty is of marginal value if one can control the two most powerful social entities ever invented: corporations and the nation-state. It is possible that other tools could also have been invented and used to allow the wealthy to control the world's resources and human labor for profit. This is why macro structural solutions to social problems, while necessary, are not sufficient to control the most serious systemic problems the world faces.

*Corporations as persons*

One of the most critical points in the evolution of the corporation as a powerful tool for the wealthy is the 1886 Supreme Court decision granting corporations the legal status of a person. This decision gave corporations the power, among other things, to invoke their right to free speech (the first amendment of the constitution) in order to be able to make political donations to politicians and political parties. As is sometimes expressed, the rest is history. The consequences of corporations being able to make political donations are very important. Members of the house and senate must weigh the potential loss of campaign funds for every decision they make. As expressed many years ago by a former congressman of Oklahoma, Michael Synar, every decision he makes is a thirty thousand dollar decision. The dollar amount could now be double or triple what it was then.

The 1886 Supreme Court decision was reinforced and used 114 years later when the 2010 Supreme Court in *Citizens United v. Federal Election Commission* ruled that Corporations, as persons, had a first amendment right to provide unlimited funds to political candidates during an election. Many congressional members are outraged by this decision, recognizing that in the future elections will be owned by corporations even more than they are owned by them today. While the mainstream media pundits accuses concerned citizens of promoting conspiracy theories, the wealthy corporate owners meet regularly through think tanks and other closed venues to strategize on how to more effectively control the political system for their benefit (Pilkington 2011).

The irony of a corporation having the status of a person is that when there is criminal liability found against that corporation, typically the most that happens is that the corporation is fined. For example, when General Electric (GE) was found guilty of conspiring with the enemy during World War II, GE Corporation was fined, and then allowed to use the fine as a tax write off. General Electric then went on to become the most powerful company in the world, with one of the most extensive criminal records. GE has a long list of federal prosecutions on its record. If a real person had been found guilty of conspiring with the enemy during WWII, it is not likely that person would have avoided a very long prison term or possibly an even more severe sentence.

"Corporations" don't make decisions to violate the law and exploit everything within their grasp. The people running the corporations do that, but the conviction of a corporation as a person brings no consequences to the real people involved. Corporations cannot be imprisoned or executed for criminal activity no matter how many real people die as a result of a corporation's actions. In most states a real person cannot vote if they have been convicted of a felony (for at least some period of time). No matter how serious the crime, CEOs of corporations can not only vote, but will now be able to purchase election outcomes by providing unlimited funding to candidates that favor their interests.

Hence, the corporation is a double shield for the wealthy. It gives them incredibly magnified constitutional powers, since the corporation has extensive resources and liberties that far exceed any one individual. Additionally, however, the corporate shield also allows wealthy people to violate the law in the name of the corporation. In those rare instances where legal convictions are rendered, it is the "corporations" and not the actual decision-makers that absorb the penalty. Corporate criminal and civil penalties are typically monetary fines that can be passed on to the consumer or deducted from the salaries of workers.

### *But I saw Kenneth Lay on trial!*

On rare occasion we will see CEO's going to jail. In these situations, however, the CEO typically violates the law in some particular way that takes his/her behavior outside of the parameters of the corporate decision-making process. For example, Martha Stewart, one of the most successful business women and female CEO's in the United States during the 1980s and 1990s, did not go to jail for wrongdoing as a CEO, which was the original charge brought against her, but for supposedly perjuring herself in court. The irony of Martha Stewart's conviction is that, while she may have been guilty of a lot of wrong doing, it would have probably been ignored as standard operating procedure had she been a man. It might have also been ignored had she cooperated with the federal prosecutor who was trying to find evidence that might result in charges against the then President, William Clinton.

Another example, and one of the most vivid of the last century, was the Enron debacle that resulted in some actual convictions of corporate executives, including then famous CEO Kenneth Lay. Among other criminal activities, Enron executives were accused of bribing federal tax officials. Much of what they did was outside of typical corporate decision-making corruption because Enron was very close to being a fictitious entity, with a paper identity that had little real world representation. Much of the criminal behavior was conducted in the course of constructing the false corporate identity in order to protect its stock values for wealthy investors, and in order to protect the extremely large salaries of the corporate executives. When indictments were rendered, the CEO's did everything they could to prevent the smaller investors and company workers from getting their contractual compensations.

While corporations spend a lot of money lobbying politicians and political parties in order to control the law, which they do very successfully (as discussed in Chapter 9), the CEO's know that there are always greater profits outside the law. So the pattern is to push the law as far as possible and then still go beyond, calculating all the while what it will cost if the corporation gets caught and convicted. The truly skillful CEO, with the help of many accountants and lawyers, knows how far to push illegal activities and still stay within corporate profits if caught. At the same time, a skillful CEO also knows how to avoid being personally prosecuted for violating the law. With the maximization of profits foremost on the minds of CEOs, the just described behavior seems to be accepted in the corporate world as standard operating procedure.

### *"Just doing my job"*

The defense of every CEO, and one that resonates well in the halls of business colleges, is that CEOs are just doing their job. After shedding any remaining restrictions that government once held over them, and essentially taking control of government, corporations have been free to define themselves however they choose. So when a CEO is accused of carrying greed beyond the limits of what even devout capitalists consider reasonable, they are not exaggerating very much when they say that they are just doing their job. Their job has become defined strictly in terms of maximizing profits, as many business and economics professors would tell you. This means that all other considerations: human lives; non-human lives; the quality of air; the availability of food and water; decent housing; safety from violence, radiation, depleted uranium, carcinogens, and war; massive destruction of rainforests; elimination of species of life; unemployment; starvation; homelessness; destruction of education; and so on … are not the CEO's responsibility in any way.

If by doing one's job harmful effects occur, that is technically not the CEO's fault because that is the way large powerful corporations have chosen to define themselves, and the surrounding world. The propaganda surrounding their self-definition has been sufficiently effective that many people defend the self-created privileges of corporations with great vigilance. What would be the consequences for average people if the decisions made in the course of doing their job resulted in the deaths of thousands of people? The sentence would most likely be life in prison or death. That is not what happens to the CEO's who make decisions that force governments to go to war in order to generate greater corporate profits; nor does it happen to the CEO's who decide to export poisonous or otherwise harmful products to other countries because the products have been banned in the United States.

CEOs make decisions everyday that rob the earth of its precious non-renewable resources, and not just oil, coal, and natural gas. How does one pretend to replace a 700 year old tree? Planting a seedling that will most likely be "harvested" in fifteen years is not renewing the resource of an old growth forest. Water quality, air quality, soil quality, and many other aspects of the earth's condition are becoming important environmental issues. The earth's soil is continuously being contaminated with chemicals and depleted uranium. Millions of people around the world, and many other forms of life, are suffering and/or dying because of the decisions made under the pretense of "just doing my job."

*Social responsibility*

The point being emphasized is that the above examples are not the work of amorphous institutions that somehow automatically make decisions void of human contact. Humans do make these decisions. The socialization and education of the decision-makers do not give them the background necessary to make decisions in the best interest of all concerned. Corporate executives sitting in board rooms calculate how they can best control and avoid the law. They do not fully understand or relate to the concept of "social responsibility." Social responsibility involves examining all the possible short and long-term effects of one's decisions, and acting accordingly. Examining short and long-term effects necessarily requires understanding, and consideration of, the root causes of the problem under consideration. Making socially responsible decisions means making choices that may cost decision-makers financially in the short run, but which will benefit the decision-maker directly and indirectly in the long run. A simple notion like leaving a healthier planet for future generations (possibly one's children and grandchildren) should bring sufficient satisfaction to decision-makers who act in a socially responsible manner.

Related to the concept of social responsibility is the well known popular term "common decency," which means putting the needs of others, at the very least, before one's own wants. It means acting out of compassion and cooperation rather than greed and exploitation. In the life of the corporation there is no place for the notion of common decency. Common decency, like greed, is a term typically ignored in academia because it is a term that conveys a judgment related to human values. Many sociologists have been taught that it is wrong to incorporate values into sociological analysis. What is missing from this position is the understanding that all research and analyses of all types, not just sociological, have some grounding in human values. The important question is always, "whose values are being protected and why?"

Most large powerful corporations are a serious problem for the welfare of all forms of life in the world. They are a dysfunctional damaging component within the broader social structure of the global social system. It is useful to ask the difficult question of how they came to be so dysfunctional. What is the root cause? If we eliminated corporations altogether tomorrow, would the problems caused by corporations disappear? It is not likely that they would. It would most likely be a short period of time before something else was invented by corrupt wealthy people to allow them to maintain and expand their wealth. Repairing a social structure is a lot like repairing any other type of structure. If the root cause of the damage is not attended to, the time spent on repairs could be wasted. If your car stalls and your lights won't work, you might discover that your car has a dead battery. You can change the battery only to find that the same thing happens again within a few days. After changing the battery a second time you realize that the battery is not the root cause of the problem. A more careful analysis reveals that the alternator/generator has gone bad. The battery won't hold a charge because there is nothing to provide the charge. Without a charged battery, there is no current to the spark plugs, no spark, no combustion, and hence, no engine power.

It is no different with social structures. Corporations are merely a tool for people raised and trained to attain and hoard unlimited amounts of wealth. Removing the corporation without doing anything deeper will not permanently solve the problems currently created by corporations because corporations are not the root cause of the problems they represent. One must ask, "What is the motivation behind the corporation?" Therein one finds the source of the systemic problems associated with corporations. Without addressing decision-maker motivation for making corporations what they are today, the problems will persist indefinitely.

## What does Corporate Greed Mean?

Corporations are not the greed itself. They are merely one of the symptoms and tools of the greed. When we speak of corporate greed, we are not speaking of the institution as much as the people who run it for their own wealth related purposes, and for the purposes of their collusive associates. Perhaps the most important lesson we can learn related to how greed operates in a laissez-faire capitalist system where corporate greed rules completely unchecked, is that for this economic system to work well for those at the top, which is who the system is designed by and for, people at all levels must maintain a high amount of self interest. The greed of those in the lower income levels supports the greed of those in the income levels above them. The imperative self-interest of those in the lower income categories makes it difficult for those people to recognize the systemic problem of greed within the contemporary corporation. As discussed earlier, learning to be "competitive" at an early age is an important part of the process of legitimizing greed as a basis for decision-making.

If people of relatively modest incomes cannot see the contradictions in their lives, how can one expect wealthy people to see the contradictions in theirs? Studying the social psychological processes through which these contradictions are nurtured and rationalized is an important part of solving global social problems. What three point structures can be constructed to represent the contradictions in the thinking of wealthy people and in our own thinking, and what adjustments are made to help one tolerate or eliminate any corresponding dissonance resulting from those contradictions? Observe what should be a pretty simple example, but which actually becomes somewhat complicated: being a Christian and a laissez-faire capitalist at the same time.

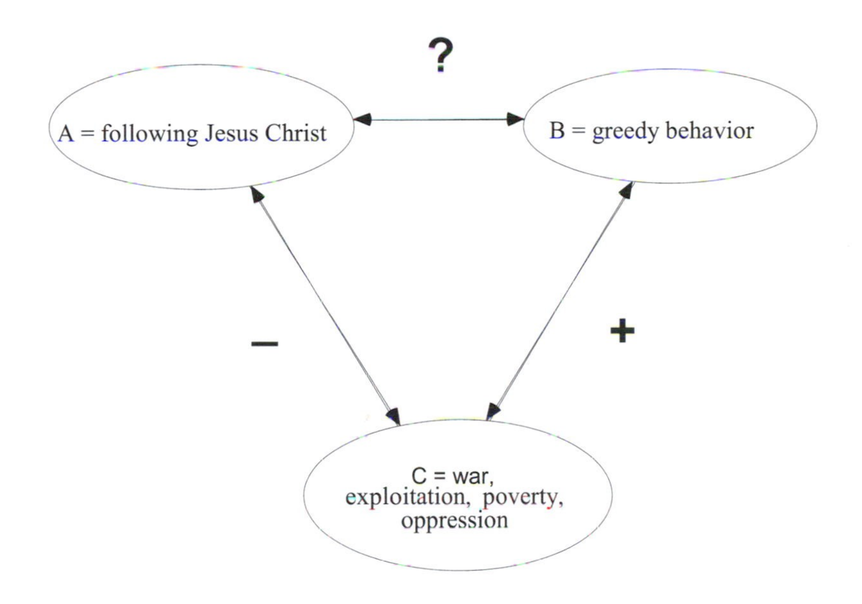


**Figure 10.1 Follower of Jesus Christ**

Anyone who is truly a follower of the teachings of Jesus Christ, based only on what Christ reportedly said and did, would have to be opposed to greed as well as war and all of the other related problems listed below war (each could be identified within separate three point structures, but all turn out the same). It is pretty easy to see that Figure 10.1 could only be balanced if the third sign, represented by a question mark between items A and B, became negative, since the product of two negative signs and one positive sign is positive. This makes perfectly good intuitive sense as well. Someone who is seriously following what Christ said would not want to be greedy, which is the basis for war and many other negative "unChristian" qualities. I use Christ and Christianity for this example because Christianity is most familiar to me, but I suspect a similar figure could be drawn using just about any religious framework.

*Redefining the situation: language as an important tool*

Once the negative sign is placed in the above mental structure represented in Figure 10.1, the holders of this thought pattern, as part of the mainstream United States economy, have a problem. How can they follow Christ and support war at the same time? Whether people are proud of their greed or not, they have to behave motivated by greed at some level in order to practice capitalism successfully. Furthermore, they must also have some way of accepting war and rationalizing away the various negative residual effects, because it is through war that resource holdings and labor pools are expanded—the two essential components of successful laissez-faire capitalism. Hence, Figure 10.1 is obviously not a preferred model if one wants to practice laissez-faire capitalism. Yet, one cannot change the sign between items A and B to positive because that would create an imbalanced structure, as represented by the product of the signs being negative, and would result in cognitive dissonance. That is, one cannot follow Christ and knowingly and overtly behave in a greedy manner. That is too obvious a contradiction to bear comfortably. So what do Christian capitalists do?

Figure 10.2 shows the power of language in controlling our mental and physical behaviors. Obviously Christianity, as it has evolved since Christ, does not oppose war—albeit the preferred term is "national defense." It doesn't matter if "defense" may sometimes mean striking first, as in the 2003 United States attack on the nation-state of Iraq. That complication is sufficiently removed from first order dissonance. And clearly Christianity (as most often practiced) and capitalism are strongly connected, with most of the Christian churches being major stock holders and, at some level of institutional governance, supporting the proliferation of capitalism around the world.

Hence, the question-mark in Figure 10.2 would have to be converted to a positive sign for balance to be achieved. Inserting a positive sign with the new language would create balance in the structure in every respect, and the holders of this thought process can be comfortable with who they are and what they believe they know. They are free to rationalize the just nature of a war as outlined in the criteria provided by their particular Christian Church. Who can be opposed to "freedom" as in "free markets" and certainly people are not to be blamed for defending themselves, as in "national defense." Yet, Figures 10.1 and 10.2 represent essentially the same phenomena.

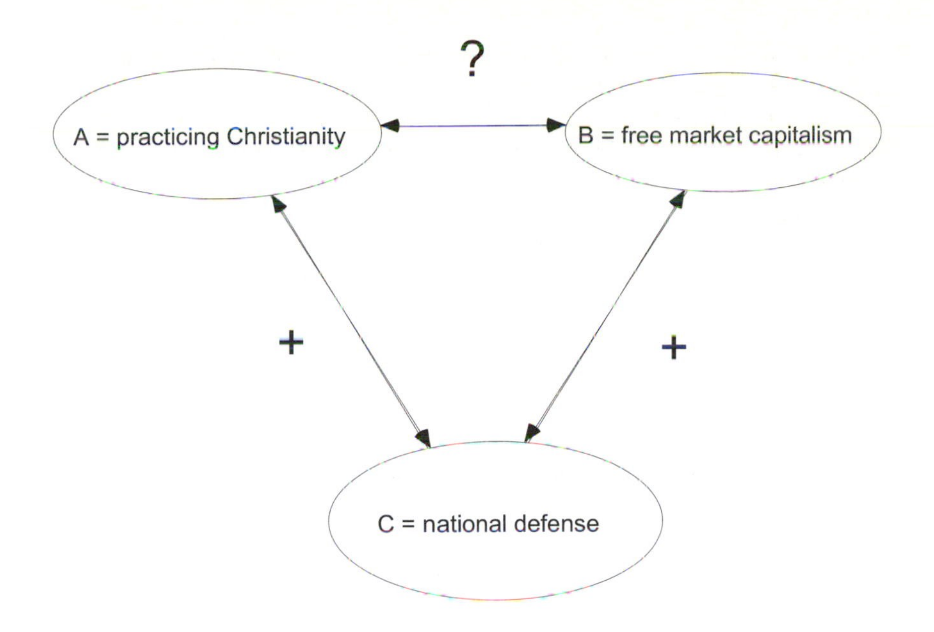


**Figure 10.2 Practicing Christianity**

An important tool, therefore, in the process of re-socializing people into a more humane state of existence, is the ability to cut through the surface language and expose the cold hard ugly steel beneath the flowers. Some religious scholars question whether Christ would be a "Christian" if he were alive today. "Free Market Capitalism" is another term for uncontrolled greed, and "national defense," as we now know it, is primarily international offense against any resistance to United States intervention on behalf of corporations (Perkins 2004, Parenti 1995).

Students at all levels of education and citizens in general should all have the necessary skills to identify and inform others of the underlying structural realities of how humans think about the social world. A massive education process would be required to carry out the re-socialization of a nation-state deeply lost in the deceptive rhetoric of corporate greed, and it could be done.

There are many individuals and organizations working to change the role that corporations play in the social lives of humans and all species of life. Some, like Marjorie Kelly, focus on the importance of changing the concept of the corporation itself. Do corporations drive the behavior of wealthy and powerful people, or are corporations simply tools for the motivation to hoard resources? I have presented the latter argument. It is, however, possible that there is a reciprocal relationship between the two. That is, the way in which corporations are structured as social entities may contribute to the ease with which greed is carried out by those who attain wealth and power. Changing the way corporations are able to operate could help reduce the negative impact of corporations on the world, but without a major adjustment in the way humans think about economics and social relations, we have to question whether such change will have a lasting effect.

## What Would Marx Say?

It is within this debate about a very practical issue that we can return to the theoretical contributions of Karl Marx. What would Marx say about this issue? Based on what we have discussed about the work of Marx we would have to see the corporation as a replaceable tool for the interests of the wealthy. While the corporation is an effective tool in the struggle of the wealthy to accumulate more surpluses and thus more wealth, it is a means to an end and not the end in itself. In the class warfare depicted in the works of Marx, those in the upper classes have the advantage of using their resources to create still other tools as needed to protect what they have and to attain more.

The piece that is missing from Marx's works, and the likely reason his predictions for the future have failed, is that revolutions and take-backs of any kind by the lower classes are of no long-term value unless ultimately the vast majority of all who remain agree that what we have is a reasonable state of existence. Such an agreement necessarily means agreeing to change our institutions, like corporations, but it also means a critical mass of people from all backgrounds accepting the reasons why such changes are important. If the motivation to become wealthier at the expense of others continues to be strong, people with the means to make that happen will continue to do so. This is where re-socialization becomes an important part of social change, and it is the part that macro social thinkers, like Marx, tend to overlook.

## The Secret Government: A Chicken and Egg Dilemma

It is difficult for people brought up in the United States to believe or even consider that the government that is supposed to be *their* government could somehow be an instrument for unethical, immoral, and illegal activities. Yet, the evidence to that effect, based on declassified federal documents alone, is overwhelming. Additionally, written and videotaped testimonies of government insiders make the case for government abuses almost impossible to refute. The involvement of the United States government in the destruction and control of peoples and their resources all over the world has been well documented by former CIA operatives and officials, such as Philip Agee (1975), Ralph McGehee (2002), and John Stockwell (1984), all of whom have written extensively about their experiences. United States interventions into other countries have also been directly linked to the demands of wealthy capitalists representing and being represented by, multinational corporations. The United Fruit Company was one of the earliest international companies for which the Central Intelligence Agency worked, causing numerous third world interventions throughout the 1950s and 1960s. There have been many multinational corporations driving our foreign policy since that time (Clark 2010, Perkins 2004, 2010, Chomsky 1993, 2005, Parenti 1995, Moyer 1987).

The initiation of violence and destruction on behalf of corporate owners by agencies of the United States government has a long history predating the CIA. United States intervention into other countries by use of force and espionage has been traced back as far as 1852. Our first documented entrance into Nicaragua, which has an important recent history of intervention as well, was in 1853. Henry Cabot Lodge stated in the 1890s that the United States should build a canal in Nicaragua to help expand United States based commerce and then move on to control other countries like Hawaii, Samoa, and Cuba (Zinn 1980).

### *The Central Intelligence Agency*

In 1947, under the newly established National Security Act, the Central Intelligence Agency (CIA) was established. While its purpose is generally stated as national security, the CIA's primary function, as part of the United States government, is to further enhance and expand the ability of corporations to use the United States government as a tool for extracting resources from and creating markets within other countries. It did not take long for the CIA to begin its work on behalf of United States corporations and sometimes British corporations. In 1953, the CIA orchestrated the overthrow of a popular Iranian prime minister by the name of Dr Mohammad Mosaddeq. Mosaddeq was planning to nationalize the oil of Iran and this was a threat to the British and United States oil companies that had taken over Iran's oil supply. The CIA created negative propaganda about him, including that he was moving the country toward communism, even though he had no connections to the communist party. The United States wanted someone in control of Iran that could be controlled (a puppet) on behalf of the United States corporations that had financial interests there. So the United States, relying on the work of the CIA, installed the Shah of Iran, a ruthless dictator. He killed and tortured tens of thousands of innocent people in order to keep Iran safe for the United States and British oil companies. He was thereby permitted to also accumulate tremendous wealth for himself (Parenti 1995, Moyer 1987).

The next CIA target was Jacobo Arbenz, the democratically elected president of Guatemala. Arbenz, quite popular with the Guatemalan people, was elected with 65 percent of the votes. He had a well thought out plan to nationalize transportation, major food supplies, electrical power, and much of the farm land in Guatemala. In other words, Arbenz wanted to make it possible for the Guatemalan people to survive independently as much as possible, a reasonable goal for anyone to have for their community or nation-state. Arbenz, gave up a large amount of his own land under his land reform program. Unfortunately, one of the largest land owners in Guatemala was the United Fruit Company and it was based in the United States. United Fruit Company owned approximately 500,000 acres of prime land, much of which was undeveloped. The land nationalization program targeted undeveloped land and the United Fruit Company had to sell approximately half of its land back to Guatemala under the nationalization program. It didn't take long for then President Eisenhower to put the CIA into action on behalf of the United Fruit Company. In 1954 a CIA-led political coup removed Arbenz from power and installed a puppet that reversed all of Arbenz's programs. The list of CIA-led interventions on behalf of United States corporations is quite long (Perkins 2004, Parenti 1995, Moyers 1987), and the same corporations are sometimes involved in multiple interventions. For example, the United Fruit Company, mentioned above, was also a prime mover in United States intervention activities in Cuba (Parenti 1995, Moyers 1987).

The United States government, under the pretense of spreading democracy and freedom has caused the destruction of democratic governments and led to the imprisonment, torture and death of millions of people all over the world (Perkins 2010, de la barra and dello buono 2009, Perkins 2004, Parenti 1995, Moyers 1987). How do these actions relate to inequality around the world and within the United States? Who are the people that benefit from these interventions and who are the people that lose and ultimately suffer? The answer to those questions should now be reasonably clear.

## The Iran-Contra Crime: A Case Study

In the 1980s the Reagan Administration funded a CIA operation in Nicaragua to overthrow the Sandinista government. The Sandinista government was the result of a people's revolution in Nicaragua. Since it was a government for the common people, it could not be supported by the United States government as controlled by multinational corporations representing the upper classes. The Sandinistas were a threat to United States corporations since the goal of the Sandinista government was to nationalize its resources for the people of Nicaragua, limiting the availability of Nicaraguan resources to external agents except through mutually agreed upon trade. The pattern is similar to the many other situations where the United States has over-turned the governments of other countries on behalf of corporations. What was different about this case was that a bombing action taken by the CIA resulted in the deaths of a number of innocent people. The public attention that was given to this bombing action aggravated members of the United States Congress. The Congress responded by cutting funds for the United States supported mercenaries, referred to as the Contras. Under the Congressional Boland Amendments the Defense Department, Central Intelligence Agency, and all other branches of government were prohibited from funding the Contras.

Upon learning of the congressional ban, President Reagan asked the director of the CIA and other White House advisors if there wasn't anything that he could do unilaterally to get around the Congress. The director of the CIA and a number of White House advisors came up with a plan run by the National Security Council that involved creating a separate organization outside of the federal government that would be totally unaccountable to anyone. It would, however, be operated by the National Security Council officers who were also close White House advisors. This organization became known as the *Enterprise*, and it was overseen by White House advisor John Poindexter. The CIA also continued to be involved.

*The Enterprise*

How would the Enterprise be funded since it could not receive funds from the United States government? The Enterprise raised money from wealthy business people. Additionally, the Enterprise sold arms to Iran, which was actually considered an enemy of the United States government at the time. Arming the enemy is supposed to be considered treason. Selling arms to the enemy was the basis for the legal finding against General Electric during World War II. In this case, arming Iran was part of a secret Reagan Administration deal to get United States hostages released, an issue on which Reagan was elected president, since United States hostages were being held by Iran at the time of the 1980 election. Reagan swore to the American people in his campaign that he would never make any deals for the hostages in Iran (Columbia Encyclopedia 2010).

Whose arms was the Enterprise selling? They were arms paid for by the United States taxpayer, and donated by the CIA to the Enterprise without taxpayer (congressional) consent. The money that was raised was supposed to be for supplies to the Contras who were fighting the Sandinistas. However, very little of the money was actually sent to the Contras. Since this was a totally illegal operation, there was no accountability, and the money ended up in the pockets of scam artists and the various people associated with the Enterprise. Congressional hearings were held which revealed evidence through testimony implicating the highest positions in government, including the president of the United States. White House advisor John Poindexter stated in his testimony that he was trying to create a situation that would allow the president to deny any involvement in the matter. Lieutenant-Colonel Oliver North, was a main player in this initiative. "North said he believed President Reagan was largely aware of the secret arrangement, and the independent prosecutor's report (1994) said that Reagan and Bush had some knowledge of the affair or its coverup (sic)" (*Columbia Encyclopedia* 2010: 1).

Yet, the president of the United States was never called before the hearings for testimony. About ten years later another president, William Clinton, was actually investigated and interrogated via a special prosecution process, and eventually impeached by the House of Representatives, for essentially what amounted to having consensual sex with a woman in the oval office of the White House. The woman involved did not file a harassment complaint against the president. Initially she claimed to be in love with him. The president's testimony about the incident was less than straightforward, but not exactly perjury. However misguided this latter president (perhaps in a variety of ways), having consensual sex with a woman in the oval office does not compare in magnitude with conspiring to circumvent a congressional decision for the purpose of illegally invading another country and overthrowing the government of a sovereign nation.

By encouraging the creation of an unaccountable entity to act in the name of the American people without the consent of the American people via Congress, President Reagan violated and seriously compromised the integrity of the United States constitution. Additionally, these described actions of President Reagan, as well as his order to invade Granada, constitute an act of war without the consent of Congress. Such actions, which have been committed by other presidents as well, including President Clinton, constitute a serious violation of the United States constitution: Article I, Section 8, Clause 11, which grants Congress, not the president, the power to declare war. Furthermore, it would seem that the creation of an organization (Enterprise) using United States resources for the purpose of circumventing the laws and constitution of the United States might even be considered still another form of treason.

Something that happened in the 1980s and 1990s may not seem relevant to a contemporary reader. However, following President George W. Bush's invasion of Iraq, he was accused of misleading the Congress, the American public, and much of the international community, with false information about Iraq and why it was to be invaded. The false information and corresponding invasion of Iraq allowed multinational corporations to seize control of that country's rich oil reserves. The most prominent of those multinational corporations is Halliburton, the company for which Vice President Cheney had been the CEO.

Hundreds of thousands of people have been killed by the United States government and the Iraqi resisters who want the United States military to leave. Millions of other Iraqi people have been displaced. While thirty-five articles of impeachment against President George W. Bush were entered into the United States congressional record, the Congress refused to consider them primarily because of concern about political fallout that might affect elections. President Obama has kept his campaign promise to withdraw combat troops from Iraq, but we have been increasing imperial combat forces in Afghanistan. This invasion is also based on a false reality: that the alleged leader of the 9/11/01 attacks against the World Trade Center, Osama Bin Laden, was in Afghanistan and had to be captured.

Most of the people who participated in the 9/11 attacks were from Saudi Arabia, as was Osama Bin Laden himself. Bin Laden's location was unknown for 10 years and in 2011 the military claimed to have found and killed him in Pakistan. Whether he is alive or not, one has to question whether attacking the country he was thought to be hiding in is an appropriate and justifiable response. If a murderer was hiding in your neighborhood would you want the government to blow up your entire neighborhood to capture that person? We have now sufficiently aggravated the Afghanistan people with our bombings and occupation of their country that we have actually dramatically increased our enemies there. There are more Taliban fighters resisting our presence now than when the war started ten years ago.

## The Imperative of Imperialism

Why would a president be impeached for having sex in his office and not for violating the constitution through unsanctioned acts of war, and other serious misdeeds? The answer to that question is contained within the answer to yet another important question: "What is imperialism?" For that answer we turn to one of the world's leading experts on imperialism, Michael Parenti. "By 'imperialism' I mean the process whereby the dominant politico-economic interests of one nation expropriate for their own enrichment the land, labor, raw materials, and markets of another people" (1995: 1). It is not possible, however, to fully understand imperialism without also understanding the true nature of the nation-state.

Nation-states (commonly referred to as countries, nations, or states) are still a relatively new phenomenon in the history of the world with most originating within the last one thousand years. The Roman Empire existed about two thousand years ago, but was for the most part, still a collection of loosely controlled cities. Roman emperors frequently fell in and out of control of these territories. Prior to the existence of nation-states as we now know them, there were predominantly what is called city-states. City-states were local communities developed around food supplies, natural transportation routes (mainly water ways), and protection via natural barriers, such as mountains, cliffs, the sea and so on. The city-states of what eventually became known as "Greece" are often identified as exemplar of how small aggregates of people organized themselves in the European territories six hundred or more years ago.

City-states often had to defend themselves against invaders from both near and far. Wars between city-states, however, are no match for the massively destructive wars that took place once city-states were combined to form nation-states. Wars between nation-states are ongoing as corporation run nation-states with great military power, like the United States, invade and exploit weaker nation-states to colonize them "... for their own enrichment ..." as Parenti puts it. *Colonization* is the process of co-opting a social entity through the use of physical or economic force to make that entity readily available for resource and labor extraction. " ... there is little question that, in one way or another, war played a decisive role in the rise of the state. Historical or archeological evidence of war is found in the early stages of state formation in Mesopotamia, Egypt, India, China, Japan, Greece, Rome, northern Europe, central Africa, Polynesia, Middle America, Peru, and Colombia, to name only the most prominent examples" (History of the Culture of War 2010).

The reason President Clinton was impeached for having sex and he and President Reagan were not impeached for committing serious violations of the Constitution, is that the imperative of the state is imperialism. That is why nation-states exist: to help the wealthy become wealthier by controlling as many of the world's resources and labor supplies as possible. Even so-called religious wars are not usually about religion at their core. They are about who gets to control what resources. Wars are most often redefined as something other than what they are, which is a strategy used by powerful wealthy people acting through corporations to gain control of resources and labor outside of the area they already control (Sanders 2009, Butler 1935). Indeed, the most likely reason President Clinton's sex life became front page news is that his loyalties to the wealthy were split. Despite his having free trade agreements (NAFTA and GATT) passed through the United States Congress, he was not accelerating imperialism in some parts of the world as rapidly as some wealthy people would have liked. Those people eventually received the support they wanted when George W. Bush was installed as president of the United States in 2000.

Why is imperialism so important and to whom is it important? The next section addresses that question by focusing on the function of the nation-state relative to the broader social structure of global economic wealth.

## The Origin and Economic Function of Nation-States?

The conquering of city-states to combine them into more convenient nation-states was, indeed, an early form of imperialism. When it comes to imperialism, we tend to think only of isolated peculiar examples like the Roman Empire or the British Empire, but nearly all nation-states are empires of a sort. They are all aggregates of people and communities molded by force or possibly other means into one political and economic social entity. As stated by Chomsky, "… the nation state in the modern form was largely created in Europe over many centuries. It's so unnatural and artificial that it had to be imposed by extreme violence. In fact that's the primary reason why Europe was the most savage part of the world for centuries. It was due to trying to impose a nation state system on cultures and societies that are varied and if you look at them had no relation to this artificial structure" (2005: 1). When we look at nation-states that way we see the process of imperialism as a continuous one, not an either/or set of circumstances. Once nation-states were forced on people of a general region the consumption of weaker units by stronger units did not stop—hence, modern imperialism as defined by Parenti (1995).

Prior to the formation of nation-states, city-states represented a significant inconvenience for wealthy business interests. Transporting goods from one place to another was often perilous since one had to do so through many different political and economic terrains. Water ways, for example, were not always free for the complete route that merchants wanted to travel in pursuit of new markets, resources, and labor. Controlling all of these different local interests and correspondingly maximizing one's profits was difficult for aspiring entrepreneurs and future capitalists.

The movement toward aggregating city-states into larger political entities that eventually became nation-states came about primarily as a result of the motivations of wealthy people who wanted an easier way to control labor supplies, resources, and transportation routes for importing and exporting materials and products.

Local resistance had to be eliminated which meant that all local capacity for physical violence had to be brought under centralized control. Hence, Max Weber's definition of the state is "… the claim to the monopoly of the legitimate use of physical force within a given territory …" (Dusza 1989: 75). "Outside of Europe, European states encountered traditional empires (Inca, Chinese, Ottoman, Persian, etc.) and a wide assortment of tribal peoples. These entities of politico-military rule were not recognized by Europeans as states in the European sense, nor were they accorded the privileges of sovereign statehood. There was no homogeneous interstate society at this time. Gradually, European states partitioned the globe into spheres of influence for trade and, finally, established colonies throughout" (Opello and Rosow 2004: 12).

Many of the wealthy people at the time when nation-states were first emerging were also the powerful city-state rulers who were trying to expand their own wealth and the wealth of their supporters. It is not much different today, however, when we see high level government officials who are acting on behalf of the corporations in which they invest or the corporations they led before taking public office. The important issue related to the time of city-states, which is an important issue now as well, is that the average person typically had nothing to do with the creation of the nation-state. The exception would be the soldiers fighting in the war, but doing so without understanding for what they are actually fighting. Masses of people did not come together and say, "Hey, why don't we create a larger political entity by forcing the people of another city to become part of our territory?" There were no mass demonstrations that we know of to promote imperialism and to colonize other peoples' territories. People most likely tolerated and sometimes participated in nation-state building activities for the same reasons they do today. Those with wealth and power convinced "their" people that the "other" people were their enemy. Demonizing the "other" is the stuff from which racism, xenophobia, and empires are built.

On the other hand, history is replete with mass demonstrations to try to stop imperialist actions by governments. Such actions take place by average citizens from the attacking imperial nation-state as well as from the nation being attacked. During imperialist interventions the average person is typically the pawn who suffers from being subjected to changing political rules, new forms of taxation, and shifting required loyalties. This can be seen in the early part of the twenty-first century with the United States occupation of Iraq: hundreds of thousands of innocent people were killed and millions of people displaced. Iraq is a territory that was forced into a nation-state for the financial convenience of the British in the early part of the twentieth century. Many of the same religious and cultural differences within that region which made the British want to unite the region into a centrally controlled state, are the basis for the many systemic conflicts and acts of resistance to United States occupation of Iraq in the early twenty-first century.

*What do nation-states have to do with empires?*

Today when we pledge allegiance to the flag of the United States of America, what exactly are we doing? We are pledging ourselves to be loyal to a nation-state created by and for the wealthy. That might make sense if we are wealthy, but even then it is a rather peculiar behavior. Furthermore, it is clear that the wealthy, as a group, have no loyalty to anything but their own wealth (Derber 1996). Nation-states are economic entities created for the convenience of capitalists, in order to increase profit maximization. Look at the United States for example, which is still one of the newer nation-states in the world. The destruction of native cultures and the collection of territories into one nation made it easy for corporations to import slaves and eventually other forms of human labor without worrying about crossing state or city boundaries.

Political consolidation within the United States eventually created industrial centers that were fed by all parts of the nation-state. Labor was easily recruited from the south in the 1950s once the farms were automated, and iron ore was easily transported from Northern Minnesota to the steel mills in Pittsburgh. From Pittsburgh the steel was then shipped to the auto manufacturers in Detroit and Flint Michigan where cars were produced and easily transported across the nation, and all of this was done with minimal inconvenience to the corporate owners.

Now many of the industrial cities that were created to maximize corporation profits no longer have the industries that were the original basis for recruiting labor and creating excessively dense populations of people. The people are still in these large cities, but the capitalist ventures have moved on. We now have large densely populated cities with nothing for many of the people who live there to do. Part of massive unemployment in the United States is by economic design directly, but other parts of unemployment are the residual effects of profit maximization decisions of some time ago. Many people are stuck in impoverished urban slums as corporations have gradually (and at times abruptly) moved their resources to other countries (Derber 1996, Goldsmith 1996).

It is out of city-states that nation-states emerged, and it is from nation-states that modern empires were built and imperialism has grown. Nation-states are the result of imperialism and also serve as the home base so to speak for expanding imperialism. By having delineated boundaries that represent a person's country, it is possible to socialize that person to have allegiance to that nation-state. Such allegiance is significant because when corporations want to invade other lands they need to be able to have the support of the people who are paying for the war and who are doing the fighting. Viewing ourselves as the heroes fighting evil can only happen if we have a sense of "us" that is conveniently grounded in some geographical location. We are further prepared for this mentality by interschool competitions based on home town loyalty, and so forth. Preparing "us" to be pitted against "them" as corporations expand their imperial holdings, is the primary function of what we call patriotism.

Nation-states have been little more than tools for enhancing profit maximization. As frequently happens with tools, nation-states have lost their usefulness, and the wealthiest people have devised still other ways of building their fortunes. The wealthy tend not to internalize the typical socialization of United States citizens to become good patriots (Derber 1996). When it comes to maximizing profits there are no loyalties among the large corporate CEO's. The process of evolving imperialism is ongoing.

The United States evolved out of the colonization of Indian and Mexican territories: first by the British and then by the independent nation-state that eventually became known as the United States of America. Once the United States established a powerful standing military force, United State interventions (imperialism) began on behalf of corporation wealth expansion. Interventions included the establishment of puppet governments to assure "business friendliness" among the invaded territories and their peoples (Perkins 2004, Parenti 1995). Initially this process was designed primarily to allow for the extraction of the resources and the establishment of markets to sell products to people who don't really need them. As time has gone on, however, corporate CEO greed, made manifest through profit maximization, has taken imperialism to yet another level. The 1980s saw still another stage of imperialism, out of which came what has become known as the globalization of the economy.

## Globalization: When Profit Motives Dwarf Nation-State Boundaries

In the post 1980 phase of imperialism (accelerated with the presidency of Ronald Reagan), nation-states are viewed in the same manner as city-states were viewed a few hundred years ago. In this era of what has become known as "globalization," one might sarcastically describe the multinational corporation view of nation-states as pesky little boundaries with annoying little rules, like constitutions, that get in the way of completely "free" enterprise. Nation-state public citizens, in trying to serve the common good, will occasionally pass laws restricting environmental degradation and human exploitation. These laws get in the way of corporate decision-makers being able to truly maximize their profits. When nation-states were the primary tool of the wealthy, the corporate owners had to continuously think about how they could expand the labor pool in the United States in order to reduce their labor costs. United States based unions sometimes made this objective more of a challenge than the corporations wanted.

With nation-states no longer thought of as the investment boundaries of modern corporations, the nature of corporate labor strategy changes. Now, instead of bringing labor to the industrial plants in the United States, wealthy corporate owners are bringing their plants to the lowest cost labor wherever it happens to be at the time that they need it, thereby reducing production of exportable products within the United States. Hence, one of the numerous negative effects (for the United States) of corporate globalization is that the United States, reduced primarily to a consumer nation, is sinking more and more rapidly into debt and the value of the United States currency has been notably diminished. Additionally, numerous other countries are working together to replace the United States dollar as the world's reserve currency. Knowing that this action could lead to the collapse of the United States economy, wealthy United States capitalists are, nonetheless, already investing in the currencies of other nation-states (Huff et al. 2010).

### *The 2008 financial institution bubble and near economic collapse*

The financial crisis of 2008 was not an unpredictable or fortuitous event. It was the conclusion of the corporate race to the far corners of the earth for the cheapest possible labor before a less politically friendly administration took over Washington. Believing the Obama administration would withdraw support for completely open globalization and would begin to reinstate corporate regulations, wealthy investors knew it was time to take the money and run. Divest and sell became the new name of the corporate game, resulting in record mergers and government bailouts.

*Wall Street bonuses: this time with tax money* The bailout funds of the waning months of the Bush Administration were not reinvested in the corporations, but treated simply as more money with which to party and run (Moore 2009). Only those corporations taken over in the first days of the Obama administration were propped back into production and saved as sources of employment. Stimulus money was pumped into local economies to create still other jobs and rebuild infrastructure: roads, bridges, and so forth. Had President Obama not acted as he did the entire economy would have collapsed as the wealthiest people maximized hoarding and coveted their ultimate treasures of billions of dollars. It is important to keep in mind that corporations are essentially owned and operated by wealthy people who do not want to share their wealth with anyone. Speaking of corporations is most often the same as speaking about the wealthy. Regardless of how bad the economy is for the average citizen, the truly wealthy will most likely always have ways of protecting their wealth and making it grow. Strict regulations on how wealthy people can use corporations to grow and protect their wealth are an important piece of the puzzle in solving the most serious social problems. This piece will be examined more carefully in Chapter 12.

Failure to regulate corporate behavior and hold corporations to their original social function has been matched consequentially by the deregulation of banks and financial institutions. Many analysts are saying the housing bubble caused the financial crisis because the loss of homes led to the collapse of family nest eggs and the reduction of spending. They go on to say that without consumption there is no incentive for corporations to produce so they have to layoff workers. Some commentaries have gone so far as to directly blame the people who took out the home loans, saying they should have known better. The housing bubble is indistinguishable from the financial bubble in terms of where it falls in the chain of events. Corporations moving to other countries predate the toxic loans to lower working class people.

As a result of completely uncontrolled and unregulated globalization, corporations are now hoarding billions of dollars with minimal investment in production or jobs of any sort. Their "profits" are skyrocketing because they have reduced expenditures (payout to employees and production investments) to a bare minimum. Banks are also sitting on their money as they scramble to justify millions of foreclosures, many of which have been determined to be illegal (Goldfarb 2010, Vieth 2010). The housing bubble is not the cause of the financial crisis, it is simply part of the same large scale effort on the part of the wealthy to take as much from the middle and working class people as possible for as long as possible. After making extreme wealth from a forced global labor pool, irregular trading and investment strategies, and toxic loans, they deliberately brought the entire economy to a sudden halt when a president was about to be elected who was not under their complete control.

Production and distribution companies in the United States alone are sitting on nearly a trillion dollars. As of this writing, they are enjoying their sixth highest quarter earnings in history (Alden 2010a), and Wall Street is expected to have a record breaking payout to its employees for the second year in a row (Alden 2010b). After squandering the government bailouts on CEO bonuses, exorbitant Wall Street salaries and bonus packages continue to be generously provided. Essentially wealthy people continue to reward themselves for their past dysfunctional behaviors, which include extensive and possibly irreparable national and international damage to environments, cultures, and economies throughout the world. Much of this destruction was done by carefully creating the false reality that globalization, as planned by corporations, would be a positive contribution to the world.

What does the current low production wealth growth mean in light of massive unemployment, homelessness, home foreclosures, and poverty around the United States and around the world? This is class warfare in its rawest form. The wealthy are holding their wealth and standing by as middle and working class people fall prey to high priced propaganda in the form of media events staged as "news" and "information" programs. The Supreme Court members, the majority of whom were appointed by presidents controlled by the wealthy, made a landmark decision in the Citizens United case that allowed corporations to give unlimited funding to political candidates. President Barack Obama described the decision as, "'a major victory for big oil, Wall Street banks, health insurance companies and the other powerful interests that marshal their power every day in Washington to drown out the voices of everyday Americans'" (Liptak 2010).

The Republican Party, long known for its allegiance to the wealthy, has steadfastly refused to support anything President Obama has tried to accomplish. Even proposals traditionally known to be Republican agenda items, like tax breaks for small businesses, have been rejected. These actions and decisions by the wealthy and their carefully controlled support agents (the Supreme Court majority, Republican Party, and many well funded Democratic legislators) are designed to make average citizens believe that the people *they* chose to put in political office are not really trying to help them. The passage of a national health care plan, badly needed in the United States (Moore 2007) was fought vehemently by wealthy insurance company owners and their political representatives, thereby greatly weakening the resulting legislation. Heavily funded disparagement of the health care program has been so great that many people who will benefit continue to oppose the program and the legislators that voted for it.

A political "group" emerged during the interim 2010 United States election campaign known as the Tea Party. This loosely organized mostly far right group led a highly charged campaign against the health care bill that included implied suggestions of violence against those legislators who supported the bill. A congresswoman who very publicly supported the health care bill was shot a couple months after she narrowly won the election in Arizona. The shooter was a young man who many believe was heavily influenced by the emotionally charged rhetoric of the election campaign (Daily Mail Reporter 2011, Marcotte 2011). The efficacy of allowing all citizens to carry fast re-load automatic weapons on the streets was also raised following this shooting. This issue is doubly pertinent since the Tea Party "members" are avid second amendment rights proponents, as are most Republicans.

Many Democratic legislators are also owned by the wealthy, but the Democratic Party continues to have some allegiance to labor unions and the organizations representing the poor. The current general goal of the wealthy is to regain complete control of all branches of the political system so that they can repeal all recent regulatory laws and once again use their corporations to operate without any government interference whatsoever. In the 2010 interim election they made considerable progress toward that goal at both national and local levels.

What is being witnessed in the United States at the time of this writing is one of the most bitter reality control struggles between the wealthy and non-wealthy that has ever occurred in the United States. It has not been since the early twentieth century labor revolts that this much overt struggle for the social control of reality has been seen. Important differences today are that the wealthy have much more control of the mainstream media than they did 70–100 years ago, and there now exists a new medium in the form of the internet.

The long term goals of the wealthy within the United States include: 1) the elimination of all labor unions so that labor is readily available and inexpensive; 2) the ability to claim resources everywhere in the world at no or very low cost to themselves; 3) the maintenance of a strong tax funded military to assure realization of number 2; 4) the elimination of all alternative (non-capitalist, non-corporate) means of sustaining oneself throughout the world so as to maximize the size and dependency of the international labor pool; 5) privatize and eventually eliminate social security and all retirement programs—initially to gain control of the billions of dollars invested in these programs, but ultimately to force people into the labor pool until they die. This latter goal is currently the norm in many parts of the non-

Western world. For example, in many parts of Africa people typically die shortly after they can no longer work. This is true even among some of the more highly educated people. 6) A sixth goal is to privatize education so that it becomes more closely aligned with job preparation. A successful conversion in this direction would eliminate wealthy people's problem of liberally and critically educated people questioning the status quo and challenging the motives and behaviors of wealthy people. An added bonus of privatized schools is that the wealthy can profit from having people pay them to become trained for the labor force of the wealthy. 7) The seventh goal is to create as many opportunities as possible for free or nearly free labor in the United States. Currently this means expanding the criminal justice system and the privatized prison system so that large segments of the population can be converted to free labor, largely at tax payer expense. The wealthy, while pretending to oppose illegal immigrants in the United States, do not want them stopped or legalized, since illegal immigrants are a major source of low cost labor for industries, especially the agricultural and garment industries.

These two important sources of low cost labor came together recently in a draconian Arizona anti-immigration bill. The new bill, currently being challenged in the courts, treats Mexican immigrants basically as enemy combatants and rather than deporting them sends them to prison. Other states are indicating they intend to pass similar bills. Under these bills prison labor will expand and all Mexican immigrants, including children of immigrants born in the United States, will become part of the low cost below minimum wage labor force. Why send the excess laborers back to Mexico when they can be converted to cheap prison labor? The most interesting and revealing part of this legislative phenomenon is that the bills are being written by people in the prison industry (Foley 2010). Perhaps the wealthy in the United States will find still other ways of exploiting desperate Mexicans as they attempt to cross the border that they believe crossed them.

### *Implications for Europe and the United States*

It is difficult for the wealthy in the United States to achieve their goals when other Western countries, namely European countries, have more effective labor unions, stronger pension plans, and retirement programs that are government sponsored. In many parts of Europe people can comfortably retire at 60 years of age. In the nineteen eighties the Reagan administration raised the age for full social security from 65 to 66 or 67, depending on when you were born. At that time the United States government was under what might be called a severe austerity program, and that program has essentially continued through the presidency of George W. Bush. It is currently being challenged in small ways by President Obama who was put in office largely by energized unions and progressive organizations opposed to the purpose of austerity programs. Government services and support programs have been heavily cut and/or privatized. As more United States citizens have become aware of the more positive conditions in Europe, the United States corporate government has pressured Europeans to institute their own austerity programs.

The crisis in the world economy, largely triggered by the near shut down of the United State economy, has provided a rationale for European governments to institute austerity programs of their own. French President Sarkozy is now bearing the fruit of Frances austerity program as millions of people take to the streets in protest. Whatever media attention the protests are getting focuses on the specific issue of Sarkozy wanting to change the French retirement age from 60 to 62, but the austerity program and corresponding protests/strikes are about much more than that. Considering the magnitude of what is happening, the media are only giving modest coverage to the protests. To learn anything about the activities on a reasonably regular basis one needs to access the alternative media. Contrary to what one might be led to believe in the scant mainstream media coverage here in the United States, 70 percent of the French public support or are sympathetic to the protests (Wolff, R. 2010). The French public, under the leadership of labor unions that can legally organize general strikes (unlike unions in the United States), is protesting the widespread problems that laissez-faire economics have brought on the French people, and the expectation that the French people should bear the burden of fixing those problems. They believe that the problems have been created by wealthy capitalists and should thus be fixed by those same people. Rather than finding ways of indirectly taxing the average citizens, it is widely believed that the wealthy should be taxed more heavily (Wolff, R. 2010).

Similar protests are occurring in Greece and other countries where the austerity programs tend to focus on cutting social services and jobs without holding the wealthy accountable for their reckless and greed-driven behavior patterns (Hamseyeh.net 2010). In Greece, under direct pressure from the International Monetary Fund, jobs and pension programs have been cut and taxes have been raised on the working class rather than targeting the wealthy, which is what the middle and working class people believe should be done (Hamseyeh.net 2010).

The same belief exists in many parts of the United States, but the mainstream media does not widely disseminate that information. In Minnesota, for example, Mark Dayton was elected governor campaigning almost exclusively on the idea of raising taxes on the wealthy in order to restore public services. What is unusual about this situation is that he is the heir of Dayton-Hudson Corporation and is himself quite wealthy. He accumulated his wealth from capitalism, so it is difficult for his opponents to call him a socialist or communist as they have done to previous candidates who have promised to raise taxes on the wealthy. It is also unusual that he is a wealthy person wanting to raise taxes on the wealthy. There are other wealthy people who realize the problems created by laissez-faire capitalism and who want to fix them, but few among the rich betray their class. On the other hand, the effectiveness of upper class propaganda techniques results in literally millions of middle and working class people religiously supporting programs and polices that hurt themselves and contribute to the wealthy becoming wealthier at their expense. Most of the seven goals of the wealthy identified above represent the current working plan of the Republican Party, which is supported by millions of middle and working class people. While the platform of the Democratic Party, influenced by labor organizations, tends to be focused on helping the non-wealthy segments of the population, many elected Democrats do not follow their party's platform because their campaigns are funded by corporations.

Britain has also begun an austerity program which is much broader and more sweeping than the programs in France, Greece, and in the United States. While cutting all social programs except for medical coverage, they are also cutting the military and increasing taxes that more heavily target the wealthier segments of the population (Chu 2010, O'Rourke 2010). While Britain is being applauded by many throughout the world as doing a more balanced austerity program, the part that is not receiving a lot of attention is their commitment to privatizing public service jobs once the economy recovers. This is a major victory for the British capitalists. What is important to keep in mind is that all austerity programs are really efforts to correct for the run away greed of wealthy corporate owners. They are programs designed by the wealthy (through the control they have over politicians) that make the non-wealthy pay for all or the majority of the environmental, social, and economic damage done by the wealthy over an extended period of time.

## Back to the Enterprise

By now the relevance of the Iran-Contra criminal activities should be clear to the purpose of this chapter. While there have been many CIA led interventions in the history of United States imperialism, the case study used in this chapter demonstrates the lengths to which the United States government will go to help make other places in the world comfortable for multinational corporations. The imperative of imperialism, most recently in the form of globalization, has trumped the nation-state constitution. In the process of making this happen, hundreds of thousands of lives have been lost and long standing ways of life and local economies have been disrupted all over the world. People around the world can no longer sustain themselves independent of working for the multinational corporations, and the global labor pool is so large and desperate that the majority of the people fortunate enough to have a job work for wages that cannot be considered livable with respect to health and cultural needs.

The competition for world resources and labor is the most important, far reaching, and devastating source of inequality, both in the United States, and in the world at large. One must remember that the United States is not the only nation-state involved in imperialism. It is, however, militarily the most powerful and, thus, the most successful imperial nation-state in the world. When the global economy began to collapse, the terrible conditions created by globalization here and around the world became worse. Jobs are harder than ever to find and are paying less than they have for a long time—possibly since the great depression of the 1930s.

Who is available and who has the power to protect the rights of all people and the constitution of the United States? Unfortunately, there is only the general public and most people in the general public are uninformed about the nature and magnitude of inequality as identified in this chapter. Occasionally people from inside the government or inside corporations become whistle blowers for the common good. They are typically discredited in a variety of CIA media maneuvers. They often lose their jobs and are scorned by others in their respective communities.

An unfortunate lesson of the Iran-Contra hearings is that the corporation controlled government doesn't have to worry about being secretive nearly as much as initially thought. The criminal activities of the Reagan administration went largely unattended following a full-scale congressional investigation. "A number of criminal convictions resulted, including those of McFarlane, North, and Poindexter, but North's and Poindexter's were vacated on appeal because of immunity agreements with the Senate concerning their testimony. Former State Department and CIA officials pleaded guilty in 1991 to withholding information from Congress about the Contra aid, and Caspar Weinberger, defense secretary under Reagan, was charged (1992) with the same offense. In 1992 then-president Bush pardoned Weinberger and other officials who had been indicted or convicted for withholding information on or obstructing investigation of the affair" (Questia 2010:1). Nothing happened to correct the wrongs done, and there was very little punishment for even those who admitted wrongdoing. President Reagan continues to be heralded as one of America's most successful and valued presidents.

The Enterprise was not the only way the Reagan administration attempted to illegally fund the Contras. The United States government, largely through the work of the CIA, has been heavily involved in protecting illegal drug trades and even participating in the distribution of drugs, many of which ended up in South-Central Los Angeles during the late 1980s and the 1990s (Webb 1999, Stockwell 1984).

### *From Watergate to Irangate to Plamegate*

An interesting twist to the use of the CIA for corporate exploitation of other countries occurred during the desperate efforts of the Bush/Cheney administration to find evidence of weapons of mass destruction in Iraq in order to justify invading that country. They never found any but in the process of looking, a former ambassador, Joe Wilson, was sent to Niger to determine if there was evidence of uranium being funneled to Iraq for nuclear bombs. When Wilson reported that he found nothing and that the Bush Administration was attempting to construct false evidence, he was attacked and publicly discredited by the Bush/Cheney White House. Even worse, upon discovering that Wilson's wife, Valerie Plame, was an undercover CIA operative, a White House top aid, Scooter Libby, deliberately leaked Plame's identity and CIA position to the press. After an elaborate cover-up scheme and Libby's indictment, Libby confessed that the leak was authorized by President Bush (Waas 2006) and this claim was later verified by White House correspondent Scott McClelland (Goodman 2008). This seems like a simple case of treason, but it is far more than that. It shows the lengths to which corporate politicians will go to protect corporate interests in other countries. Halliburton, the company for which Vice President Cheney served as CEO, wanted access to Iraq's oil fields. Vice President Cheney and President Bush were prepared to bomb hundreds of thousands of innocent people and take the United States to war to make that happen. Anyone who got in the way of their goal would have to be eliminated, including a CIA operative.

It is ironic that the sanctity of CIA secrecy, an imperative for creating social disorganization around the world, was so carelessly disregarded by the same corporate politicians that employ the CIA to carry out planned international disruptions. However, Plamegate was not just about Valarie Plame. It was more so about the massive information fraud imposed upon the world publics to justify bombing Iraq and sending soldiers to war under false pretenses.

## Conflict Theory

What sociological sense can we make of all of this? What theories help us understand modern day imperialism and its various components? Much of what exists related to corporate greed is evidenced in the case study of the Iran-Contra crime. At the most general level we see clearly a classic war being conducted between the common people of Nicaragua (as represented by the Sandinistas) and the wealthy people of the United States and Nicaragua, as represented by their corporations and their United States government forces (primarily the National Security Council and the CIA operating through hired mercenaries known as the Contras). The haves and have-nots are struggling for control of resources. On the one side there are the wealthy people who have attained their wealth through international exploitation of resources and labor, and on the other side there are the masses of regular people trying to create a more hopeful and positive life for themselves. One would be hard pressed to deny the importance of conflict theory in understanding this social circumstance.

When we look at the United States corporate intervention into other countries around the world we see the exact same pattern of class warfare as took place in Nicaragua. Mosaddeq represented the masses of common people in Iran when corporations used the United States government to overthrow him. Arbenz represented the masses of common people in Guatemala when CEO's used the United States government to overthrow him. And Ho Chi Minh represented the masses of common people in Vietnam when, once again, wealthy capitalists, working through their corporations, forced the United States government to overthrow Ho Chi Minh and the Vietnam government. These, and many more cases, are irrefutable examples of class warfare clearly depicting the basic principles of Marxist conflict theory. They tell us a great deal about how inequality is created, maintained, and increased.

**Feminist Theory?**

Feminist theory is relevant to the Iran-Contra crimes because the activities involved in these crimes are gendered in nature and, hence, not surprisingly carried out primarily by men. Unfortunately, in those rare situations where women are involved in these kinds of activities it is only because they have shown themselves to be "manly" enough to do so. Women are socialized to be less greedy and less violent than men, as indicated by their long standing greater support for social programs and their greater opposition to war. The behavior of the men in the Iran-Contra crimes is a social problem, and so is the exclusion of women from the various decision-making circumstances surrounding and leading up to the Iran-Contra crimes. Had equal numbers of women been involved in the processes leading up to the Iran-Contra crimes, and not just as token male-like women, the situation may have turned out quite differently. In matters of aggression, violence, and war, women tend to have a more balanced and reasoned disposition. Men tend to become overly emotional and irrational.

**Structural Functionalism**

What we also see in the provided case study is the functional interdependence of the component parts of the social structure leading up to and containing imperialism. We start out with a speculative estimate of what most likely transpired leading up to an early form of capitalism as discussed in Chapter 6, or what I have labeled a pre-capitalism economic state of existence. This pre-capitalism stage, still governed predominantly by city-states, transitioned into capitalism as a result of wealthy people forcing the aggregation of city-state run territories into nation-states. The existence of nation-states allowed for more systematic transportation of resources, labor, and produced goods. Without the transition into nation-states the industrial revolution could not have taken place as it did. Figure 10.3 illustrates the structure and probable flow of events leading to our current corporate greed based imperialism and the interdependence of those events.

Figure 10.3 is the extension of Figure 5.3 found at the end of Chapter 5. It represents additional relationships between some key concepts discussed in this book since Chapter 5. The United States government could be any imperial nation-state. Since the United States is currently the world's foremost imperial power, however, it is appropriate that the model contain the United States rather than some other country or no specific country at all.

As was the case in Figure 5.3, the arrows in Figure 10.3 represent flow in terms of time and directional causality. A single arrow with a head on both sides indicates that it is not possible or not useful to determine a causal time lag. Where there are two separate arrows connecting two concepts, the causal time lag is thought to be determinable and significant. For example, on the social psychological level the relationship between self esteem and greed is ongoing (single arrow). Success

**Figure 10.3 Interface of micro and macro structural representation of imperialism and social disorganization**

makes people more satisfied with themselves, and success is most often defined in terms of accumulation or steps toward accumulation: new car, better paying job, bigger house, big investment return and so on. On the other hand, capitalism creates and determines the corporation and eventually the corporation acts back to support and further develop capitalism (two arrows).

## Combining Social Psychology and Macro Sociology

As can be seen from Figure 10.3 the network of factors surrounding imperialism is multifaceted and complicated. Of particular importance is the convergence of the social psychological and the macro sociological into one integrated social structure. We should also now have a greater understanding of how this integration takes place with the help of the various media. This model is somewhat unique in that it does not ignore the micro determinants of capitalism and imperialism. People keep capitalism and imperialism alive in their thoughts and behaviors and have motivations for doing so. Laissez-faire capitalism and imperialism are the primary sources of most of our systemic world problems. It is not realistic to expect to get rid of capitalism and imperialism, however, without people changing the way they think about themselves and the world around them. Trying to eliminate laissez-faire capitalism and imperialism without thinking about how to change future generations of people and their motivations is like treating corporations as if they truly are giant mysterious individuals without real people within them making the decisions.

As social change activists work to expose and eliminate the actions of corporate decision-makers that are harmful to most of the people of the world, it is a mistake to think strictly in terms of class warfare. Class warfare exists, but the upper class way of viewing the world is now part of everyone's view of the world, even the very poor. That has to change in order to truly address the root causes of inequality. The aspiration of all people to be rich cumulatively creates and maintains the current imperialist system by demanding the availability of labor and resources purely for capital growth.

To create a sustainable and healthy world, labor and resources should be used for improving living conditions for all people and all forms of life, and not for creating unneeded surpluses for a few wealthy people. The result does not have to be communism, socialism or capitalism. In order to best serve the long-term interests of all people and the world, however, the result does have to be something that communities of people can agree upon without being tricked or coerced by external powerful forces.

### *Anarchist thinking*

This is where anarchist thinking becomes useful. The intent is not to promote a particular ideology, because anarchist thinking does not really embrace a single organized ideology. Anarchists foremost promote the notion that people should maintain control of their own communities and local environments, which they can only do if they are fully informed about the forces that work to control and oppress people. Forces like unquestioned patriotism for a nation-state that has become little more than a tool for the wealthy, keep people from being able to democratically control their own lives and their own environments. The misinformed commitment that most people now have to the nation-state they live within comes with an ideology and corresponding way of thinking that will most likely take several generations to eliminate in its entirety. It is important, however, that people who are aware of these issues find ways of educating and re-socializing others. There are some key starting points that can make a significant, albeit very gradual, difference in the way people view the world. Contrary to the rhetoric of some anarchists, government per se is not a problem. Government (collective decision-making) that is not controlled by, and responsive to, the vast majority of people it impacts is, indeed, dysfunctional to social organization, and thus a problem. Anarchism is any system people can devise where they are truly self governing. Most nation-states are a long ways from self governance by the vast majority of the people impacted by those nation-states.

Imperialism cannot be dismantled quickly. It will have to be approached strategically and gradually from all directions. The anarchist way of proceeding is not a quick fix way. It is a well informed, gradual, and lasting way that is grounded in a critically aware population of people. Identifying key components to address is the first step toward bringing about lasting movement away from corporate domination and imperialism. As with government, corporations are not necessarily a problem, and there are well run socially responsible corporations. Like government, corporations are a problem when they are misused and not controlled by the people most impacted by them. This issue will be addressed more systematically in Chapter 12.

## Where do we Drive the Wooden Stake?

If we look at Figure 10.3 as a living organism, as some structural functionalists might like to do, we have to ask ourselves, "What is the heart of this beast?" "If I could remove one component that would most likely assure its transformation, what would it be?" There probably is not one certain answer, and we cannot afford to assume that there is. It is important to keep working on all of the components. Notwithstanding, one's best chance of ending this dysfunctional system would most likely be the removal of the greed component. That is probably where the wooden stake belongs. Capitalism and imperialism, which are the manifest root causes of the most serious world problems, will be reinvented under some other method if people continue to act on greed. Greed is not a natural human motivation as some capitalists might argue. It is a learned condition just as most other motivations are learned. Before we can effectively deal with greed in general, we must first deal with it within ourselves, which may be the hardest step in the process.

There have been and continue to be many groups of people, not to mention other forms of life, that have lived without greed. Many indigenous peoples around the world lead lives built on cooperation rather than greed. Additionally, we see increasing numbers of people around the world turning to religions like Buddhism as a way of life more so than as a religion. Buddhism leads to cooperation and finding happiness from within rather than trying to find happiness in material objects at someone else's expense. There is no perfect social arrangement and most likely never will be, but people can learn from others who have been more successful at finding peaceful and healthy ways of living.

Moving into the last two chapters it will be useful to keep in mind that effective re-socialization can only come about if humans fully understand the current mechanisms in place that are used to produce the false realities protecting laissez-faire capitalism and imperialism.

# Chapter 11
# Political Economy and Social Change

**Increasing Productivity: What does that Really Mean?**

Who hasn't picked up a newspaper to see a headline that reads something like: "PRODUCTIVITY HAS INCREASED OVER THE LAST TWO QUARTERS"? Typically this headline is given as a positive proclamation that somehow we (the people of the United States or perhaps some other country) are better off than before the increase. When productivity increases some people are better off. These are generally people with large direct investments in businesses or large investments in stocks somehow mysteriously associated with businesses. This group of people is a fairly small segment of the population—less than ten percent of all United States citizens. Most people in the population are not benefiting by increases in productivity. An increase in productivity means that the amount of output per worker has increased. This condition can only exist under one, or some combination, of the following circumstances: existing workers working harder to produce more output, fewer workers producing the same or more output, new technology assisting existing workers so they can produce more.

If we look at these options carefully we see that only the last represents any real benefit to the average citizen. Furthermore, the last option seldom, if ever, occurs. Advances are often made in technology in ways that could benefit the worker, but benefitting the worker is not the intention behind advances in technology. Technology advances are most often used to allow employers to operate with fewer workers and thus greater profits (Noble 1995). This use of technological development throughout history is what has led to the periodic rise of anti-technology worker movements. People who resist letting technology take over their jobs are known as luddites, named after the early British resistors to the creation and widespread use of textile machines in the early 1800s. The term luddite came from the name of one of the supposed early revolutionaries named Ned Ludd, now believed to be a mythical legend rather than an actual leader of the revolt. Whether Ned Ludd existed or not there is no doubt that British workers united to prevent their jobs from being replaced by machines. The matter was sufficiently serious that the British military was used to control the workers. There have been more recent activities of a similar nature with people in some industries, like journalism, rebelling against being replaced by computers (Simon 2009, Noble 1995).

To understand why technology is not used to simply make working conditions better for workers one need only remind oneself of the most fundamental principle of modern capitalist thinking: the first priority of any corporation is profit maximization. From the standpoint of CEOs and corporate boards, their primary and only responsibility is to drive up stock values for their major shareholders, which just happens to be themselves and a very small segment of the United States (not to mention world) population.

Sometimes "innovative" management strategies or organizational changes are credited for increases in productivity. These claimed successes are typically output increases resulting from employers finding ways of getting workers to do more work. In other words, the concepts of effective innovative management and organizational restructuring seem like they have nothing to do with actual people, and they therefore seem to be quite innocuous. The reality is, however, that productivity does not typically increase without some people losing their jobs and/or some people working harder. So is increased productivity good? It depends on whether you are receiving the profits or creating them. If you are receiving the profits higher productivity is great news. If you are creating the profits, higher productivity simply means you are working harder in some important respect.

*Productivity as a social problem*

One might question why so much time is being dedicated to the issue of productivity in a chapter about capitalist solutions to capitalist problems. There is a two pronged response to that question. "Low" productivity is socially constructed as a serious social problem. Social Problems textbooks don't cover it as such, but it is treated as a serious social problem by most of the important institutions of the United States. That is why higher productivity is celebrated with: newspaper headlines; entire business colleges existing for the purpose of teaching people how they can help increase productivity; criminal laws being used to force people into prisons for labor; employment being kept to a minimum by all corporations; military/police forces being used against their own people to prevent or destroy labor strikes; and wars being fought to increase corporate productivity at extreme costs to tax payers and life itself. The imperative of socially constructing "low" productivity as a social problem is also why Milton Friedman's (1970) notion that corporations have no social responsibility beyond increasing profits continues to be a widely held disposition among many economists. Nothing must get in the way of higher productivity because higher productivity is the primary ingredient of higher profits, and profit maximization is the ideological fuel of capitalism.

This brings us to the second prong of the response to the question of why the concept of productivity is so important to the discussion of capitalist solutions to capitalist problems. If profit maximization is the driving force of capitalism and increasing productivity is a primary means by which profits are raised, what is the true role of productivity in the identification of social problems? Is "low" productivity really a serious social problem? Is it a social problem at all? As was discussed throughout earlier chapters of this text, profit maximization requires greed and greed causes waste for some and deprivation for others. Hence, the most serious social problems related to productivity are those that result from institutionalized efforts to keep productivity ever increasing. Eventually we will want to address the question of whether an economic system dependent on the creation of deprivation can solve social problems without changing its fundamental operating premise. For now, we need to look further at how reifying the notion that "low" productivity is a social problem actually creates social problems.

*Reducing labor costs for increased productivity*

Reducing the cost of labor can be done in more than one way. The most obvious way of reducing the cost of labor is to force people to work for you. Such is the approach of defining certain groups of people as inferior (possibly less than human), capturing them, and forcing them to work under threat of physical punishment or death. This is what we generally call slavery. Most citizens of the United States associate the word "slavery" with the early period in the United States up through the first half of the nineteenth century. During that time Africans were captured and brought to the United States to work, primarily but not exclusively, in the cotton fields of the South. What most people in the United States don't realize is that there is far more slavery in the world now in the early twenty-first century than there was during the time when slavery was openly conducted in the United States. Furthermore, some of that slavery is still taking place in the United States. The process is slightly different since slavery is now illegal. People in other countries are tricked into coming to the United States under false pretenses and then, because they are not legal citizens, cannot speak English, and are immediately plunged into debt to their employer, they are held captive and forced to work without pay (sometimes these work environments are referred to as sweatshops as mentioned above). Such was the case for millions of immigrants who were brought to the United States from other countries during the last part of the nineteenth century and much of the early part of the twentieth century. A version of that same process is still in place in the United States and in other parts of the Western world.

## Increasing Labor Pool Size

If one cannot physically force people to work for nothing or close to nothing as described above through direct slavery and sweatshops, another strategy is to create large enough labor pools that result in people feeling fortunate to have a job with any income whatsoever. This is the strategy associated with the globalization of the economy. The globalized economy first and foremost creates an extremely large world-wide labor pool.

The corporate strategy of bloating the labor pool size to increase productivity and profits did not start with globalization. It started with the above mentioned early twentieth century massive importation of immigrants to the United States (largely recruited for labor). As immigrant populations in the United States continued to grow throughout the early and mid parts of the twentieth century there were far more laborers than there were jobs, and the cost of labor was exceptionally low. Many of the imported laborers also became soldiers in the various twentieth century wars, only to return to poor paying jobs or no jobs at all. The shear number of laborers relative to the number of available jobs caused workers to compete with each other for low paying jobs—often times setting entire ethnic groups against each other, such as the Irish and the Italians. This problem for the workers was exacerbated by the automation of agriculture in the South, forcing large numbers of workers, especially African American descendents of slaves, to migrate to the northern mines and steel mills. Newer immigrant and migrant groups were despised for taking jobs away from the existing groups, and thus social movements emerged to suppress immigration and oppress the latest immigrants. We now see this same phenomenon occurring again in the United States, especially toward the Mexican workers who are hired for many of the seasonal agricultural jobs, as well as other types of manual labor.

Labor conditions in the United States became so bad in the nineteenth century that the laborers eventually united across groups and successfully formed labor unions to protect themselves from further exploitation. The unionization of the United States labor force was a long process starting in the nineteenth century, but the institutionalization of stable labor unions in the United States didn't happen until the early twentieth century, reaching a peak just past mid twentieth century. Institutionalized collective bargaining in the United States has a very short history of success. When the unions were growing and becoming stronger, they were quite successful in creating livable wages, benefits, and security for workers. Maximum union success was reached during the 1960s and through most of the 1970s. Successes in unionization were the single significant mitigating factor in stabilizing somewhat the wealth gap between the social classes in the United States, as well as in other parts of the world. But unions by themselves have proven to be no match for the combination of wealth, power and greed that was quickly and systematically turned against them.

Prosperity for workers began to diminish most dramatically with the presidency of Ronald Reagan, who committed himself to full support for the wealthy and their corporations. As previously mentioned, Ronald Reagan was also responsible for significantly advancing the globalization of the economy—often in places where Western countries like the United States, Britain, and France had already destroyed existing local economies. Expansion of the labor pool through globalization is a serious issue related to many systemic problems: destruction of local cultures and economies, environmental degradation and devastation, destruction of human and non-human habitats, and inhumane working conditions at home and abroad. The more workers there are available, the more corporations can expect from each worker hired and the less they have to pay them, because each worker is reminded that there are many workers out there waiting to take their job if they do not work hard enough for the small amount of pay that is offered.

## Place-Bound Industries

Not all industries can be moved to other countries to take advantage of desperate people in countries targeted by Western corporations. Some industries, like agriculture and service industries, must continue to find ways of bringing low cost labor to their United States-based work places. The place-bound limitation faced by these corporations, forces them to rely on older place-bound labor induction strategies, which typically means importing the desperate people to the United States workplace instead of taking the workplace to the desperate people—that is, early twentieth century induced immigration strategies. The issue of immigration for labor represents a dilemma for politicians heavily indebted or committed to corporations. On the one hand many politicians during the time of this writing want to represent their average citizen constituents, many of whom do not like immigrants. These are people who believe the United States borders should be basically closed, especially to poor people. On the other hand, these same politicians want to continue to provide low cost labor for their sponsors in the corporate world. The result is that we maintain laws forbidding large scale immigration from places like Mexico, but sort of look the other way so millions can come over and provide the low cost labor desired by corporations. Periodically there will be crackdowns and Mexicans will be arrested/deported, and periodically there will be amnesty granted so the "illegal" workers can stay and continue to provide their labor. Efforts to arrive at meaningful immigration laws typically fail because of the competing interests within the political forces that must deal with the immigration issue.

All of these strategies result in what might be called exploited labor: those people forced to work unreasonably hard in order to survive and/or live modestly comfortable lives—something many (if not most) never achieve. The term "exploited labor" also refers to the millions of people in the United States and the millions of people elsewhere who do not have an opportunity to work at all, and are thereby relegated to poverty, homelessness, and various other forms of material, social, cultural, and psychological deprivation. Exploited labor is a social problem that results directly from the reification of "low" productivity as a social problem—that is, the false perception that high productivity is a social good in itself and the absence of high productivity is socially bad.

## Productivity and the Value of Stock

An economist might argue that when productivity is down stock values are down, and when stock values are down everyone loses because all of our retirement benefits and savings are tied up in stock values. First of all, at the time of this writing only a small portion of the population of the United States has meaningful retirement options based in stock values. Many people have no viable retirement program whatsoever other than social security. The reason for this social condition is that the highest productivity comes with the lowest number of workers at the lowest possible pay. Many people are without jobs and many of the jobs that people do have are not livable wage jobs with retirement benefits. So the purported economic demand for higher productivity is by its nature self defeating: the higher the productivity, the lower the number of people with any stock investments whatsoever. In terms of annual capital gains from stock, only about 10 percent or less of the population of the United States reports income from that source.

Secondly, stock values, whether on individual stocks or the stock market in general, are contrived artificially on a daily (if not hourly) basis and have little to do with any kind of objective actual value of a product or the company producing that product. Most important in the determination of the value of stock is the perception of how well a company may be doing, and hence, the interest there is in owning that particular stock. It is like buying a house. If everyone in town wants a particular house the value of that house will be perceived to be very high and people will be bidding on it. If suddenly word gets out that something serious is wrong with the house, whether it is true or not, the value of that house is going to drop dramatically. A week prior to this writing Microsoft stock value dropped significantly because the long time successful CEO of the company announced his retirement.

That is basically how the stock market operates. The just described mass psychology related to stock values makes it possible for the market values to be rapidly climbing one moment and dropping the next. This particular understanding of how the stock market operates is becoming increasingly recognized by economists from some of the most highly respected universities in the United States, such as Yale, Stanford, and Harvard (Amadeo 2007). Much of what we hear otherwise from economists is illogical and contradictory. Among most traditional economists there is a pretense of science attributed to understanding and predicting stock market changes that has little, if any, grounding in reality.

When a few of the world's largest investors make significant changes in their stock buying and selling patterns, the stock market can be impacted because of the alteration in stock values vis-à-vis what these investors buy or sell, but more importantly because of the perceptions created by the signal that is sent to all other investors. Similarly, if for some unknown reason thousands of people start buying a particular stock, the value of that stock will most likely increase. The reverse would also be true. This sort of mass shift in the buying and selling of stocks does happen, and is what is sometimes referred to as a herd mentality.

Could reports of productivity levels be factored into stock trading decision-making? Yes, they could, but not necessarily in any real sense based on what the company is actually worth, which is largely unknown during stock trading in any objective sense. Reports of high productivity simply make people feel good about investing without any real knowledge of what the stock will be worth tomorrow or the next day. One of the important lessons of the Enron Corporation Scandal/Crimes that took place in the early part of the twenty-first century is that stock values can be fairly easily manipulated by people in the right positions to do it.

A footnote to that lesson is that stock values have no actual direct substantive counterpart in the real world, especially in the modern age of paper and electronic companies that may not actually produce anything. The 5,800 point drop in the Dow during 2008 had nothing to do with actual productivity, which couldn't possibly change that fast. Indeed, the stock buying and selling patterns themselves have a significant effect on the perceived value of stocks the moment after the "trading" occurs.

The primary social function served by the CEO's of Enron Corporation (Kenneth Lay and Jeffrey Skilling) being arrested and prosecuted in the early part of the twenty-first century was making the public feel that what happened with Enron was due only to the illegal activities of those particular individuals, and that there was nothing wrong with how the stock market component of the capitalist system operated. Lay and Skilling argued they were not doing anything outside of what the economic system dictated. They were doing whatever had to be done to make the stock value of their company seem high, falsely claiming value where value was low or indeterminate, and in effect lying to their workers and investors. Their problem was not that they did something unusual. Their problem was that they did it unusually well and without sufficient pretense of normalcy. They forced a public viewing of the underbelly of the beast, and it was not pretty.

### *Stock values as self correcting*

A term that gives away the largely irrational, and possibly at times contrived, depiction of how the stock market operates is the notion of "self correction," a term used by economists to rationalize/normalize notable drops in the stock market. Economists who use this concept argue that periodically the market adjusts itself to correct for inaccuracies in the stock values. The basic idea behind using this concept is to suggest to the public and business student: 1) that most of the time the value of stock is somehow accurate; and 2) that there is nothing wrong with a sharp drop in the stock market value. As a "correction," it is supposedly a normal part of the investment process and should not be cause for concern. Indeed, some economists promote celebrating the so-called corrections in the stock market. One investment expert writes, "Stock market correction is usually when the stock market, usually the Dow Jones Industrial Average, declines 10% or less in a relatively short period of time … A stock market correction can help the stock market catch its breath and hit even higher peaks" (Amadeo 2007: 1). It is rare that economists speak of increases in the stock market value as corrections. Indeed, increasing values are what is expected on a daily basis. There is nothing rational provided in the discussions of stock market corrections—no real explanations, no formula for prediction, only seemingly whimsical expressions of relief that corrections sometimes occur.

Perhaps most telling is the reference in the above quote to the stock market catching its breath. This statement symbolizes the manner in which markets in general are viewed by people religiously dedicated to capitalism as a way of life.

There is continuous reference to "when the market does this" and "when the market does that," all within the context of a breathing living being somewhere out there acting on its own initiative.

Finally, a system that depends on any kind of exploitation is a seriously flawed system and needs to be examined for dramatic changes. Even if it was true that stock values were directly driven by productivity levels, it would not make sense to pursue higher stock values through higher productivity if the quality of life for millions of people would be diminished by doing so. In actuality, higher productivity increases profits shared directly with the CEO's through higher salaries, benefits, and bonuses. It also makes the company more valuable for resale. It is common for companies to buy one another since laws governing mergers and monopolies have been relaxed since the early 1980s. When a company is sold, it is the primary stock holders only who enjoy the benefits of the sale. Other people who "own" stock in the sold company, stock they most likely attained through a mutual stock investment program for their retirement, are probably unaware of gaining anything. The sell means little to them in terms of known income, and yet their money is an important part of the wealth that represents the value of that company when it is sold. Ironically, little if any of the money invested in a company's stock is ever actually invested directly into the company to improve its operation. It is more likely that the money is used for other investments. The average workers of a sold company, who may also be token stock holders, may lose some or all of their retirement stock investments. It is also common that they lose their job.

### *Ever higher productivity as oscillation*

The quest for higher productivity is a process forced upon the general public that enables a few people to gain more from the work of others. Because of the competitive nature of unregulated capitalism, companies are continually striving to have higher productivity than one another and, hence, greater profits than one another over time. The quest for ever higher productivity creates an oscillation effect that spins ever more people into unemployment, underemployment, or over-employment. That is, fewer workers must produce more goods, and do so with less time and money. Getting paid less requires working multiple jobs. People who have second jobs often times actually feel fortunate since many people have no job at all. Working multiple jobs is typically accomplished by accepting undesirable low paying jobs.

One might conclude, therefore, that higher productivity does not solve a social problem, but instead creates many of the conditions we do normally talk about as social problems: poverty, hunger, homelessness, absence of medical insurance, psychological problems related to stress, deprivation, and many other residual effects. Going back to the definition of a social problem given early in this book, one finds the following:

> A social problem is a condition that involves harm to one or more individuals and/or one or more social entities, has at least one social cause and/or at least one social effect, and consequently has one or more social remedies.

Indeed, the just mentioned conditions resulting from the perpetual quest for higher productivity do fit this definition with respect to all of its specifications: harm to individuals, a social cause, and a social remedy. The social cause is the employment strategies embedded in free market capitalism that are used to create higher productivity, and the social remedy is to remove the higher productivity/profit maximization imperative from the foundation of our economic system.

On the other hand, low productivity does not bring harm to anyone since the people who benefit from high productivity already have a great deal of wealth and live well beyond the means of most people in the world. An exception might be a small business person who needs to increase productivity in order for her/his business to survive. That is not, however, the context in which we typically see public information about high or low productivity. High and low productivity information is usually provided within the context of what is happening within large corporations. It is not even possible to measure productivity with reasonable accuracy within all the various small businesses around the United States.

It is also important to differentiate between low productivity and stable productivity. Strong unionization of workers within large corporate enterprises creates what might be thought of as stable productivity. When I worked in the steel mill as a grinder in my home town in Pennsylvania I was expected to grind eight cylinders a day: no more and no less. This was a requirement contractually agreed upon by the company and the union. This agreement, and many others like it, did not result in low productivity, since the steel mills made more than enough money to maintain their plants and substantial profits. When the mills began closing in the late 1970s, it was not because they were not making a profit. It was because high level corporate owners and CEO's could make a larger profit investing their money in other ventures in other places.

What is low productivity? One is hard pressed to even find a definition of the concept. Presumably it is when labor units are not producing enough output to make the desired profit, since productivity itself is defined in economics as the amount of output per unit of labor. How is the amount of desired profit determined? One would hope that it would be based on the amount needed for a reasonable livable wage for all involved with the company after all expenses, including costs to the environment, were covered. Unfortunately, the "amount of *desired* profit" is determined by the amount of profit last quarter. If profits are not higher this quarter, then productivity has to be considered too low. The quest for ever higher profits based on ever higher productivity is not a rational, let alone humane, economic viewpoint. It makes economics the determinant of social life in general rather than the other way around. The quality of social life in general, based on a relatively stable physical and cultural environment, should be what determines economics.

## Globalization and Labor

Through globalization corporations profit from the use of extracted resources from other countries and sometimes simultaneously profit from the sales of weapons (and/or military supplies) to the United States military or other countries. Large sums of United States tax-payer dollars are spent on purported reconstruction activities in invaded countries, many of which are staged essentially for the purpose of spending money and attaining more (St. Clair 2006). From the standpoint of the United States, when we use the term "military" we are referring to the largest financial component of the United States government, and the single largest source of the worlds environmental destruction (Sanders 2009). Globalization through the use of the military requires United States citizens as soldiers to find and secure low cost labor in other parts of the world that will eliminate those soldier's jobs here in the United States. When they return they are assured of very little other than a high probability of unemployment.

Unions have been systematically destroyed through globalization and when workers in other countries try to organize they are quickly suppressed. This occurred in one Ford auto plant in Mexico where workers stood at their machines and refused to work. Ford hired thugs to force the employees to work at gun point, killing one man and injuring others (USLEAP 2010). Abuse and exploitation are common in plants located in other countries. Sometimes these plants are owned by corporations from one part of the world and contracted to be run by people/corporations from another part of the world so that ownership and responsibility are not immediately apparent.

### *Labor pool size and productivity*

The expansion of profits by increasing the size of the labor pool is not necessarily independent from increasing productivity. Corporations can continue to find ways of getting more work out of fewer workers even after the labor pool has been increased. In fact, acceptability of strategies for greater productivity increases with the increased size of the labor pool since workers feel "lucky" to have a job in the face of high amounts of unemployment. The few remaining unionized workers in the United States (about 8 percent of the workforce) have no choice but to allow themselves to be worked at a much faster pace than they did when 33 percent of the workforce in the United States was unionized in the late 1960s and early 1970s. Working conditions in most important respects have not improved in the United States since the early 1970s. Along with the expanded labor pool and the destruction of unions has been the emergence of what some call neo-Taylorism, which has been a primary managerial tool for creating work speedup (Crowley et al. 2010). The current labor pool condition can thus be described as an oscillating feedback process. The larger the labor pool, the greater the leverage for increasing productivity. The greater the productivity, the greater the excess labor pool, and again, the greater the leverage for increasing productivity even more … and so on.

### Market "Solutions" to Social Problems

Most people in the United States are religiously devoted to capitalism as a way of life. They defend capitalism simultaneously with patriotism to their country. Devout capitalist economists, market economists, tell us that the principles of capitalism have built into them the means by which all social problems can be solved. If there is a need, that simply means a market exists (a demand) to correct that need. The argument continues with the idea that clever entrepreneurs will then come forward to compete on ways to satisfy the need while making money at the same time. Yet, one is pressed to understand how the process can work given other more fundamental principles of capitalism. Entrepreneurship within our current economic system is supposedly motivated by the endless desire for more, or what many capitalists now openly call greed.

If I am operating on the principle that greed is a positive behavioral motivator and that the maximization of profits for my company (and myself) is my sole responsibility, what are the limits of my behavior toward the objective of increasing corporate profits? One can easily witness various existing forms of enslavement, as described above and elsewhere. But where do I draw the line and say that I could not behave in a particular way because it would be immoral or that, more pragmatically, my behavior might lead to the destruction/denigration of the long term welfare of the human and non-human world and corresponding environments? Would I, for example, promote the expansion and use of prisons for my own profits under the pretense of solving the "problem of crime"? If I am willing to promote war, which results in the deaths of hundreds of thousands of innocent people, is there anything that I would not do? Even if markets *could* solve individual social problems, the complexities of life and physical environments guarantee the creation of other problems in that process: given the structural nature of the capitalist economic system.

#### *The problem of crime or the problem of socially unacceptable behavior?*

It is common to see reference to "the problem of crime." Is that a proper label for the circumstances being referenced when that phrase is used? Do the Amish, for example, have a "crime problem?" The Amish have problems with people who do not choose to live strictly by their beliefs and expectations. They do not have a crime problem because they do not have a legal system. Yet, their problem is no different than everyone else's problem. Some people act the way we think they should and others do not. When people behave in a way that is harmful to others a problem clearly exists, and it is a problem for everyone touched by it. Undesirable behavior is only a "crime problem," however, if the behavior is defined as a crime. When behaviors are defined as criminal, the nature of the social problem changes from helping people behave in a socially acceptable manner to catching and punishing people who violate laws. With a focus strictly on laws and law enforcement, the true nature of the social problem of harmful behavior is lost to the massive criminal justice system, a system that continues to escalate out of control.

Why the dramatic increase in imprisoning United States Citizens? Why have the laws become so punitive, and why has law enforcement become so arbitrary and capricious? These are more serious social problems than the "crimes" purportedly being addressed by the criminal justice system. As of 2007, 750,000 people in the United States were part of a prison labor force making a wide range of products for well known United States-based corporations. For-profit privatized prisons have mushroomed around the United States in the last 20 years and represent what might be considered a separate growth industry (Jean 2007).

As indicated in Chapter 9, most people in prison are poor and have been convicted of non-violent crimes, with a high percentage related to drug possession. For-profit prisoners are often paid less than 50 cents an hour with no benefits (Jean 2007). From a corporate labor standpoint, prisons are better than slave camps. State and federal governments pay for the "room and board" and corporations have nearly free production once the prisons are retrofitted with the production facility.

The general economy of the United States is sufficiently bad that local communities are vying for the right to build prisons, arguing that they bring jobs (Hallinan 2001). There are profits to be made from the development of the property and temporary jobs created from the construction of the prison and the corresponding houses that are built to accommodate the inward migration. There are also permanent jobs available for people in the corrections industry. It wasn't that long ago that people saw prisons in their backyard as a scourge, an eyesore, and a danger. While community satisfaction surveys related to recently built prisons are positive in some areas, they also show important areas of concern (Courtright et al. 2007). Research is also showing that the rural prison boom is not as economically advantageous as communities believe them to be (Genter and Hooks 2010, Hooks et al. 2004), and actually may lead to unanticipated problems.

Regardless of whether community perceptions are accurate or not, the overriding issue related to the prison boom is whether they are a response to the "crime problem" or possibly a response to financial greed.

## Does Capitalism Address the "Crime Problem"?

The profits being made from prison labor make prisons one of the hottest commodities on Wall Street. People with money to invest want to invest in prisons. Companies want to buy into existing prisons or build new ones, and communities can't wait to get one in their location. What is the connection between the economics of prisons and solving important related social problems? Staunch capitalists would tell you that the promise of making money from prisons is solving the social problem of crime by making sure criminals are incarcerated. As discussed earlier, however, defining behavioral social problems in terms of crime does not address the social problem of unacceptable or harmful behaviors. Treating unacceptable behaviors as a "crime problem" simply creates additional problems, especially now that there is a heavy focus on imprisonment. Some of those problems are:

1. There is a serious conflict of interest problem when it becomes profitable for some people to identify others people as criminals so as to make money from their labor;
2. Communities now perceive prisons to be desirable financial partners, providing jobs and stimulating the local economy. Crime is thus financially helpful to struggling communities—another serious conflict of interest;
3. Imprisonment affects entire families, not just the imprisoned individual. Families are broken by long term imprisonments leaving children without parents and loved ones without their partners;
4. Prisons and the criminal justice system in general are a huge tax payer expense for the creation of more laws, increased law enforcement, increased security costs related to the real behavioral social problems remaining unaddressed, and the creation and maintenance of police and prison facilities (it costs more to keep a person in state or federal prison than it does to send them to an expensive private college or university);
5. The lives of imprisoned individuals are being lost to the criminal justice system with little hope of recovery into a relatively "normal" and happy existence;
6. Corporate crime, which costs the public far more than all other types of crime combined in all important respects, goes relatively unattended. Violating upper class normative economic principles seems to be taken more seriously than violating legal or common ethical principles. For example, the reason there were high level convictions related to the Savings and Loan crimes of the 1980s and 1990s and the Enron crimes of the turn of the twenty-first century, is that they began to lose other wealthy peoples' money. Corporate violations seldom result in CEO convictions (Goodman 2010) unless the questionable behaviors negatively impact other corporations or wealthy people.

## Summary of Major Issues

It is clear that capitalism does not and cannot address the "crime problem"; nor can it address any other social problems. The first priority of capitalism is profit maximization. By marketing what is claimed to be a solution to one problem capitalists often times create or exacerbate other problems, which is theoretically an endless oscillating process with ever new problems spun out of supposed capitalist solutions. Furthermore, in free market capitalism, solutions are only as good as the profits they make. If profits are not great enough, the solution can be compromised or even abandoned altogether. Pacific Lumber Company serves as a good example. The company had an environmentally sensitive production policy until profits slipped. The company then abandoned its environmental program and cut down its old growth forests.

Companies that want to do what is right for the environment and life in general cannot reconcile the common conflict between profits and social responsibility. Under our current economic system profits must always come first, regardless of what compromises need to be made in the production of goods and services, and regardless of residual consequences. Milton Friedman maintained to the end that corporations have no social responsibilities. They are simply to make money. Yet, as legal persons, corporations protect the CEOs from *their* social responsibilities as well. There are thus no motivations or incentives for wealthy people behaving in a socially responsible or even legal manner when it comes to making corporate decisions. Nothing matters but profits. Given this somber reality it is incredible (almost beyond belief) that free market capitalists maintain that social problems can best be solved through the profit motive alone. Hopefully this chapter demonstrated the fallacy of that thinking.

Some economists are rightfully rediscovering the work of John Maynard Keynes, who had a healthy distrust of anything that smacked of a pure model, like the belief that markets were self regulating. He understood how economic systems interacted with other human systems to create large margins of economic predictive error and market volatility. Additionally, some highly regarded economists are lamenting the conversion of Economics into a discipline of mathematical modeling void of meaningful purpose and any inclination to make the world a better place (Krugman 1998, 2009). Modern Friedman economics is a political ideology with a clear agenda for supporting the goals of the wealthy. One of the pillars of that agenda is the irrational proposition that collectively created government and corresponding regulations are somehow public enemies. Aside from defending short term financial gains for the wealthy, such claims show a lack of understanding of the function of government as a form of collective decision-making (Krugman 1998).

### *Changing the face of economics*

Indeed, a primary lesson of this chapter is that populations of people cannot rely on laissez-faire capitalism to solve systemic problems created by laissez-faire capitalism. It is illogical to argue that such could be the case. In order for human populations to solve their problems they must be able to do so in a systematic manner based on as much information as possible. All relevant variables should be entered into the decision-making, and that certainly includes the nature of the economic system. The purpose of an economy should not be to promote excess wealth at other peoples' expense. Ever higher productivity should not be considered a positive value and economic goal. A healthy economy is one that facilitates a healthy lifestyle, and a healthy lifestyle by any set of reasonable standards is one that includes leisure time and time for family and friendship relationships.

Change in the current economy is inevitable if humans are going to survive as a species. Like the hard lesson of the Swiss watch makers in the mid-twentieth century, Western world leaders need to realize that other paradigms are possible, and in this case, desirable. What should the new economy look like, and how do we get there?

# Chapter 12
# Micro and Macro Solutions to Global Problems

## Be the Change

"You must be the change you wish to see in the world." This famous and popularized quote from Mohandas Gandhi expresses part of the intent and purpose of this chapter. Gandhi was one of the greatest activists the world has known. He was nonviolent, insisted that those who worked with him remain nonviolent, and he lived the life he talked about. More importantly, he led social movements that resulted in the removal of oppressive and exploitative governments. There have been other great activists who made great strides in improving conditions for oppressed people and other living beings. One of the best known in the Western world was Jesus Christ—even though Jesus was not from the West. Most people who practice what has become known as a Christian religion (of which there are many) believe that Jesus Christ was the son of God. What we know about Christ's life is that he spoke out against violence, he was opposed to money lenders in the Temple, and he believed that all people should be treated equally.

Christ, like Gandhi, was a social activist who wanted to make the world a better place. He led others in that effort in word, deed, and by example. I don't have to believe in Christ as the son of God to recognize his work as a social activist. Jane Addams, mentioned earlier in this book as a founder of Applied Sociology, was instrumental in bringing public service and relief to those in need. An exemplar civic and social justice minded person, she was awarded the Nobel Peace prize in 1931 for her work in identifying ways of fostering peace and avoiding war. Addams came from a fairly affluent family background, but did not choose to live her life in the comfort available to her.

There are many women and men who, like the above mentioned individuals, have made a significant difference in the world by first living a life that exemplified what was needed from everyone, and then by leading others wanting to follow their example. The message is straightforward. In order to expect the world to be a better place one must be willing to improve one's own behaviors. We have to be the change we wish to see in the world. In the complete adaptation of that statement, where everyone takes that expression seriously, solutions to most social problems could be solved at the micro level. There would not need to be macro solutions to most social problems. How do we take that expression seriously? There are a number of approaches one can take to make the world better. One doesn't have to be a Gandhi, a Christ, or an Addams in order to make an important contribution. Positive changes in the way one interacts with the world on a daily basis can make a difference, and the more people there are who recognize this reality, the more profound the social change becomes.

*Where to start*

The University for which I work recently went through the process of determining what values best represent the culture of the University. I participated in this process which culminated in a values statement that tells others who we are and reminds those within the institution what is expected of a person as a member of this organization. This is the second University for which I have participated in identifying a core set of values. Increasingly businesses are doing the same, and even large corporations sometimes have a statement of organizational values. It seems reasonable that all social entities should spend some time focusing on identifying their values, and then finding ways in which they can help everyone live by those values. Articulating values is the first step toward creating positive social change.

What do we believe is important for ourselves, for our communities, and for others in the world? Do we value peace? Do we value fairness? Do we value clean air, clean water, and food free of contaminants? Do we value a biologically diverse environment free of toxins? Do we believe that all communities should have the right of maximum possible self determination? If we could ask everyone in the world whether they embrace the above stated values, there are probably relatively few people who would not respond in the affirmative to all of them. Indeed, these values are not only represented in foundation documents of the United States as a nation, but can be found in important international documents such as: The Universal Declaration of Human Rights, The Earth Charter, The United Nations Convention on the Rights of the Child, the United Nations Convention on the Elimination of Racial Discrimination, The United Nations Convention on the Elimination of Discrimination Against Women, the Hague Agenda for Peace and Justice, and many more (Andrzejewski et al. 2009).

So then, why is it so difficult to attain fulfillment of the above basic values? What would fulfillment of those values look like, and how does our own individual behavior impact that fulfillment? The answers are not easy, and some seem simpler than what they actually are. If we go back, for example, to the discussion of Tolstoy's work in Chapter 8, we see that he argues that the only way for peace to ever occur is for people to refuse to fight. He provides a letter, also printed in Chapter 8, showing how one person refused to report for military duty while fully recognizing the negative consequences of that decision for him. Herein resides the true challenge to people's values. How can people consistently uphold their values without sometimes suffering negative consequences? Most likely it is not possible. If people are not willing to suffer some negative consequences in the immediate to support their values, there is little hope of those values ever being realized to an appreciable extent.

Once an organization has identified its values, goals and objectives are subsequently set accordingly. In other words, the behaviors of the people within the organization should in some way follow from the stated values. Individuals outside of organizations can adhere to the same principle for living in general. The important understanding related to values is that if the values of an organization, or a community or a nation-state are not followed now, there will most likely be serious negative consequences for that social entity in the future. The earth is now in that future. The United States and a number of other Western nation-states have set a course that is now being followed by many developing nation-states, which is to superimpose aggressive economic values over all others. Through this superimposition, people come to believe that all of the values mentioned earlier can be achieved by first adhering to yet another set of values: greed is good, profit maximization comes before everything else, wealth in the hands of a select few is good, and producing lots of material objects to sell at a fast rate is good. In support of these values there is the corollary value of the earth and most working people serving as resources to be used in fulfillment of the just stated values.

*Values and free market economics*

You will recognize the later mentioned set of values as what we have identified throughout this book as laissez-faire free market economics. The most ardent believers in this economic system are firmly convinced that it is good and that all good things follow from it. As this book is being written, the world economy is in trouble. Those with most of the wealth are no longer investing because they do not see the profit in doing so. Without the investments of the wealthiest individuals in the world, there is not enough money available for the rest of the economy to operate. The last four presidential administrations established the foundation for the 2008 economic crisis, but it was the anticipated election of a progressive president (someone strongly committed to the first set of values) that most likely triggered the massive disinvestments of the super wealthy. To avoid a complete financial collapse of the magnitude of the great depression of 1929 the newly elected president put billions of dollars of federal money into local economies for infrastructure projects. Millions of jobs were created by this project.

The so-called bailouts of multibillion dollar corporations that President Bush enacted at the very end of his term have done little to help the economy since the wealthiest of the wealthy apparently see no benefit in reinvesting their resources. Very little of the bailout money was reinvested in production and much of it was squandered on CEO bonuses. Greed has prevailed and forced a literal stalemate between those that have and those that do not have. This is a direct form of class warfare, with the super wealthy starving out the rest of the world to reestablish their preeminence and complete control of labor and resources around the world.

The most appropriate analysis of this condition is traditional Marxism. The superstructure of laissez-faire economics as the savior of the "free" world has been exposed as a false reality. That is, the listed superimposed values that make up that concept have not led to the fulfillment of people's true values: peace, fairness, clean air, pure water, and healthy food for everyone. The infrastructure of competition and struggle has once again emerged as the true reality. According to Marxism and corresponding conflict theory, a revolution should be eminent. We are at this time seeing revolutionary activities in various parts of the world. Protests and government violence are now occurring in the Middle East. As austerity measures, poverty, and desperation increase we are likely to see more uprisings.

## A Different Kind of Revolution

Is it possible to have a different kind of revolution … not a violent revolution, but the opposite. What if more people refuse to participate in acts of violence, as suggested by Leo Tolstoy and as exemplified in the successful work of activists like Mohandas Gandhi and Martin Luther King? Massive non-violent protest is taking place in many countries at this time. People can make that choice, especially people who have access to resources, such as anyone who might be reading this book. I encourage anyone who has an inclination to help make the world a better place to access the website: betterworldhandbook.com. Most of us cannot imagine how we can make a positive difference in such a big and complicated world. This inability to visualize an alternative reality within which we can make a contribution sometimes leads to what the Better World Handbook describes as the cycle of cynicism. The cycle of cynicism is represented as an eight step process that eventually leads to total discouragement and apathy (Jones et al. 2007: 3). The identified steps are as follows:

*Cycle of cynicism*

1. finding out about a problem
2. wanting to do something about the problem
3. not seeing how you can help
4. not doing anything about it
5. feeling sad, powerless, angry
6. deciding that nothing can be done
7. beginning to shut down
8. wanting to know less about the problem

The recommended alternative to the cycle of cynicism is the cycle of hope that is represented by six steps (Jones et al. 2007: 3) Those six steps are as follows:

*Cycle of hope*

1. taking personal responsibility for being a good person
2. creating a vision of a better world based on your values

3. seeking out quality information about the world's problems
4. discovering practical options for action
5. acting in line with your values
6. recognizing you can't do everything

Most of the above items feed off of each other and enhance one another in a cyclical fashion. In the journey from the cycle of cynicism to the cycle of hope there are a number of traps along the way, which are also nicely described in the Better World Handbook (Jones et al. 2007). Rather than provide yet another list, I will discuss some of the traps.

*Traps on the way to the cycle of hope* The first trap is to fall into the pattern of simply thinking "that is just the way the world is." This is a common trap built on the lack of recognition that the world has changed a great deal as a result of the actions of many people over time: more rights for women and peoples of color in the United States; and more rights for other excluded groups, such as people with disabilities. The anti-littering campaign mentioned earlier in this book is another good example of what can be done if people are properly informed and motivated. And there are countless smaller examples of local citizen groups taking action to make a difference, such as dead lakes being brought back to life, corporations being forced to stop polluting local rivers, and animal abuse being stopped. Indeed, a great deal is possible if everyone is willing to do their part and act in a responsible manner. To avoid this trap and others one must continually envision a better world with respect to some particular problem, and then proceed in accordance with the cycle of hope. All change must start with a vision that is better than the current reality.

Two other traps are to think one person cannot make a difference or that it is not my responsibility to do so. As citizens of a nation-state, and more importantly as citizens of our communities, everyone has a responsibility to make life better for others as well as for ourselves, which ultimately makes life better for the world. Changing our lives to improve the world takes effort initially because we have to discipline ourselves to change our habits, but once accomplished, it does not necessarily take more time and energy than we were spending before we changed. Most people don't think of themselves as activists. However, once people change their lives in small ways to improve conditions in the world, they have become activists. The example you have set for others in response to the question of why you are doing what you are doing becomes a simple act of social change.

The key to being a positive force in the world around us is being informed about the issues, which to many people seems like an overwhelming task. Much of what we have to learn is unavailable in the mainstream media news and talk shows; nor is it taught to us throughout most of our education. With the availability of the web we now have at our fingertips a wealth of information about almost any topic. It is important to learn to cross check sources with one another and learn which sources can be trusted. There are numerous non-profit organizations we can join for small amounts of money that will provide us with regular newsletters about the important issues related to the work they are doing. This latter step takes us into the next level of creating social change: the macro level. Before discussing that level, I would like to give some examples of personal changes that are consistent with the cycle of hope and which can make a positive difference in the world around us.

*Personal citizenship projects*

Teachers and university professors can develop personal citizenship projects for their classes to show young people what is possible when people apply themselves. I have done this in my classes, but not nearly as extensively and in as well thought out a manner as Andrzejewski (shared unpublished teaching materials), who uses the Better World Handbook as a guide. She also uses non-religious Buddhist principles taken from Bodhisattva Peace Trainings conducted by Lama Shenpen Drolma (2003), a student of Chagdud Tulku who is a well known and widely respected Buddhist lama.

Andrzejewski created nine categories of possible actions for better citizenship, and there are 86 items distributed across the nine categories. Students are asked to pick one item a week and work on making improvements in their lives related to that item. Each week they are adding a new item without stopping the progress on the items started in previous weeks. By the end of the semester the students have undertaken a fairly long list of changes in their own personal lives that make a positive contribution to the people around them and to the world in general. Oral progress reports are given periodically throughout the semester and both written and oral reports are given at the end of the semester. This is a project that has given new hope to hundreds of students that they can change the world by first changing themselves.

The list of personal change activities is too long to include here, since it would require several pages. I will identify a few that I believe to be among the more important and/or useful.

*Sample personal action items for change*

1. Antidote judgment, bias, pride, and self-righteousness with equal regard and care for others.
2. Watch less or no corporate television especially manufactured "news," and junk media that wastes your time, constructs false "realities" (reality shows), fosters "humor" based on stereotypes and oppression (many sitcoms), fosters violence (action shows and many dramas), increases feelings of inadequacy (makeovers), desensitizes us to violence, encourages materialism (money and prize shows), and so on.
3. Value all life. Try not to harm anything, even beings you are taught to dislike.

4. Become a vegetarian, vegan, or eat substantially less meat and dairy.
5. Buy and consume organic, non-genetically engineered, non-irradiated locally grown food.
6. Use only what you need: reduce your ecological footprint on the world.
7. Buy from small and/or local companies, groups or individuals, organic farmers, food coops, etc.
8. Resist being stupefied (as used by Tolstoy) through mind altering/deadening drugs and media.
9. Respect the habitats of other species and strive to preserve them.
10. Educate yourself about destructive consequences of consuming and using pornography and sexually violent movies, music and advertisements (for example, objectification and commodification of others).

The above short list of action items focuses on what people can do to help improve conditions in the world with little organized involvement with others. These are only 10 of the 86 listed in Andrzejewski's exercise. It is likely that one could think of still many more personal change activities if one was inclined to do so. Personal action steps might seem silly, foolish or impractical, but they are not. The smallest positive action of one individual can have far reaching implications for life around that person. Unfortunately, the same is true of the smallest negative action (Tolstoy 1885).

In addition to personal activities that can be done without others, there are also many activities that focus on working with others to bring about macro level social change in a more direct manner. All individual separate self improvement behaviors, when combined over a long period of time, do make a significant difference in the world. There are, however, bigger steps a person can take in order to work for social change more systematically and in concert with other people. I will provide five examples out of many from Andrzejewski's list.

*Sample collective action steps for change*

1. Support movements to prevent or stop imperialism and war, and the violent extraction of land, labor, and resources from peoples of color and animals around the world.
2. Work to challenge corporate policies that put greed and profits above the earth and its inhabitants. Educate yourself/others about "free" trade agreements, World Trade Organization, World Bank, IMF, and their consequences for ordinary people, workers, indigenous peoples, animals, and the environment.
3. Examine how public tax money is being spent, and join organizations working for a fairer distribution of wealth nationally and globally.
4. Challenge corporate welfare and excessive CEO salaries while millions of people lose their jobs.

5. Understand how unions counter corporate greed. Learn about and challenge myths about unions, and support the right of people to organize themselves for their own protection.

For an extensive list of action steps and models specifically related to peace and nonviolence see Andrzejewski (2009).

## Re-Socialization Revisited

In Chapter 6, I alluded to the importance of a re-socialization process consistent with basic common values in order for people to be open to and sustain macro level changes. Personal citizen action projects, like those used by Andrzejewski and others, are exercises in re-socialization. As a result of taking courses like the one Andrzejewski teaches, students go out into the world aware of the relationship between their actions and the problems in the world around them. They also go out into the world aware of the root causes of problems and are prepared to work for organizations that help address those root causes. Education for citizenship does not have to be restricted to isolated classes within schools. It should be part of public service broadcasts, like the "no littering campaign" of the nineteen sixties and seventies. It should also be a part of workplace programs, where both employers and union leaders work together to educate employees about how to act as responsible citizens to make the world a better place for subsequent generations.

Religious leaders are socializing and re-socializing agents through their ministries from the church pulpit and beyond. Like teachers and professors, they can choose to be socializing agents for positive change or apologists for the corporate status quo. Churches also have schools and camps for children which can be used for positive socialization activities. Where is it more appropriate to encourage children to have positive values than in a religious organization? It is unfortunate that some religious leaders actually instill hatred in their parishioners and children toward a particular group of people. This is socialization at its worst.

### *Early childhood socialization*

Re-socialization can take place in a variety of ways. Just as important as re-socialization programs are early childhood programs that serve as original socializing agents. Pre-school and elementary school programs have the opportunity and capacity to build a strong early commitment to the values previously discussed—values that most humans around the world would consider important. Simple concepts like sharing and supporting one another, making sure everyone has safe water and healthy food, the importance of protecting the environment, nonviolence, eliminating problems related to greed, and the importance of respect for all forms of life, should be taught often at every grade level and with careful attention to the important reasons we have these values.

The most important years for socialization are the first few years following birth, which typically takes place with a parent or parents. These years are not only important because of the lasting effects of what children learn at that age, but also because there are critical biological and sensory contact needs during those early years (Repetti et al. 2007). Early developmental experiences of children impact interpersonal relations, which in turn impact mental and social health in adult life (Laible and Thompson 2007). Effective socialization of children is not a process of information injection, but more so one of contact and relationship. The sensory emotional contact and ensuing interactional bond make information sharing and transmission possible.

It is somewhat of a sidebar to say, but extremely relevant to the content of this book, that few parents today actually have the needed quality time and resources to effectively socialize their children. There is long standing and extensive research showing that family stress impacts on the socialization of children, not only from material deprivation itself, but also from the quality of interaction that takes place within and around the environment of family stress (Conger and Dogan 2007). The high productivity, high unemployment, high debt, multiple low paying job culture that greed driven laissez-faire capitalism has created is leaving children in the United States without the kind of care and socialization needed to become healthy well informed self actualizing adults. Indeed, it is difficult to entertain how children can become socialized into actively involved citizens for a better world when socializing them into mentally healthy individuals is a substantial challenge in itself.

There are other related challenges, such as the role of violent video games and other damaging violent forms of media entertainment, which increase in use as parental time and energy diminishes. It would be useful if churches would integrate parenting issues into their marriage classes: under what conditions should people consider having children and what challenges will they face in the modern world? There are tens of thousands of children on behavior control drugs today in the United States, with some estimates as high as 20 percent of the country's children on some form of behavior control drugs (Acu-Cell 2010). Parents are not to blame, but family stress from profit maximization in the corporate work world most likely plays an important role. There is also pressure from the pharmaceutical companies and drug oriented clinicians to medicate children with behavior problems (Acu-Cell 2010, Petit-Zeman 2003).

With many parents out of time and at wits end from either working too many hours or being unemployed, the schools and other social institutions have an even greater responsibility. Yet, maintaining adequate support for the schools in the face of a push by the wealthy to privatize education is a constant struggle (Rogen 2009). The world needs healthy well socialized children in order to have adults that will one day fix the problems of the world: systemic problems that currently make it difficult to have healthy well socialized children. This is a classic circular dilemma.

Because the micro and macro social problems are highly interrelated it is not possible to work on one in isolation of the other in hopes of getting needed results. Both micro and macro solutions have to be addressed simultaneously. Improved and more intensive socialization practices have to be developed, but changes in the socio-economic structures will facilitate those changes, which in turn will enhance the socio-economic changes further. Working with micro change and macro change together has the potential for creating an oscillation effect where improvement at both levels can be witnessed at multiplicative rather than additive levels. Unfortunately, it also works in the opposite direction, which is what we have witnessed over the last 30 years. The simultaneous degeneration of both our broader socio-economic structure and our socialization processes has created an oscillation effect that is rapidly spiraling in a negative direction. That needs to be turned around, and it is clearly possible to do so.

## Community Organizing: An Honorable Profession

During the general presidential election campaign of Barack Obama he was sometimes criticized by his opponents for having been a community organizer before going into politics. One of his opponents asked in a nationally televised speech something like, "all he has been is a community organizer; what is that?" A full time community organizer is someone who usually works through a non-profit organization, or perhaps more than one, to bring about positive change to a community. They help people in communities organize to attain the services they need from agencies, businesses, and government. They sometimes help local communities bring about change within the service organizations, businesses, and government offices themselves. Community organizers could be involved in helping people of a community prevent something harmful from happening to their community, like an eight lane highway going through the center of town, or a community park being sold to a developer.

Community organizers are people with special skills for bringing people together to accomplish common goals. People are not necessarily born with these skills, but develop them over time, as is the case with most skills people have. Community organizers often times also have knowledge attained through education or special experiences that is useful in solving community problems. President Barack Obama was an attorney who was graduated first in his class from Harvard University, one of the most prestigious universities in the world. He could have gone on to work in almost any law firm that he chose, but instead he decided to be a community organizer so that he could focus his energy on making the world a better place for others. He used his knowledge about the law and his status as an attorney to help people who lacked the resources to help themselves. One of the interesting consequences of having a community organizer become president of the United States is that it will now be difficult for people who oppose the work of community organizers to negatively label people who do that work. Community organizers have sometimes been portrayed as trouble makers, revolutionaries, or social deviants. During the George W. Bush presidency many were considered terrorists.

*Saul Alinsky*

Saul Alinsky is sometimes given credit for being the founder of modern community organizing, and he established a reputation for being the most effective community organizer of his era within the United States. He grew up and did his work during the first half of the twentieth century and into the early 1970s. He was Jewish and the son of immigrants. Alinsky understood oppression first hand and identified with the disadvantaged people of Chicago, where he lived and worked. He was a sociologist who never completed his graduate education in Sociology. He practiced and wrote about what he considered to be a Marxist version of community organizing, whereby the goal was to expose inequities in such a way that public outrage would be directed toward people in positions of power, the people who could do something about the inequities. The goal was to unite people with a common cause against visible "enemies" and continually pressure those enemies until they changed their laws, policies, or existing practices in favor of disadvantaged excluded people (Alinsky 1989).

Alinsky thought he was getting to the root causes of the problems he addressed by dealing with power imbalances. Power imbalance is not the root cause of social problems like poverty, homelessness and hunger. The root causes of the most serious social problems are the attitudes, values, and beliefs that people have about how to live with other beings and the earth. These attitudes, values, and beliefs are what ultimately create motivations for behaviors on a daily basis. Power imbalance is an intervening variable, something that acts as an in-between catalyst for an outcome, but something that is not really the original cause of that outcome. Placing a high value on money and material gain no matter what the cost to others and the environment is an attitudinal disposition that leads some people to be highly motivated to do whatever it takes to accumulate large amounts of wealth. Some people having a lot of wealth and others having little is what creates the power imbalance that leads to further exploitation, oppression and deprivation.

*Short term vs. long term change*

It is sometimes possible to remove the power imbalance for a period of time, as Alinsky and others have demonstrated. However, people with power and wealth do not require a lot of time to figure out how to regain their power and continue their wealth accumulation if that is what is motivating their behavior. If that is not what is motivating their behavior they would not resist, as they do, requests for more equitable arrangements that would distribute wealth in a humanitarian manner. Alinsky recognized the flaws in human character when he occasionally saw people who were poor and disadvantaged attain power and mistreat others just as they had been mistreated. His methods could not deal with this aspect of human behavior because they dealt only with the structural imbalances between groups and not the motivations behind what causes those structural imbalances in the first place—the root causes.

As we look at successful and unsuccessful revolutions over time, the most successful are those that have implemented a quick and effective socialization process, typically through some form of mass education system. It has been true in the United States at various stages of its development, but certainly in conjunction with the industrial revolution. It has been true in Cuba where, despite heavy external pressure and intervention, a reasonably strong socialist government has been maintained. Mass education does work as an effective socializing agent. The "news" and entertainment media have also become strong socializing agents within most developed and developing countries.

If people want to create more just communities and nation-states, it will be necessary to be able to effectively socialize people into behavior patterns and ways of thinking that will maximize the likelihood of cooperation and peaceful coexistence. Achieving such a socialization process means creating educational systems that teach/socialize students/people of all income levels about the damage done to the environment, other species of life, and each other if humans maintain a disposition of greed and crude materialism. Moving our educational system away from preparing children for laissez-faire capitalism will not be easily accomplished, but like eliminating littering, it can be done if recognized as a public service. Attention now turns to the macro level where the actual serious damage is being done. Where should the socialization process take us and what might that place look like?

## Root Problems and Corporations

In reviewing Figure 10.3 in Chapter 10, the reader will notice that the proposed near starting point of the entire process, the root cause of the many connections that follow, is greed. In the late twentieth century and early twenty-first century systematic efforts have been successfully made to change greed to a positive value. This transformation has quickly exacerbated the serious systemic problems that stem from greed. One of those problems, seen further along in the flow of Figure 10.3, is the expansion of capitalism specifically through the growth and autonomous power of corporations.

Recall from earlier discussions that the original intent of corporations was to serve a public good. The earliest corporations dating back to the seventeenth century were non-profit organizations. Eventually they were redefined to be able to make a profit, but were still intended as a means by which a public good could be served. The public good did not happen through the profits, but through the activities and products generated. Corporations were, and still are, chartered by the state, and that charter should be removed if the corporation does not comply with its intended objectives. Corporation removal does not happen because corporations have gained control of the political system that has the power to revoke charters. Through that control they have also been able to change the public perception and understanding of what corporations are supposed to do. President Obama is the only president in modern history who has taken any initiative to control corporations—however modest that initiative may have been.

## Corporate Design

It is not likely that capitalism as a primary form of the Western economy is going to be completely eliminated in the future, but elimination would be welcomed if a better economic system could be created—one based on cooperation and long term benefits to the environment and future generations. Short of a totally new economic system, it is possible to significantly change capitalism to meet the needs of current and future life on the planet. If at the micro level we are instituting programs to reinforce people's attitudes and values to create a more humane disposition toward one another and life in general, at the macro level a logical starting point would be to change corporations back to their originally intended purpose. That means establishing and enforcing principles of corporation use that meet the needs of the public.

I previously referred to the work of Marjorie Kelly, co-founder and long time publisher of *Business Ethics* magazine. She also wrote *The Devine Right of Capital*, which laid out some of the critique of capitalism used in this book. Kelly is the co-founder (along with Allen White) of a project called Corporation 20/20. This initiative is for the purpose of re-designing corporations back to their originally intended social purpose. One of the important outcomes of this project has been the identification of six principles of future corporate design:

1. The purpose of the corporation is to harness private interests to serve the public interest;
2. Corporations shall accrue fair returns for shareholders, but not at the expense of the legitimate interests of other stakeholders;
3. Corporations shall operate sustainably, meeting the needs of the present generation without compromising the ability of future generations to meet their needs;
4. Corporations shall distribute their wealth equitably among those who contribute to wealth creation;
5. Corporations shall be governed in a manner that is participatory, transparent, ethical, and accountable;
6. Corporations shall not infringe on the right of natural persons to govern themselves, nor infringe on other universal human rights (Kelly and White 2007: 6).

You will notice that these principles are quite different than what has been taught in many Business and Economics programs across the United States and in other countries as well. It is not uncommon that students in business and economics courses are taught that the only purpose of the corporation is to maximize profits for shareholders. Often enthusiastic free market capitalists will end their statement about the purpose of corporations being profit maximization by emphatically saying the word, "period!"

*Friedman vs. corporate design*

Friedman (1962, 1970) mocks the notion that corporations should act in a socially responsible manner. He ignores the original purpose of corporations as social units created and chartered to serve some public good. Friedman's message, publically and consistently delivered in the 1960s and 70s, is that social responsibility is a form of socialism and socialism is against individual freedom. Therefore, social responsibility is against individual freedom. Friedman ignores the millions of people around the world denied their freedom by the actions of corporations. He also ignores the existence of democratic socialist states, where people vote democratically to share wealth and put restrictions on corporations for the common good. Friedman talks about the importance of separating government from business to avoid socialism. This mandate is contradicted by Friedman and his students being funded with tax payer money through the CIA to spread Friedman's free market form of capitalism to other parts of the world (Klein 2007), an economic system designed to effectively increase the personal freedoms of people who already have wealth and decrease the freedoms of those who do not. Using the word "socialism" in the way that Friedman does is reminiscent of the red scare that took place in the hunt for communists and socialists during the early post-World War II period in the United States, a period of heightened unnecessary fear known as the McCarthy era.

Problems arise when people are confused by misinformation about the value of the common good, the meaning of individual freedom, and how both of those qualities can best be fulfilled. If an owner of a corporation, acting through the "person" of that corporation, reduces the freedom of another person, nobody's freedom has actually been well served. All human groups have restrictions on human behavior and most of those restrictions relate to the harm that one person might do to another. It doesn't matter if the harmful "person" is representing a corporate board of directors, corporate stockholders, or the role of a CEO, socially agreed upon rules are needed to assure that one person's freedom is not another person's prison.

The rules and assumptions that Friedman made up and convinced others to follow so that wealth could grow unencumbered by long standing cultural values have little to do with freedom in a general sense, and represent no regard for the original intent, purpose, or positive capabilities of corporations.

*What do the corporate design principles mean?*

The corporate design initiative starts with the assumption that, however corporations came to be the way they are, we now know they represent a serious problem in the world. Recall that unnecessary wars have been fought on behalf of corporations and many lives have been lost. Corporate deaths have occurred, not only through wars and violence on behalf of corporations, but also through marketing dangerous products, and human and non-human habitat disruption. Corporations in their current state represent one of the greatest problems the world has ever seen. As one looks at the six new principles of corporate design one sees that there is little that is controversial about them. The first principle is simply a statement of what the original intent of corporations was supposed to be. It isn't new at all.

Milton Friedman would most likely agree with the first half of the second principle, which reinforces the notion that corporations have an obligation to the people that invest in them. However, the second principle then goes on to qualify that objective by adding a phrase to the effect that a corporation cannot benefit at the expense of others. This is a simple notion, but an economically interesting and controversial notion as well. The strict notion that maximization of profits is the only driving principle of corporations and capitalism is now brought to question by this principle. One cannot restrain corporate behavior relative to harming others if one is operating on the basis of greed being a positive value. Principle two is telling us what most of our grandparents would have told us. It is a basic principle of life that does not require a Nobel Prize or even a high school education: to knowingly gain at the expense of others is greedy and unethical behavior. It does harm to others, and because of the complexity and interrelatedness of all life, it will most likely eventually do harm to the social actor expressing the behavior: either directly or through its impact on generations following that social actor (see principle three). As we face the sixth mass extinction of species on earth, and the first caused by human behavior, we now know that all aspects of the earth (human and non-human, living and non-living) are delicately connected and interdependent. It is a positive reflection on the intelligence of humans that such an understanding can be reached, although it may be that other species of life have known this for a longer period of time than we have. It will reflect poorly on human intelligence if we cannot solve the systemic problems humans have created by severely disrupting the balance among and between living and non-living phenomena (such as chemicals and basic elements).

*Painless extinction*

Principle three tells us that harming life in the future is as unethical as harming life in the present. Humans who exist now are not only connected with one another, but they are connected with humans in the future, just as they are connected with humans in their past. In its most basic form this means that I am part of my father and mother, and my children and grandchildren will be part of me. This is most likely why we feel such strong connections with, and work so hard to protect, our children and grandchildren. This is the mysterious part of the preservation of the species. It is, however, most likely more complicated than that. Our DNA is not only connected to the DNA of our direct relatives, but to the DNA of other humans and other forms of life as well. The differences between all forms of matter are exaggerated for conceptual short term conveniences. Yet similarities between forms of matter do not allow, without serious consequences, casually disrupting the order of phenomena that has gradually evolved over the millennia. Such disruptions are what result in toxins in our air, water, and food.

We can probably assume that humans will eventually be extinct. Over 99 percent of all species that have ever existed on earth are now extinct. What is important, however, is that evolution of life toward extinction takes place in a relatively balanced gradual manner, so that no single generation experiences notable pain.

*Startup and shutdown effects of corporations*

Extremely large corporations, created for efficiency and greater profits, result in massive social disorganization for the communities in which they locate. Additionally, those communities develop a dependency on the company that makes the company's movement or closure an even greater disorganizing factor. After establishing community dependency, companies will often extort additional benefits from communities in the form of tax exemptions or additional land acquisitions in exchange for not relocating or closing. Multinational corporations have this same ability to extort benefits on a larger scale from nation-states, since their closure would result in massive social disorganization in many communities. It would seem consistent with principle three that the size of corporations be limited so as to reduce their startup and shutdown impact on the social organization of local communities.

Anarchist thinking becomes useful in this situation because it tells us that local communities should be able to plan and govern themselves to the maximum extent possible without negatively impacting on the wellbeing of other communities. Such planning and self governance becomes seriously challenged if a community is pressured to reorganize itself around a large industrial plant. What communities must continuously consider is that a sudden influx of jobs via one plant means a possible equally sudden loss of jobs in the future. This often occurs after the community has increased its population through inward migration due to the new plant's arrival. With inward migration the local community has more people and fewer jobs than it did before the plant arrived. Another possible solution to this problem is enforcing the ability of local communities to declare eminent domain rights over the plants facility since the wealth of the plant was built on the local labor and tax/land incentives provided by that community. Not only has eminent domain not been upheld by state and national government, local communities that have offered to purchase large plants to keep them operating for their unemployed citizens have been denied that right because the company that was moving did not want to have to compete with the same plant it was closing. Most often plants do not close because they are not making profits, but because the owners can make bigger profits somewhere else. It is common practice for profits to be disguised by clever accounting practices for tax avoidance purposes and for filing bankruptcy purposes.

*Quest for equity*

The fourth principle is the most controversial since it involves what ideologues might categorize as socialism. Indeed, principle four could have been written by the great social theorist and critic, Karl Marx. Marx's criticism of industrialization and the corresponding form of capitalism that was emerging out of the industrial revolution was that the people who did the work to create the industrial products were part of a socially created labor pool. This labor pool was, and from a Marxist Conflict Theory perspective still is, used solely for the purpose of making maximum profits for the owners of the companies. As has been discussed throughout many sections of this book, maximizing profits means minimizing labor costs. Labor costs are often times the most expensive part of the production process. Unions were organized in the United States during the early part of the twentieth century as a way to offset the raw exploitation of company owners who treated their workers, especially their immigrant workers, like slaves. Unions protected the workers from gross exploitation, but after they were targeted to be systematically eradicated by the Reagan administration and the administrations that followed, union membership was reduced from about a third of the workforce to less than 10 percent of the workforce.

With the exception of a few professional unions, like the nurses and public employees unions in certain states, working conditions have moved backwards. In many ways labor conditions for the working class in the early part of the twenty-first century became similar to what they were during the late nineteenth and early twentieth centuries. This is especially true of labor conditions in other countries where there are no effective unions. Production industries were moved to other countries as one of the strategies to avoid and destroy unionization in the United States. As one could easily predict, once those labor markets were exploited and investors became extremely wealthy, the flow of capital stopped. It was inevitable that eventually the output/input ratio of profits to production investment would begin to become larger rather than smaller and the perception or prediction of decreased profit would bring everything to a halt, which is what happened in 2008. Such manoeuvring makes a lot of wealthy people wealthier while the rest of the world's population moves toward desperation.

Corporate design principle four says that all who participate in the production of wealth should have an equitable share in that wealth. Determining income equity is not an easy matter, but it has been attempted in other countries. The ten-times rule, which states that CEOs cannot make more than ten times their workers is one method of sharing the wealth in a more equitable fashion than has been done in the past within most nation-states. Many CEOs of major corporations make over 500 times their workers and they still blame their workers for reductions in shareholder profits. There are two general ways of actualizing the ten-times rule. One is to allow the corporation to make as much profit as it can and thereby increase everyone's wealth. This approach risks continued rapid depletion of the earth's resources and environmental degradation. The other approach is to set limits on the amount of wealth that can be accumulated using the natural resources of the earth—resources that should belong to all life challenged with survival on this planet. Going back to principle number three the latter option seems advisable, since sustainability is also an important consideration.

*Democracy and transparency*

One of the hallmarks of Western nation-states is that they use democratic procedures for making decisions about what actions should be taken relative to the business at hand. Elections are conducted to determine who will serve as government officials and meetings within most organizations operate using something like Robert's Rules of Order, which means that those present have a voice and a vote on matters requiring decisions. Unions are required by state and federal law to operate according to democratic practices. Yet, some multinational corporations control more resources and/or wealth than many nation-states. With the globalization of the economy, following "free" trade agreements, corporations have the power, through representation on appointed international decision-making committees, to override the laws and constitutions of sovereign nations. Powerful corporations are not held to any standards of democracy or transparency. Decisions are typically made by boards of directors and CEOs behind closed doors. Shareholder meetings that are attended by a few interested stockholders are a facade for democracy and transparency, but are not where the decisions actually get made. They often turn into opportunities for stockholders to complain about the decisions that were made secretly behind closed doors.

Kelly and Allen are proposing that corporations, allowed to exist as tools of the state for the common good, should be required (just like unions and other social aggregates) to operate democratically and in full daylight. In this way the corporation can be held accountable for violations of the letter or spirit of any of the six corporate design principles. It is also the way in which the public can be assured that corporation leaders will behave ethically and that they will be held accountable for their decisions. For example, we now know that many corporations that have closed or moved their plants had made that decision literally years in advance of the action taken. During the time between the decision to leave and the time of actual departure the corporation decision-makers continue to extort benefits from the local community and the workers in exchange for not leaving, knowing all the while that they had already set a date for closing the plant. This is unethical behavior and could not occur if all meetings were open and all decisions were made democratically within the entire corporate organization, meaning the workers as well as management should be involved in the decisions.

*Respect for other ways of living*

Principle number six is one that is of utmost importance during a time when the globalization of the economy has reached preeminence. The amount of destruction to local economies, to life of all forms, and to corresponding communities around the world is much greater than most people realize. Millions of people have been killed by military interventions to secure property and resources for corporations. Massive amounts of destruction to human and non-human habitats have occurred that will have a long term impact on the ability of life to survive on this planet. Kelly and Allen are proposing that corporations no longer be able to impose themselves over the rights and cultures of affected groups of people.

This principle would theoretically eliminate corporate lobbying and paying for political leaders who will use government military power to interfere with the affairs of other peoples in other places around the world. In terms of macro social structural change, principle six is the most far reaching in that it addresses issues related to global stratification and inequality. One of the great contemporary social theorists, Emanuel Wallerstein (1974), developed an area of sociological study known as world systems theory, which addresses issues of how individual nation-states are related to one another vis a vis global capitalism and global stratification. Wallerstein maintains that it is not true, as most people in Western nation-states believe, that capitalism has advanced humans beyond the previous economic and resource distribution systems that existed in earlier time periods.

The question humans must face now is, "where do we go from here?" Part of the answer might be found in the cultures, values, and living practices of many of the indigenous and peasant peoples around the world who currently are discounted and often ridiculed/displaced by Western capitalists (Smith 1999). What is it like to live without greed as a value? What is like to live within a strong cultural value of balance and sustainability with other forms of life (LaDuke 1996, 1999), and how do we move closer to a cultural blend of who we are and what other much older and wiser cultural traditions have to offer?

## Anarchism Revisited: Gradual Diffusion of Corporate Nation-State Economies

What is it that people need? What is it that people want? What makes for healthy functional social units and communities: social organization rather than social disorganization? None of these questions are effectively answered with large corporations. The early sociologists of the nineteenth century understood that when they saw industrialization unfolding with all of its inevitable problems and systemic social disorganization. Large impersonal factories where humans are small assembly line cogs in a giant wheel: the Charlie Chaplin silent movie *Modern Times* rings true.

What is happening across the United States today, and in other parts of the world as well, is the emergence of literally thousands of small businesses producing useful products for people right there in their home towns. Using predominantly local environmentally friendly materials, local workers, and local markets, people are creating sustainable micro economies based on what they and their neighbors need and want for a balanced high quality life (BALLE 2010). Many, if not most, of these businesses are worker owned and operated with decision-making shared by all involved in the operation. This is modern day anarchism: people living in relatively independent local communities to whatever extent the parameters of the outside world will allow.

Fixing corporations through a corporate redesign project as described above is a laudable endeavor. They certainly need to be fixed, and we know they are not going to disappear anytime soon. Others who share most of the views expressed in this book might disagree on this point (Korten 2010). As human cultures move increasingly toward lifestyles revolving around a common set of positive values: peace; justice; fairness; equality; pure air, water, food; and so on (Andrzejewski et al. 2009), a new economy will emerge that will eventually make giant multinational corporations rare and limited in their social and environmental footprint. Many people do not realize that most workers today do not work for large corporations. They work for small businesses. Continued exposure of the social problems related to the use of multinational corporations will move communities increasingly toward alternative economic models and a new economy based on the needs of all people and ecological systems—not just on what is needed to make a few people wealthy (Korten 2010).

Perhaps the hardest lesson for community organizers and social change agents to learn is the importance of including all forms of life into the planning and transition toward a new economy and way of life. The various animal production industries (meat, pets, fur and so on) are unsustainable, and any culture that includes them will be unsustainable as well. As humans grapple to rediscover and reclaim their core values two central issues are: a) what humans should eat and why, and b) how humans should view and treat other forms of life (Alessio 2008). Speciesism is the foundation of all the isms. A transition to a peaceful, nonviolent, and more sustainable world will not occur if the economic function of the isms does not disappear, and the economic function of the isms cannot disappear if speciesism is not addressed.

**President of the United States for a Day**

*Values enhancement through re-socialization: micro level change*

If you were able to be president for a day, how would you, as a global citizen/leader, use what you have learned from this book to make the world a better place for all life on earth? You might start by putting in place educational and other re-socialization systems that would help people reclaim the important values that bring people and other forms of life together, rather than setting them apart through competition and structurally created systemic conflict. You might set as your goal the establishment of a means by which our communities can successfully foster behaviors modeled after the ten items identified earlier in this chapter under the section titled "Sample Personal Action Items for Change." Just as the George W. Bush administration established a task force to eliminate alternative and justice related curricula from the schools, you might do the same in the opposite direction. That is, establish a task force to make recommendations on how sociologists can be used to help establish information systems and interaction systems that would produce cooperative behavior patterns and positive relations among children as they grow to adulthood. The task force could advise educational standards for a more inclusive school curriculum, one that included the benefits and contributions of labor unions, non-Western civilizations, Latino/Latina Americans, African Americans, Women, LGBT people and so on.

A task force could also explore educational programs for fostering better relations in all adult workplaces using positive reinforcement programs, and providing information about the impact of various types of interaction. Again, the goal could be the enhancement of behaviors like those listed under "Sample Personal Action Items for Change." The Department of Education and the Department of Health and Human Services could have these behavioral and attitudinal changes as their top priorities for an informed and healthy United States population. I previously pointed to the progress made during the Johnson Administration in the nineteen sixties in the area of controlling littering. Educational programs in the schools and re-socialization programs through the media elevated the value of non-littering to a sufficiently high level that everyone adopted a non-littering attitude and disposition toward their community and work environments. Greed and harmful competition could be eliminated in the same manner. I still remember those anti-littering public service announcements on television. We could be seeing those same announcements directed toward socially harmful behaviors and values.

*Changing social structures: the macro level*

Once you had programs in place to socialize and re-socialize people into more cooperative living and working arrangements, you could then focus your attention on the macro level by assigning a task force to study and find ways of implementing the above discussed six principles of corporate design. This would be the primary responsibility of the Department of Labor and the Department of Commerce. A joint task force, co-chaired by the two cabinet members representing those departments, could develop a plan that would bring corporations back to their original purpose in a way that would stabilize them around the six principles. Accomplishing this objective would go a long ways toward stabilizing the United States economy, improving our international relations and thereby stabilizing the economies of the world.

There are also many other areas where there is work to be done, but the above mentioned actions alone would make major contributions toward solving what are now the most serious social problems in the United States and possibly in the world, given the influence and presence of the United States throughout the planet. Going back to Figure 10.3, controlling corporations will drive the wooden stake into the second heart of the beast. The first heart was greed that leads to excess accumulation, hoarding, and conflict, and the second is the large corporations that have become the primary vehicles of that greed.

## You don't have to be President

The good news is that in order to work on the above tasks a person doesn't have to be the president. Being an average citizen is sufficient to make a significant difference in the world. People can, indeed, be the change that they seek. They can decide to change their own life and thereby influence others to do the same. They can decide to contact their political representatives and encourage them to support initiatives based on, or similar to, the six principles of corporate design. They can explore possibilities from the section titled "Sample Collective Action Items for Change," or they can come up with still other ideas and proposals that will help make the world a better place. There is much to be done.

Serious problem solvers are needed to advocate for a more humane criminal justice system—one that recognizes current discriminatory practices and which resolves to imprison fewer instead of greater numbers of people, reserving prisons for serious acts of violence. Pressure could be placed on the Secretary of Justice to focus more on prevention methods, working with the Department of Education and the Department of Health and Human Services—decriminalizing drug use and developing socialization campaigns to stop the abuse of all kinds of substances. Activities along these lines, with opportunities for people to make a comfortable living legally, could dramatically change the way we view crime and justice in the United States and in the world in general.

On the brink of the sixth mass extinction and the meltdown of the Arctic ice caps, one might focus directly on the environmental problems facing the earth and all forms of life on it. What kinds of programs can be implemented to reverse our course of self destruction? What sources of energy can be tapped and how can we convince the public and the government that our current course is oscillating out of control. These are all important points of intervention to bring about needed social change, and we need progressive social scientists in government who are able to use their understanding of human interaction and social structure to help make improvements in all of these areas. It is clear, however, that without a corresponding revitalization of basic human values and an effective way to make corporations work for the public good, rather than continuing to make the public and government work for corporate profits, current social problems will continue to worsen. By reinstituting early core human values and corresponding social programs, human social life and the social lives of non-human beings have the potential and capacity to be positive and healthy long into the foreseeable future.

# References


Access Project. 2010. 2009–2010 Federal Poverty Guidelines. [Online]. Available at: http://www.atdn.org/access/poverty.html [accessed July 7 2010].

Acu-Cell. 2010. ADD/ADHD & behavioral problems: Nutritional causes, preventions and therapies. [Online: *Acu-Cell Disorders*]. Available at: http://www.Acu-Cell.com/dis-add.html [accessed November 6 2010].

Agee, P. 1987. *On the Run*. New York: L. Stuart.

Alden, W. 2010a. Companies hoarding 1 $ trillion in cash. [Online: *The Huffington Post*]. Available at: http://www.huffingtonpost.com/2010/10/27/corporate-cash-hoarding_n_774559.html [accessed October 30 2010].

Alden, W. 2010b. Wall street may break pay record – again. [Online: *The Huffington Post*]. Available at: http://www.huffingtonpost.com/2010/10/12/wall-street-pay_n_759068.html [accessed October 30 2010].

Alessio, J.C. 1990. A synthesis and formalization of heiderian balance and social exchange theory, *Social Forces* 68(4) 1267–86.

Alessio, J.C. 1996. Common myths about crime, in *Oppression and Social Justice: Critical Frameworks*, edited by Andrzejewski, J. 5th edition. Needham Heights: Simon & Schuster Custom Publishing, 75–84.

Alessio, J.C. 1999. Using discriminant analysis to predict professorial rank by gender. *Journal of Applied Sociology* 16(1) 123–43.

Alessio, J.C. 2007. Increasing stratification by gender: The results of a gender equity adjustment, in *Transforming the Academy: Struggles and Strategies for Women in Higher Education*, Volume II, edited by R. Martin. Tehachapi, CA: GrayMill Publications.

Alessio, J.C. 2008. Being sentient and sentient being: The animal rights movement and interspecies boundaries. [Online: *Green Theory & Praxis: The Journal of Ecopedagogy* 4(2) 67–86]. Available at: http:greentheoryandpraxis.org/journal/index.php/journal/search/titles [accessed October 9 2010].

Alinsky, S. 1989. *Rules for Radicals*. New York: Vintage Books.

AllBusiness. 2010. The definition of a corporation. [Online]. Available at: http://www.allbusiness.com/legal/contracts-agreements-incorporation/529-1.html [accessed August 28 2010].

Amadeo, K. 2007. Stock market correction. [Online]. Available at: http://us economy.about.com/od/glossary/g/Market_Correcti.htm (p. 1) [accessed January 11 2009].

America's Army. 2010. America's AA army. [Online]. Available at: http://www.americasarmy.com/ [accessed August 2 2010].

Amnesty International USA. 2010. Death penalty and innocence. [Online]. Available at: http://www.amnestyusa.org/death-penalty/death-penalty-facts/death-penalty-and-innocence/page.do?id=1101086 [accessed November 13 2010].

Andrzejewski, J. 2007. Alternative press, in *Encyclopedia of Activism and Social Justice*, edited by Anderson, G.L., Herr, K.G. London: Sage Publications, 78–84.

Andrzejewski, J. 2009. Education for peace and nonviolence, in *Social Justice, Peace, and Environmental Education: Transformative Standards*, edited by Andrzejewski, J., Baltodano, M. and Symcox, L. London: Routledge, 99–120.

Andrzejewski, J. and Alessio, J. 1999. *Education for Global Citizenship and Social Responsibility.* (Monograph). Burlington: John Dewey Project for Progressive Education, University of Vermont.

Andrzejewski, J., Baltodano, M. and Symcox, L. (eds) 2009. *Social Justice, Peace, and Environmental Education: Transformative Standards.* London: Routledge.

Antrobus, P. 2004. *The Global Women's Movement: Origins, Issues and Strategies*. New York: Zed Books.

Aslam, A. 2005. U.S.: Pay gap widens between CEOs and workers. [Online: OneWorld.Net]. Available at: http://www.commondreams.org/headlines05/0412-10.htm [accessed July 17 2010].

Baker, A. 2010. Judge cites discrimination in N.Y. fire department. [Online: *The New York Times*]. Available at: http://www.nytimes.com/2010/01/14/nyregion/14fire.html [accessed October 26 2010].

BALLE. 2010. *Business Alliance for Local Living Economies*. [Online]. Available at: http://www.livingeconomies.org/ [accessed November 3 2010].

Banfield, E.C. 1970. *The Unheavenly City*. Boston: Little, Brown and Co.

Barlett, D.L. and Steele, J.B. 1994. *America: Who Really Pays the Taxes?* Riverside, NJ: Simon and Schuster, Inc.

Bassett, L. 2010a. Income gap between rich and poor is highest in decades, data show. [Online: *The Huffington Post*]. Available at: http://www.huffingtonpost.Com/2010/07/08/income-gap-between-rich-a_n_639984.html [accessed July 17 2010].

Bassett, L. 2010b. Extending Bush tax cuts WON'T create jobs, says leading economist. [Online: *The Huffington Post*]. Available at: http://www.huffingtonpost.com/2010/07/28/bush-tax-cuts-extending_n_662743.html [accessed January 9 2011].

BBC News. 2010. Rich-poor divide 'wider than 40 years ago'. [Online]. Available at: http://news.bbc.co.uk/2/hi/business/8481534.stm [accessed July 15 2010].

Beaubien, J. 2010. As the drug war rages on, will Mexico surrender? [Online]. Available at: http://www.npr.org/templates/story/story.php?storyId=129009629 [accessed August 9 2010].

Bedau, H.A. 1998. *The Death Penalty in America: Current Controversies.* New York: Oxford University Press.

Beirne, P. 2009. *Confronting Animal Abuse: Law, Criminology, and Human-Animal Relationships*. New York: Rowman & Littlefield Publisher, Inc.

Berry, B. 2004a. International progress and regress on animal rights. *The International Journal of Sociology and Social Policy* 24(9) 58–75.

Berry, B. 2004b. Nonhuman animals as victims: Victimology and the animal rights movement, in *Victimizing Vulnerable Groups: Images of Uniquely High-Risk Crime Targets*, edited by Coston, C.T.M. London: Praeger Publishers, 244–254.

Berry, B. 2007. *Beauty Bias: Discrimination and Social Power.* London: Praeger Publishers.

Berry, B. 2008. *The Power of Looks: Social Stratification of Physical Appearance.* Aldershot: Ashgate Publishing Limited.

Best, J. 2008. *Social Problems*. New York: W.W. Norton and Company.

Best, S. and Nocella, A.J. (eds) 2004. *Terrorists or freedom fighters? Reflections on the liberation of animals*. New York: Lantern Books.

Blau, P.M. 1964. *Exchange and Power in Social Life*. New York: Wiley.

BLS (Bureau of Labor Statistics). 2010. The employment situation – 2010. [Online: US Department of Labor]. Available at: http://www.bls.gov/news.release/pdf/empsit.pdf [accessed October 25 2010].

Bowden, C. 2010. U.S.-Mexico 'war on drugs' a failure. [Online]. Available at: http://www.cnn.com/2010/OPINION/03/31/bowden.ciudad.juarez.cartels/index.html [accessed August 9 2010].

Boyer, W. 2003. *Myth America: Democracy vs. Capitalism*. New York: Apex Press.

Brady, D., Fullerton, A.S. and Cross, J.M. 2010. More than just nickels and dimes: A cross-national analysis of working poverty in affluent democracies. *Social Problems* 57(4) 559–85.

Brezina, T. 2008. What went wrong in New Orleans? An examination of the welfare dependency theory. *Social Problems* 55(1) 23–42.

Brown, J.C. 1997. What the heck is an e coli? [Online]. Available at: http://people.ku.edu/~jbrown/ecoli.html [accessed November 3 2010].

Buhi, E.R., Marhefko, S.L. and Hoban, M.T. 2010. The state of the union: sexual health disparities in a national sample of U.S. college students. *Journal of American College Health* 58(4) 337–346.

Butler, S. 1935. *War is a Racket.* New York: Round Table Press, Inc.

Butler Byrd, N. and Jangu, M. 2009. A past is not a heritage: Reclaiming indigenous principles for global justice and education for peoples of African descent, in *Social Justice, Peace, and Environmental Education: Transformative Standards*, edited by J. Andrzejewski, M. Baltodano and L. Symcox. London: Routledge, 193–315.

Carlton, J. 2011. Dallas man declared innocent after 30 years in prison. [Online]. Available at: http://www.nbcdfw.com/news/local-beat/Dallas-Man-Declared-Innocent-After-30-Years-in-Prison-112880414.html [accessed January 8 2011].

Carus, F. 2010. UN urges global move to meat and dairy-free diet. [Online]. Available at: http://www.guardian.co.uk/environment/2010/jun/02/un-report-meat-free-diet [accessed July 22 2010].

Center for Genomics & Bioinformatics and Indiana University Biology Department. 2003. [Online]. Available at: http://sunflower.bio.indiana.edu and http://sunflower.bio.indiana.edu/~rhangart/plantmotion/movements/nastic/mimosa/mimosa.html [accessed January 11 2009].

Chambliss, W.J. 1964. A sociological analysis of the law of vagrancy. *Social Problems*, 67–77.

Chambliss, W.J. 2011. Toward a political economy of crime, in *The Study of Social Problems: Seven Perspectives*, edited by E. Rubington and M.S. Weinberg. New York: Oxford University Press, Inc., 255–65

*Charleston Gazette, The*. 2006. New Jersey considers hold on death penalty. [Online]. Available at: http://findarticles.com/p/news-articles/charleston-gazette-the/mi_8022/is_20060107/nj-considers-hold-death-penalty/ai_n43200011/?tag=rel.res4 [accessed September 5 2010].

Chomsky, N. 1976. The relevance of anarcho-syndicalism. [Online]. Available at: http://www.chomsky.info/interviews/19760725.htm [accessed August 7 2010].

Chomsky, N. 1986. *What Uncle Sam Really Wants*. Berkeley: Odonian Press.

Chomsky, N. 1993. *Year 501: The Conquest Continues*. Boston: South End Press.

Chomsky, N. 2005. State and corp.: Noam Chomsky interviewed by uncredited interviewer. [Online]. Available at: http://www.chomsky.info/interviews/20050518.htm [accessed August 29 2010].

Chu, H. 2010. Britain unveils radical austerity plan. [Online: *The Los Angeles Times*]. Available at: http://articles.latimes.com/2010/oct/21/world/la-fg-britain-budget-cuts-20101021 [accessed October 31 2010].

Clabaugh, G.K. 2004. The educational legacy of Ronald Reagan. [Online]. Available at: http://www.newfoundations.com/Clabaugh/CuttingEdge/Reagan.html [accessed July 4 2010].

Clark, R. 2010. Interview conducted in 2000 by Jensen, D., in *Resistance Against Empire*, edited by D. Jensen. Oakland: PM Press, 115–136.

Cobb, C.W. and Diaz, P. 2009. *Why Global Poverty*. New York: Robert Schalkenbach Foundation and Cinema Libre Studio.

Collins, P.H. 1998. *Fighting Words: Black Women & the Search for Justice*. Minneapolis: University of Minnesota Press.

Coleman, J.W. 2006. *The Criminal Elite: Understanding White-Collar Crime*. New York: Worth Publishers.

Columbia Encyclopedia. 2010. Iran-contra affair. [Online]. Available at: http://www.answers.com/topic/iran-contra-affair [accessed August 30 2010].

Condon, S. 2010. Poll: Most Americans want tax break for the rich to expire. [Online: CBS News]. Available at: http://www.cbsnews.com/8301-503544_162-20016602-503544.html [accessed January 9 2011].

Conger, R.D. and Dogan, S.J. Social class and socialization in families, in *Socialization: Theory and Research*, edited by Grusec, J.E. and Hastings, P.D. New York: The Guilford Press, 433–460.

Cooley, C.H. 1902. *Human Nature and the Social Order*. New York: Scribner.

Courtright, K.E., Hannan, M.J., Packard, S.H. and Brennan, E.T. 2007. Prisons and rural communities: Exploring impact and community satisfaction. [Online].

Available at: http://www.rural.palegislature.us/Prisons.pdf [accessed September 5 2010].

Crowley, M., Tope, D., Chamberlain, L.J. and Hodson, R. 2010. Neo-Taylorism at work: Occupational change in the post-fordist era. *Social Problems* 57(3) 421–47.

Currie, E. 1994. Crime and work, in *Crisis in American Institutions*, edited by J.H. Skolnick and E. Currie. New York: HarperCollins College Publishers, 417–426.

*Daily Mail Reporter*. 2011. Sarah Palin under fire as Arizona sheriff blames political 'vitriol' for triggering 'unstable' Safeway gunman's massacre. [Online: *Mail Online*]. Available at: http://www.dailymail.co.uk/news/article-1345460/Sarah-Palin-sheriff-Clarence-Dupnik-blames-political-vitriol-Arizona-shooting.html [accessed January 29 2011].

Davie, M.R. 1963. *William Graham Sumner: An Essay of Commentary and Selections*. New York: Thomas Y. Crowell.

Davin, D. 1999. *Internal Migration in Contemporary China.* New York: St. Martin's Press, Inc.

Davis, A. 1998. Masked racism: Reflections on the prison industrial complex. [Online: ColorLines, Fall]. Available at: http://www.thirdworldtraveler.com/Prison_System/Masked_Racism_ADavis.html [accessed October 23 2010].

Davis, A. 2003. *Are Prisons Obsolete?* New York: Seven Stories Press.

de la Barra, X. and dello Buono, R.A. 2009. *Latin America after the neoliberal debacle*. Plymouth, UK: Rowan & Littlefield Publishers, Inc.

de la Vega, E. 2005. The White House criminal conspiracy. [Online]. Available at: http://www.commondreams.org/views05/1030-25.htm [accessed August 18 2010].

DeCarlo, S. and Zajac, B. 2009. CEO compensation. [Online: Forbes.Com]. Available at: http://www.forbes.com/2009/04/22/executive-pay-ceo-leadership-compensation-best-boss-09-ceo_land.html [accessed July 17 2010].

Derber, C. 1996. *The Wilding of America*. New York: St. Martin's Press.

Doctorow, C. 2010. Canadian cops' history of agent provocateurs and the G20. [Online]. Available at: http://boingboing.net/2010/06/28/canadian-cops-histor.html [accessed August 22 2010].

Domhoff, G.W. 2010. Wealth, income, and power. [Online: *Who Rules America*]. Available at: http://sociology.ucsc.edu/whorulesamerica/power/wealth.html [accessed July 17 2010].

Draut, T. 2005. The growing college gap, in *Inequality Matters: The Growing Economic Divide* in *America and its Poisonous Consequences.* Edited by J. Lardner and D.A. Smith. New York: The New Press, 89–101.

Drolma, L.S. 2003. *Change of Heart: The Bodhisattva Peace Training of Chagdud Tulku*. Junction City, CA: Padma Publishing.

Drug Policy Alliance. 2010. Police corruption. [Online: Drugs, Police & the Law]. Available at: http://www.drugpolicy.org/law/police/ [accessed November 13 2010].

DrugWarFacts. 2005. Prisons and drug offenders. [Online]. Available at: http://www.drugwarfacts.org/cms/?q=node/63 [accessed January 11 2009].
DrugWarFacts. 2008. Race and prison. [Online]. Available at: http://www.drugwarfacts.org/cms/node/64 [accessed July 8 2010].
Du Bois, W.E.B. 2003. *The Souls of Black Folk*. New York: Fine Creative Media.
Duff, G. 2010. "AWOL Bush" NY Times coverup revealed, president "runs away" during Vietnam War. [Online]. Available at: http://www.veteranstoday.com/2010/05/26/awol-bush-ny-times-coverup-gets-revealed-president-runs-away-during-vietnam-war/ [accessed August 1 2010].
Dunayer, J. 2001. *Animal Equality: Language and Liberation*. Derwood: Ryce Publishing.
Durkheim, E. 1938. *The Rules of the Sociological Method*. New York: Free Press.
Dusza, K. 1989. Max Weber's conception of the state. *International Journal of Politics, Culture, and Society* 1(3) Fall.
Dyer, J. 2000. *The Perpetual Prison Machine*. Boulder: Westview Press.
Eitzen, D.S. and Leedham, C.S. 2004. *Solutions to Social Problems: Lessons from Other Societies*. 3rd edition. Boston: Allyn & Bacon.
Eley, T. 2008. "Working Poor" Report: Nearly 30 percent of US families subsist on poverty wages. [Online: World Socialist Website]. Available at: http://www.wsws.org/articles/2008/oct2008/work-o16.shtml [accessed July 17 2010].
eMedicineHealth. 2010. Post-traumatic stress disorder (PTSD). [Online]. Available at: http://www.emedicinehealth.com/post-traumatic_stress_disorder_ptsd/article_em.htm [accessed August 1 2010].
eRiposte. 2010. The truths behind corporate income taxes and corporate welfare. [Online]. Available at: http://www.eriposte.com/economy/tax/corporate_welfare.htm [accessed June 27 2010].
FBI (Federal Bureau of Investigation). 2009. *Crime in the United States, 2008*. [Online]. Available at: http://www.fbi.gov/ucr/cius2008/data/table_29.html [accessed August 21 2010].
FCIC (Financial Crisis Inquiry Commission) 2011. *Conclusions of the Financial Crisis Inquiry Commission*. [Online]. Available at: http://webcache.googleusercontent.com/search?q=cache:http://c0182732.cdn1.cloudfiles.rackspacecloud.com/fcic_final_report_conclusions.pdf, p. xvii [accessed January 29 2011].
Feagin, J.R. 2008. The continuing significance of race: antiblack discrimination in public places, in *Social Stratification: Class, Race, and Gender in Sociological Perspective*, edited by D. Grusky. Boulder: Westview Press.
Feagin, J.R. and Vera, H. 2001. *Liberation Sociology*. Oxford: Westview Press.
Feagin, J.R., Feagin, C.B. and Baker, D.V. 2006. *Social Problems: A Critical Power-Conflict Perspective*. 6th edition. New Jersey: Prentice Hall.
Feeding America. 2010. Hunger in America 2010 key findings. [Online]. Available at: http://feedingamerica.org/faces-of-hunger/hunger-in-america-2010/hunger-report-2010/key-findings.aspx [accessed July 5 2010].
Finley, L. and Reynolds Stringer, E. 2010. *Beyond Burning Bras: Feminist Activism for Everyone*. Denver: Praeger Publishing.

Flood, M. 2010. Skilling ruling leaves much undecided. [Online: *Houston Chronicle*]. Available at: http://www.chron.com/disp/story.mpl/special/enron/skilling/7077853.html [accessed on August 22 2010].

Foley, E. 2010. Private prisons' ties to anti-illegal immigration bills. [Online: *The Washington Independent*]. Available at: http://washingtonindependent.com/101908/private-prisons-ties-to-anti-illegal-immigration-bills [accessed October 31 2010].

Foner, P.S. (ed.) 1970. *W.E.B. Du Bois Speaks: Speeches and Addresses 1890–1919*. New York: Pathfinder.

Fourier, C. 2005. Attractive labour (1822–1837), in *Anarchism: A Documentary History of Libertarian Ideas*, edited by R. Graham. Montreal: Black Rose Books, 30–33.

FRAC (Food Research and Action Center). 2009. Hunger in the U.S. [Online]. Available at: http://frac.org/html/hunger_in_the_us/hunger_index.html [accessed July 5 2010].

Francione, G.L. 2002. Animal rights and animal welfare: Five frequently asked questions. [Online]. Available at: http://www.animal-law.org/library/quests.htm [accessed November 11 2010].

Frazer, J.G. 1919. *Folklore in the Old Testament*. New York: Macmillan.

Freepress. 2009. Ownership chart: The big six. [Online]. Available at: http://www.freepress.net/ownership/chart/main [accessed August 8 2010].

Friedan, B. 1963. *The Feminine Mystique*. New York: W.W. Norton and Co.

Friedman, J. 2003. The decline of corporate income tax revenues. [Online: Center on Budget and Policy Priorities]. Available at: http://www.cbpp.org/cms/index.cfm?fa=view&id=1311 [accessed July 19 2010].

Friedman, M. 1962. *Capitalism and Freedom*. Chicago: University of Chicago Press.

Friedman, M. 1970. The social responsibility of business is to increase its profits. [Online: *The New York Times Magazine*]. Available at: http://www.umich.edu/~thecore/doc/ Friedman.pdf [accessed November 11 2010].

Fromm, E. 1941. *Escape from Freedom*. New York: Henry Holt & Co.

GAO (United States General Accounting Office). 2000. Gender equity: Men's and women's participation in higher education. [Online]. Available at: http://www.gao.gov/new.items/d01128.pdf [accessed July 22 2010].

GAO (United States General Accounting Office). 2003a. Military recruiting. [Online]. Available at: http://www.gao.gov/new.items/d031005.pdf [accessed July 22 2010].

GAO (United States General Accounting Office). 2003b. Women's earnings: Work patterns partially explain difference between men's and women's earnings. [Online]. Available at: http://www.gao.gov/new.items/d0435.pdf [accessed July 22 2010].

Geier, J. 1999. Vietnam: The soldier's rebellion. *International Socialist Review*, 9 Fall.

Gelb, M. 2007. For many Americans, hard work is badge of honor. [Online]. Available at: http://1website.be/myamerica/php/americain.php?aID=23 [accessed August 6 2010].

Genter, S. and Hooks, G. 2010. "Examining prison privatization: A quantitative comparative study of public and private prison construction and employment growth in U.S. rural counties, 1997–2004", paper presented at the Society for the Study of Social Problems Meetings. Atlanta, GA.

Gettings, J., Johnson, D., Brunner, B. and Frantz, C. 2007. Wonder women: Profiles of leading female CEOs and business executives. [Online]. Available at: http://www.infoplease.com/spot/womenceo1.html [accessed July 21 2010].

Gibbs, N. 1994. Til death do us part, in *Crisis in American Institutions*, edited by J.H. Skolnick and E. Currie. New York: HarperCollins College Publishers, 231–242

Gibson, P. 2009. Gay male and lesbian suicide. [Online]. Available at: http://www.lambda.org/youth_suicide.htm [accessed July 25 2010].

Glynn, J.A., Hohm, C.F. and Stewart, E.W. 1996. *Global Social Problems*. New York: HarperCollins Publishers.

Goldfarb, Z. 2010. Task force probing whether banks broke federal laws during home seizures. [Online: *The Washington Post*]. Available at: http://www.washingtonpost.com/wp-dyn/content/article/2010/10/19/AR2010101904845.html [accessed October 30 2010].

Goldman, E. 1996a. Syndicalism: Its theory and practice, in *Red Emma Speaks*, edited by A. Shulman. Atlantic Highlands: Humanities Press International, 87–100.

Goldman, E. 1996b. Anarchism: What it really stands for, in *Red Emma Speaks*, edited by A. Shulman. Atlantic Highlands: Humanities Press International, 61–86.

Goldman, E. 1996c. What I believe, in *Red Emma Speaks*, edited by A. Shulman. Atlantic Highlands: Humanities Press International, 48–60.

Goldsmith, J. 1996. The winners and the losers, in *The Case Against the Global Economy*, edited by J. Mander and E. Goldsmith. San Francisco: Sierra Club Books, 171–79.

Goodman, A. 2008. Headlines for May 30th 2008. [Online: *Democracy Now*]. Available at: http://www.democracynow.org/2008/5/30/headlines [accessed October 28 2010].

Goodman, A. 2010. Rotten eggs and our broken democracy. [Online]. Available at: http://www.commondreams.org/print/59745 [accessed August 28 2010].

Grameen Foundation. 2010. China. [Online]. Available at: http://www.gfusa.org/asia/china [accessed July 18 2010].

Grant, R.W. 2010 (written in 2002). Men against fire: How many soldiers actually fired their weapons at the enemy during the Vietnam War? [Online]. Available at: http://www.historynet.com/men-against-fire-how-many-soldiers-actually-fired-their-weapons-at-the-enemy-during-the-vietnam-war.htm/5 [accessed August 17 2010].

Greek, C.R. and Greek, J.S. 2000. *Sacred Cows and Golden Geese: The Human Cost of Experiments on Animals*. London: Continuum.

Greek, C.R. and Greek, J.S. 2002. *Specious Science: How Genetics and Evolution Reveal Why Medical Research on Animals Harms Humans*. New York: Continuum.

Greenwood, D.A., Manteau, B.O. and Smith, G.A. 2009. Environmental education: From International resolve to local experience and inquiry, in *Social Justice, Peace, and Environmental Education: Transformative Standards*, edited by J. Andrzejewski, M. Baltodano and L. Symcox. London: Routledge.

Greider, W. 1992. *Who will tell the People: The Betrayal of American Democracy*. New York: Simon & Schuster, Inc.

Griffis, M. 2010. The human cost of occupation. [Online]. Available at: http://antiwar.com/casualties/ [accessed August 1 2010].

Grossman, D. 1995. *On Killing: The Psychological Cost of Learning to Kill in War and Society*. Toronto: Little, Brown and Company.

Grusec, J. and Hastings, P.D. 2007. *Handbook of Socialization: Theory and Research*. New York: The Guilford Press.

Hallinan, J.T. 2001. *Going Up the River: Travels in a Prison Nation*. New York: Random House.

Hamseyeh.net. 2010. More protests in Greece and Eastern Europe over austerity program [Online: *Iran & International News*]. Available at: http://www.hamsayeh.net/hamsayehnet_iran-international%20news1751.htm [accessed October 31 2010].

Hans, J.D., Gillen, M. and Akande, K. 2010. Sex redefined: The reclassification of oral-genital contact. *Perspectives on Sexual and Reproduction Health* 42(2) 74–78.

Harding, S. (ed.) 1993. *The "Racial" Economy of Science: Toward a Democratic Future*. Bloomington: Indiana University Press.

Harding, S. 2006. *Science and Social Inequality: Feminist and Postcolonial Issues*. Urbana: University of Illinois Press.

Hattery, A. and Smith, E. 2010. *Prisoner Re-entry and Social Capital*. New York: Lexington Books.

Heider, F. 1958. *The Psychology of Interpersonal Relations*. New York: John Wiley and Sons.

Heiner, R. 2010b. *Social Problems: An Introduction to Critical Constructionism*. New York: Oxford University Press.

Hersch, J. 2006. Skin color and wages among new U.S. immigrants. [Online: SOLE 2006 Annual Meeting]. Available at: http://client.norc.org/jole/SOLEweb/Hersch.pdf [accessed October 26 2010].

Hightower, J. 2010. Two multibillionare brothers are remaking America for their own benefit. [Online]. Available at: http://www.commondreams.org/print/60107 [accessed September 13 2010].

History of the Culture of War. 2010. *Warfare and the Origin of the State.* [Online]. Available at: http://www.culture-of-peace.info/books/history/state.html [accessed September 2 2010].

Hoffman, F. 1998. Animal abuse and human abuse: Partners in crime. [Online]. Available at: http://www.all-creatures.org/sof/animalabuse.html [accessed July 21 2010].

Homans, G.C. 1961. *Social Behavior: Its Elementary Forms*. New York: Harcourt Brace & World.

Hooks, G., Mosher, C., Rotolo, T. and Lobao, L. 2004. The prison industry: Carceral expansion and employment in U.S. counties 1969–1994. *Social Science Quarterly* 85(1) 37–57.

Horton, P.B., Leslie, G.R., Larson, R.L. and Horton, R.L. 1997. *The Sociology of Social Problems*. Englewood Cliffs, NJ: Prentice Hall.

Huff, M., Phillips, P. and Project Censored. 2010. Increased tensions with unresolved 9/11 issues, in *Censored 2011: The Top 25 Censored Stories of 2009–10*, edited by Huff, M., Phillips, P. and Project Censored. New York: Seven Stories Press, 70–77.

Hurst, C.E. 2010. *Social Inequality: Forms, Causes, and Consequences*. 7th edition. Boston: Allyn & Bacon.

Illich, I. 1971. *Deschooling Society*. London: Calder and Boyers

Infact. 1991. *Deadly Deception: General Electric, Nuclear Weapons, and our Environment.* (Documentary video, dir. Debra Chasnoff). Boston: Infact.

Infoplease. 2007. "Railroad Accidents". [Online: Pearson Education, Inc.]. Available at: http://www.infoplease.com/ipa/A0001450.html [accessed July 5 2010].

IWPR (Institute for Women's Policy Research). 2010. *The Gender Wage Gap: 2009.* [Online]. Available at: http://www.iwpr.org/pdf/C350.pdf [accessed July 21 2009].

Jean, P. 2007. Prison labor: Who stands to profit in the U.S.A's most important growth industry? [Online]. Available at: http://www.digitaljournal.com/article/199622 [accessed September 5 2010].

Jericho Project. 2007. *The Crisis of Homeless Veterans*. [Online].Available at: http://www.jerichoproject.org/index.php?option=com_content&task=view&id=50&Itemid=81 [accessed August 1 2010].

Johnson, R. 2010. Gay, lesbian, bisexual, transgender and questioning youth suicide statistics. [Online]. Available at: http://gaylife.about.com/od/gayteens/a/gaysuicide.htm [accessed July 25 2010].

Johnston, D.C. 2007. Income gap is widening, data shows. [Online: *The New York Times*]. Available at: http://www.nytimes.com/2007/03/29/business/29tax.html [accessed July 9 2010].

Jones, E., Haenfler, R. and Johnson, B. 2007. *The Better World Handbook: Small Changes that Make a Big Difference*. British Columbia, Canada: New Society Publishers.

Jorgenson, A.K. and Clark, B. 2009. The economy, military, and ecologically unequal exchange relationships in comparative perspective: A panel study of the ecological footprints of nations, 1975–2000. *Social Problems* 56(4) 621–46.

JPI (Justice Policy Institute). 2008. Substance abuse treatment and public safety. [Online]. Available at: http://www.justicepolicy.org/images/upload/08_01_REP_DrugTx_AC-PS.pdf [accessed August 21 2010].

JPI (Justice Policy Institute). 2009. Pruning prisons: how cutting corrections can save money and protect public safety. [Online]. Available at: http://www.justicepolicy.org/images/upload/09_05_REP_PruningPrisons_AC_PS.pdf [accessed August 21 2010].

Katz, E., Aisenbrey, M., Baldwin, A., Cheuse, E. and Weisbrodt, A. 2005. Documenting discrimination in voting: Judicial findings under section 2 of the voting rights act since 1982. [Online]. Available at: https://www.law.berkeley.edu/files/kats_discrimination_ in_voting.pdf [accessed October 26 2010].

Kelly, M. 2003. *The Divine Right of Capital: Dethroning the Corporate Aristocracy*. San Francisco: Berrett-Koehler Publishers.

Kelly, M. and White, A. 2007. *Corporate Design: The Missing Business and Public Policy Issue of Our Time.* [Online: Tellus Institute]. Available at: http://tellus.org/documents/CorporateDesign.pdf [accessed November 6 2010].

Keteyian, A. 2008. VA hid suicide risk, internal emails show. [Online]. Available at: http://www.cbsnews.com/stories/2008/04/21/cbsnews_investigates/main4032921.shtml [accessed August 1 2010].

King, M.L. 1970 (originally delivered in 1968). Honoring Dr. Du Bois, in *W.E.B. Du Bois Speaks: Speeches and Addresses 1890–1919*, edited by P.S. Foner, New York: Pathfinder, 20–28.

Klahsen, R.L. 2008. S-corps: Recommended Reforms that Promote Parity, Growth and Development for Small Businesses. [Online: House Committee on Small Business Subcommittee on Finance and Tax]. Available at: http://s-corp.org/documents/Klahsen%20testimony%206-18-08%20Final.pdf [accessed June 27 2010].

Klein, N. 2007. *The Shock Doctrine: The Rise of Disaster Capitalism.* New York: Metropolitan Books.

Korten, D.C. 2010. *Agenda for a New Economy: From Phantom Wealth to Real Wealth.* San Francisco: Berrett-Koehler Publishers, Inc.

Kozol, J. 1991. *Life on the Mississippi: East St. Louis, Illinois*. New York: Crown Publishers.

Krugman, P. 1998. *The Accidental Theorist*. New York: W.W. Norton & Company.

Krugman, P. 2009. How did economists get it so wrong? [Online: *New York Times*]. Available at: http://www.nytimes.com/2009/09/06/magazine/06Economic-t.html [accessed November 2 2010].

LaDuke, W. 1996. A society based on conquest cannot be sustained, in *Oppression and Social Justice: Critical Frameworks*, edited by J. Andrzejewski. Needham Heights: Simon & Schuster Custom Publishing.

LaDuke, W. 1999. *All Our Relations: Native Struggles for Land and Life.* Cambridge, MA: South End Press.

Laible, D. and Thompson, R.A. 2007. Early socialization: A relationship perspective, in *Handbook of Socialization: Theory and Research*, edited by Grusec, J.E. and Hastings, P.D. New York: The Guilford Press, 181–207

Lardner, J. and Smith, D.A. (eds) 2005. *Inequality Matters: The Growing Economic Divide in America and its Poisonous Consequences.* New York: The New Press.

Lauer, R.H. and Lauer, J.C. 2007. *Social Problems and the Quality of Life.* New York: McGraw-Hill.

Leach, S.L. 2004. Slavery is not dead, just less recognizable. [Online: Christian Science Monitor]. Available at: http://www.csmonitor.com/2004/0901/p16s01-wogi.html [accessed October 24 2010].

Leakey, R. and Lewin, R. 1995. *Sixth Extinction: Patterns of Life and the Future of Humankind.* [Online]. Available at: http://www.well.com/~davidu/sixthextinction.html [accessed February 6 2011].

Lean, G. 2000. Experts link Ebola to destruction of rainforest. [Online: *The Independent*]. Available at: http://www.independent.co.uk/news/world/africa/experts-link-ebola-to-destruction-of-rainforest-634861.html [accessed July 4 2010].

LEAP (Law Enforcement Against Prohibition) 2010a. Cops, the war on drugs & race. [Online]. Available at: http://leap.cc/cms/index.php?name=Web_Links&l_op= visit&lid= 152 [accessed August 21 2010].

LEAP (Law Enforcement Against Prohibition) 2010b. LEAP statement of principles. [Online]. Available at: http://leap.cc/cms/index.php [accessed August 21 2010].

Leicht, K.T. and Fitzgerald, S.T. 2007. *Postindustrial Peasants: The Illusion of Middle-Class Prosperity.* New York: Worth Publishers.

Leon-Guerrero, A. 2009. *Social Problems: Community, Policy, and Social Action.* 2nd edition. New York: Sage/Pine Forge Press.

Levey, G. 2007. *Northern Exposure.* [Online]. Available at: http://www.salon.com/news/feature/2007/05/03/awol_in_canada/index.html [accessed October 12 2010].

Levine, A. 2009. More women than men dismissed from military for being gay. [Online: CNN]. Available at: http://articles.cnn.com/2009-10-09/us/military.gays.dismissals_1_palm-center-gay-nathaniel-frank?_s=PM:US [accessed January 1 2011].

Lewis, O. 1959. *Five Families: Mexican Case Studies in the Culture of Poverty.* New York: Basic Books, Inc.

Liptak, A. 2010. Justices, 5–4, reject corporate spending limit. [Online: *The New York Times*]. Available at: http://www.nytimes.com/2010/01/22/us/politics/22scotus.html [accessed October 30 2010].

Longley, R. 2004. Gender wage gap widening, census data shows. [Online]. Available at: http://usgovinfo.about.com/od/censusandstatistics/a/paygapgrows.htm [accessed July 21 2009].

Lyman, H. 1998. *Mad Cowboy: Plain Truth from the Cattle Rancher Who Won't Eat Meat*. New York: Scribner Publishing.

Lyman, H. 2006. *FACTOIDS AND RESOURCE LINKS*. [Online]. Available at: http://www.madcowboy.com/01_FactsMC.000.html [accessed July 5 2010].

MacLean, A. 2010. The things they carry: Combat, disability, and unemployment among U.S. Men. *American Sociological Review* 75(4) 563–85.

Maggi, L. 2010. Henry Glover case trial begins for 5 current and former New Orleans police officers. [Online: *The Times Picayune*]. Available at: http://www.nola.com/crime/index.ssf/2010/11/trial_of_5_current_and_former.html [accessed November 13 2010].

Maheshwari, J.K. 2001. Origin of AIDS virus linked to rainforest destruction. [Online: Environews, vol. 7, no. 4]. Available at: http://isebindia.com/01_04/01-10-1.html [accessed July 4 2010].

Malacad, B.L. and Hess, G. 2010. Oral sex: Behaviours and feelings of Canadian young women and implications for sex education. *European Journal of Contraception & Reproductive Health Care* 15(3) 177–185.

Malinowski, B. 1922. *Argonauts of the Western Pacific*. London: Routledge and Kegan Paul.

Mandel, E. 2010 (written before 1995). Marx's theory of surplus value. [Online: International Viewpoint]. Available at: http://www.internationalviewpoint.org/spip.php?article287 [accessed November 14 2010].

Marcotte, A. 2011. The rhetoric of fear feeds terror. [Online: *Guardian.co.uk*]. Available at: http://www.guardian.co.uk/commentisfree/cifamerica/2011/jan/24/washington-state-martin-luther-king [accessed January 29 2011].

Marshall, S.L.A. 1978. *Men Against Fire: The Problem of Battle Command.* Gloucester: Peter Smith Publisher.

Marx, K., Engels, F. 1969 (written 1947). *The Communist Manifesto*. Moscow: Progress Publishers.

Marx, K. 2008. Alienation and social classes, in *Social Stratification: Class, Race, and Gender in Sociological Perspective*, edited by D. Grusky. Boulder: Westview Press, 74–78.

Maslow, A. 1954. *Motivation and Personality.* 3rd edition. New York: Harper & Row Publishers.

Mason, J. 1993. *An Unnatural Order: Why We are Destroying the Planet and Each Other: A Manifesto for Change.* New York: Continuum.

McCarthy, M. 2009. Rainforest razed so cattle can graze. [Online]. Available at: http://www.independent.co.uk/environment/climate-change/rainforest-razed-so-cattle-can-graze-1521677.html [accessed July 5 2010].

McGehee, R. 2002. *Deadly Deceits: My 25 Years in the CIA*. New York: Ocean Press.

McNamara, J.D. 1997. A veteran chief: Too many cops think it's a war. [Online: *Time*, September 1, p. 2]. Available at: http://www.time.com/time/magazine/article/0,9171,986941-2,00.html [accessed January 11 2009].

Mead, G.H. 1934. *Mind, Self, and Society: From the Standpoint of a Social Behaviorist*. Chicago: University of Chicago Press.

Mills, C.W. 1973. *The Power Elite*. New York, Oxford University Press.

Mills, C.W. 1993. The sociological imagination, in *Systemic Crisis: Problems in Society, Politics, and World Order*, edited by W.D. Perdue. Toronto: Harcourt Brace Jovanovich College Publishers.

Mirowsky, J. and Ross, C.E. 2003. *Social Causes of Psychological Distress*. 2nd edition. Piscataway, New Jersey: Aldine Transaction.

Mixon, B. 2008. Chore wars: Men, women, and housework. [Online: National Science Foundation]. Available at: http://www.nsf.gov/discoveries/disc_summ.jsp?cntn_id=111458 [accessed July 23 2010].

Montopoli, B. 2009. Poll: Many Blacks say police treat them unfairly. [Online: CBS]. Available at: http://www.cbsnews.com/8301-503544_162-5196554-503544.html [accessed October 26 2010].

Mooney, L., Knox, D. and Schacht, C. 2007. *Understanding Social Problems*. New York: Wadsworth Publishing.

Moore, M. 2004. Fahrenheit 9/11. (Documentary film, dir. Michael Moore). [Online: lead for film] Available at: http://www.fahrenheit911.com/ [accessed August 2 2010].

Moore, M. 2007. Sicko. (Documentary film, dir. Michael Moore). [Online: lead for film]. Available at: http://sickothemovie.com/dvd/ [accessed August 6 2010].

Moore, M. 2009. Capitalism: A Love Story. (Documentary film, dir. Michael Moore) [Online: lead for film]. Available at: http://www.michaelmoore.com/books-films/capitalism-love-story [accessed August 6 2010].

Moyers, B. 1987. The Secret Government. [Online: A Public Television Documentary]. Available at: http://www.youtube.com/watch?v=_sstDwKTCpM [accessed October 12 2010].

Mumola, C. and Karberg, J. 2007. *Drug Use and Dependence, State and Federal Prisons, 2004*. [Online: Bureau of Justice Statistics Special Report]. Available at: http://bjs.ojp.usdoj.gov/content/pub/pdf/dudsfp04.pdf [accessed August 7 2010].

Mueller, C. 1999. Wealth distribution statistics – 1999. [Online]. Available at: http://www.cooperativeindividualism.org/wealth_distribution1999.html [accessed July 15 2010].

Muzzatti, S.L., Dowler, K. and Fleming, T. 2006. Constructing crime: Media, crime and popular culture. *Canadian Journal of Criminology and Criminal Justice* 48(6) 837–850.

NAACP. 2010. Criminal justice fact sheet. [Online]. Available at: http://www.naacp.org/pages/criminal-justice-fact-sheet [accessed November 13 2010].

Nettlau, M. 1996. *A Short History of Anarchism*. London: Freedom Press.

NEW Leadership Nevada. 2006. History of the program. [Online: Women's Research Institute of Nevada]. Available at: http://wrin.unlv.edu/new/history.html [accessed January 11 2009].

Newman, D.M. 2009. *Families: A Sociology Perspective*. New York: McGraw-Hill.

Nibert, D. 2002. *Animal Rights/Human Rights: Entanglements of Oppression and Liberation*. Lanham, MD: Rowman & Littlefield Publishers.

Nieves, S. 2006. The "policing-to prisons" track. [Online: *The Real Cost of Prisons Weblog*]. Available at: http://realcostofprisons.org/blog/archives/2006/04/the_policingto.html [accessed January 11 2009].

Noble, D.F. 1995. *Progress Without People: New Technology, Unemployment, and the Message of Resistance.* Toronto: Between the Lines Publishers.

Nurmakov, A. 2010. Kyrgyzstan: Provocateurs seen behind ethnic clashes. [Online]. Available at: http://globalvoicesonline.org/2010/06/14/kyrgyzstan-provocateurs-seen-behind-ethnic-clashes/ [accessed August 22 2010].

NWLC (National Women's Law Center). 2008. The reality of the workforce: Mothers are working outside the home. [Online]. Available at: http://www.nwlc.org/pdf/WorkingMothersMarch2008.pdf [accessed July 21 2009].

Opello, W.C., Rosow, S.J. 2004. *The Nation-State and Global Order: A Historical Introduction to Contemporary Politics.* Boulder: Lynne Rienner Publishers.

O'Rourke, B. 2010. Britain announces sweeping austerity measures. [Online: *Radio Free Europe, Radio Liberty*]. Available at: http://www.rferl.org/content/Britain_Announces_Sweeping_Austerity_Measures/2196108.html [accessed October 31 2010].

Parenti, C. 2010. Interview, in *Resistance Against Empire*, edited by D. Jenson. Oakland: PM Press, 193–216.

Parenti, M. 1995. *Against Empire*. San Francisco: City Lights Publishers.

Parenti, M. 2011. *Democracy for the Few.* Boston: Wadsworth.

Parr, J. and Addison, S. 2010. "Blatant and shocking racism" still exists in parts of the world of work, according to a report on Tuesday. [Online: Reuters]. Available at: http://uk.reuters.com/article/idUKTRE65E2GB20100615 [accessed October 26 2010].

Parry, R. 2004. CIA's drug confession. [Online]. Available at: http://www.consortiumnews.com/1990s/consor29.html [accessed April 7 2005].

Peale, C. 2001. At work, Blacks still sense limits. [Online: *The Enquirer*]. Available at: http://www.enquirer.com/editions/2001/09/04/loc_at_work_blacks_still.html [accessed October 26 2010].

Pelaez, V. 2008. The prison industry in the United States: Big business or a new form of slavery. [Online]. Available at: http://www.globalresearch.ca/index.php?context=va&aid=8289 [accessed September 5 2010].

Perkins, J. 2004. *Confessions of an Economic Hit Man.* San Francisco: Berrett-Koehler Publishers.

Perkins, J. 2010. Is the U.S. economic model a failure? [Online: Correo Del Orinoco]. Available at: http://www.johnperkins.org/wp-content/uploads/2010/02/Perkins-CORREO1.pdf [accessed July 5 2010].

Perrucci, R. and Wysong, E. 2008. *The New Class Society: Goodbye American Dream?* 3rd edition. Lanham, MD: Rowman & Littlefield Publishers, Inc.

Petit-Zeman, S. 2003. Pills for everything. [Online: *The Guardian*]. Available at: http://www.guardian.co.uk/society/2003/jul/30/medicineandhealth.childrens services [accessed November 6 2010].

Phillips, P. and Project Censored. 2004a. 13 Schwarzenegger met with Enron's Ken Lay years before the California recall, in *Censored 2005: The Top 25 Censored Stories of 2003–04*, edited by P. Phillips and Project Censored. New York: Seven Stories Press.

Phillips, P. and Project Censored. 2004b. The destabilization of Haiti, in *Censored 2005: The Top 25 Censored Stories of 2003–04,* edited by P. Phillips and Project Censored. New York: Seven Stories Press.

Phillips, P. and Project Censored. 2009. *Censored 2010: The Top 25 Censored Stories of 2008–09.* New York: Seven Stories Press.

Pilkington, E. 2011. The billionaires are coming: Obama's richest enemies to hold summit. [Online: *The Guardian*]. Available at: http://www.guardian.co.uk/world/2011/jan/28/obama-richest-enemies-billionaires-summit [accessed January 29 2011].

Pimentel, D. and Pimentel, M. 2003. Sustainability of meat-based and plant-based diets and the environment. [Online: American Journal of Clinical Nutrition, 78(3)]. Available at: http://www.ajcn.org/cgi/content/full/78/3/660S#FN3 [accessed July 5 2010].

Pizzigati, S. 2004. *Greed and Good: Understanding and Overcoming the Inequality that Limits Our Lives.* Arlington, VA: Apex Press.

PNAC (the Project for the New American Century). 2000. Rebuilding America's defenses: Strategies, forces and resources. [Online]. Available at: http://www.newamericancentury.org/RebuildingAmericasDefenses.pdf [accessed August 7 2010].

Poverty.com. 2010. Hunger and world poverty. [Online]. Available at: http://www.poverty.com/ [accessed November 13 2010].

Proyect, L. 2009. Are worker owned companies an alternative to capitalism? [Online]. Available at: http://activistseducation.blogspot.com/2009/10/are-worker-owned-companies-alterative.html [accessed August 7 2010].

Ptacek, J. 2000. The tactics and strategies of men who batter, in *Crisis in American Institutions*, edited by J. Skolnick and E. Currie. 11th edition. Boston: Allyn and Bacon, 195–209.

Questia. 2010. Iran-Contra Affiar. [Online]. Available at: http://www.questia.com/library/encyclopedia/iran_contra_affair.jsp [accessed August 31 2010].

Quinn, B. 2008. 11,000 Troops go AWOL since the Iraq War. [Online]. Available at: http://www.telegraph.co.uk/news/uknews/1554155/11000-troops-go-Awol-since-Iraq-war.html [accessed August 1 2010].

Rashbaum, W.K. 2010. Retired officers raise questions on crime data. [Online: *The New York Times*]. Available at: http://www.nytimes.com/2010/02/07/nyregion/07crime.html?_r=1&ref=nyregion [accessed November 13 2010].

Raver, E. 2006. The Enron scandal: The crime,scandal, tragedy, and controversy of the century. [Online: Business & Finance]. Available at: http://www.associatedcontent.com/article/100479/the_enron_scandal_the_crime_scandal_pg3.html?cat=3 [accessed July 19 2010].

Reback, G.L. 2009. *Free the Market: Why Only Government Can Keep the Marketplace Competitive.* New York: Penguin Group (USA) Inc.

Reddy, S.G. and Pogge, T.W. 2005. How not to count the poor. [Online]. Available at: http://www.columbia.edu/~sr793/count.pdf [accessed July 18 2010].

Reiman, J. 2001. *The Rich Get Richer and the Poor Get Prison: Ideology, Class, and Criminal Justice.* Boston: Allyn and Bacon.

Regan, T. 2004. *Empty Cages: Facing the Challenge of Animal Rights.* New York: Rowman and Littlefield Publishers, Inc.

Repetti, R. Taylor, S.E. and Saxbe, D. 2007. The influence of early socialization experiences on the development of biological systems, in *Handbook of Socialization: Theory and Research*, edited by Grusec, J.E. and Hastings, P.D. New York: The Guilford Press, 124–52.

Robbins, J. 2001. *The Food Revolution: How Your Diet can Help Save Your Life and the World.* Berkeley: Conari Press.

Rogen, J. 2009. Schools for sale: Privatizing education in America. [Online: Orbis]. Available at: http://www.vanderbiltorbis.com/2.12253/schools-for-sale-privatizing-education-in-america-1.1611897 [accessed October 24 2010].

Rubington, E. and Weinberg, M.S. (eds) 2011. *The Study of Social Problems: Seven Perspectives*. New York: Oxford University Press.

Ryan, W. 1996. From blaming the victim, in *Oppression and Social Justice: Critical Frameworks*, edited by J. Andrzejewski. Needham Heights: Simon & Schuster.

Ritzer, G. 1975. *Sociology: A Multiple Paradigm Science*. Boston: Allyn and Bacon, Inc.

Ritzer, G. 2004. *Handbook of Social Problems: A Comparative International Perspective*. Thousand Oaks, CA: Sage Publications.

Rifkin, J. 1992. *Beyond Beef: The Rise and Fall of the Cattle Culture*. New York: Plume/Penguin Books.

Rugh, J.S. and Massey, D.S. 2010. Racial segregation and the American foreclosure crisis. *American Sociological Review* 75(5) 629–51.

Sanders, Barry. 2009. *The Green Zone: The Environmental Cost of Militarism*. Oakland: AK Press.

Schlosser, E. (2002). *Fast Food Nation: The Dark Side of the All-American Meal.* New York: HarperCollins.

Schorn, D. 2006. A Spy Speaks Out. [Online]. Available at: http://www.cbsnews.com/stories/2006/04/21/60minutes/main1527749.shtml [accessed August 7 2010].

Science News. 2007. Wealth gap is increasing, study shows. [Online: ScienceDaily]. Available at: http://www.sciencedaily.com/releases/2007/08/070807171936.htm [accessed October 15 2010].

Sernau, S. 2009. *Global Problems: The Search for Equity, Peace, and Sustainability.* New York: Pearson Education Inc.

Shargorodsky, S. 2000. Chernobyl zone: A world of radiation and death. [Online: Mindfully.org]. Available at: http://www.mindfully.org/Nucs/Chernobyl-Death-Zone.htm [accessed October 24 2010].

Shenon, P. 2004. Final 9/11 report is said to dismiss Iraq-Qaeda alliance. [Online]. Available at: http://www.nytimes.com/2004/07/12/politics/12panel.html [accessed August 7 2010].

Sherman, A. and Stone, C. 2010. Income gaps between very rich and everyone else more than tripled over last three decades, new data show. [Online: Center on Budget and Policy Priorities]. Available at: http://www.cbpp.org/cms/index.cfm?fa=view&id=3220 [accessed July 18 2010].

Shiva, V. 1995. *Biopiracy: The Plunder of Nature and Knowledge.* Boston: South End Press.

Shulman, A.K. 1996. Biographical introduction, in *Red Emma Speaks*, edited by A.K. Shulman, Atlantic Highlands: Humanities Press International, 20–40.

Siegel, L.J. 1992. *Criminology* New York: Wadsworth.

Siegel, L.J. 2007. *Criminology: The core.* 3rd edition. New York: Wadsworth.

Simon, D. 2009. Wire creator David Simon testifies on the future of journalism. [Online]. Available at: http://www.reclaimthemedia.org/journalistic_practice/wire_creator_david_simon_testi0719 [accessed September 6 2010].

Singer, P. 1975. *Animal Liberation*. New York: Avon Books.

Sirota, D. and Harvey, C. 2004. They knew. [Online]. Available at: http://www.inthesetimes.com/article/899/they_knew/ [accessed August 7 2010].

Smeeding, T. 2008. Poverty, work, and policy: The United States in comparative perspective, in *Social Stratification: Class, Race, and Gender in Sociological Perspective*, edited by D.B. Grusky. Boulder: Westview Press.

Smith, A. 1977. *An Inquiry into the Nature and Causes of the Wealth of Nations*. Chicago: University of Chicago Press.

Smith, L.T. 1999. *Decolonizing Methodologies: Research and Indigenous Peoples.* London: Zed Books.

Sonn, R. 1992. *Anarchism*. New York: Twayne Publishers.

Spiegel, M. 1997. *The Dreaded Comparison: Human and Animal Slavery.* 3rd edition. New York: Mirror Books.

Stallwood, K.W. 2002. *A Primer on Animal Rights.* New York: Lantern Books.

Stein, B. 2006. In class warfare, guess which class is winning. [Online: *The New York Times*]. Available at: http://www.nytimes.com/2006/11/26/business/yourmoney/26every.html? [accessed October 9 2010].

Stewart, S.D. and Croudep, C. 2010. Fast facts on domestic violence. [Online: Domestic Violence]. Available at: http://www.clarkprosecutor.org/html/domviol/facts.htm [accessed October 15 2010].

Stern, V. 2006. *Creating Criminals: Persons and People in a Market Society.* London: Zed Books.

Stiglitz, J.E. 2008. Globalism's discontents, in *Social Stratification: Class, Race, and Gender in Sociological Perspective*, edited by D.B. Grusky. Boulder: Westview Press.

Stockwell, J. 1984. *In Search of Enemies*. New York: W.W. Norton and Company, Inc.

Symcox, L. 2002. *Whose History? The Struggle for National Standards in American Classrooms*. New York: Teachers College Press.

Thakur, R. 2005. Social stratification in contemporary China. [Online: *IIAS Newsletter* #36]. http://www.iias.nl/nl/36/IIAS_NL36_16.pdf [accessed July 9 2010].

The Humane Society. 2009. First strike: The connection between animal cruelty and human violence. [Online]. Available at: http://hsus.org/hsus_field/first_strike_the_connection_between_animal_cruelty_and_human_violence/index.html [accessed July 21 2010].

*The Telegraph.* 2009. One billion suffer from world hunger. [Online]. Available at: http://www.telegraph.co.uk/news/worldnews/europe/italy/5580841/One-billion-suffer-from-world-hunger.html [accessed November 13 2010].

The World Bank. 2010. Overview: Understanding, measuring and overcoming poverty [Online: Poverty Reduction & Equity]. Available at: http://go.worldbank.org/K7LWQUT9L0 [accessed July 18 2010].

Tolstoy, L. 1898. How shall we escape, in *The Complete Works of Lyof N. Tolstoi,* New York: Thomas Y. Crowell & Company (within *What is Religion?* 122–133).

Tolstoy, L. 1899a. The beginning of the end, in *The Complete Works of Lyof N. Tolstoi.* New York: Thomas Y. Crowell & Company (within *Essays, Letters, and Miscellanies*, 70–71).

Tolstoy, L. 1899b. *Tolstoy's Works: Resurrection, What is Religion?* New York: Thomas Y. Crowell & Company.

Tolstoy, L. 1985. *The Forged Coupon: A Classic Tale of Crime and Guilt.* New York: W.W. Norton & Company.

Turner, J.H. 2003. *The Structure of Sociological Theory.* Belmont: Wadsworth/Thomson Learning.

US Census Bureau. 2004. Educational attainment in the United States: 2003. [Online: Population Characteristics]. Available at: http://www.census.gov/prod/2004pubs/p20-550.pdf.

US Census Bureau. 2010. Transportation: Motor vehicle accidents and fatalities. [Online: The 2010 Statistical Abstract]. Available at: http://www.census.gov/compendia/ statab/2010/tables/10s1067.pdf [accessed July 5 2010].

USDL (United States Department of Labor). 2009. Quick stats on women workers, 2009. [Online]. Available at: http://www.dol.gov/wb/stats/main.htm [accessed October 15 2010].

USLEAP. 2010. Major victory for Johnson controls workers at Mexican plant; struggle goes on at second factory. [Online]. Available at: http://www.usleap.org/major-victory-johnson-controls-workers-mexican-plant-struggle-goes-second-factory [accessed September 7 2010].

Vieth, E. 2010. An outrageous prediction regarding millions of illegal foreclosures conducted by banks. [Online: *Dangerous Intersection*]. Available at: http://dangerousintersection.org/2010/10/13/an-outrageous-prediction-regarding-millions-of-illegal-foreclosures-conducted-by-banks/ [accessed October 30 2010].

Waas, M. 2006. Libby says Bush authorized leaks. [Online: *National Journal*]. Available at: http://news.nationaljournal.com/articles/0406nj1.htm [accessed October 28 2010].

Wallerstein, I. 1974. *The Modern World-System*. New York: Academic Press.

Washington, M.H. 2007. Anna Julia Cooper, in *Black Women's Intellectual Traditions: Speaking their Minds*, edited by K. Waters and C.B. Conaway. Lebanon, NH: University of Vermont Press, 249–268.

Webb, G. 1999. *Dark Alliance*. New York: Seven Stories Press.

Weber, M. 1958. *The City*. New York: The Free Press.

West, H.C. 2010. Prison inmates at midyear 2009 – statistical table. [Online]. Available at: http://bjs.ojp.usdoj.gov/index.cfm?ty=pbdetail&iid=2200 [accessed August 21 2010].

White, D. 2010. Iraq war facts, results & statistics at August 23, 2010. [Online]. Available at: http://usliberals.about.com/od/homelandsecurit1/a/IraqNumbers.htm [accessed October 15 2010].

White, M. 2010. What the bible says – and doesn't say – about homosexuality. [Online: Soulforce]. Available at: http://www.soulforce.org/article/homosexuality-bible-gay-christian [accessed October 24 2010].

Whitman, S. 1992. The crime of Black imprisonment. *Z Magazine*, May, 69–72.

WikiLeaks. 2010. Collateral murder. [Online]. Available at: http://collateralmurder.com/ [accessed August 1 2010].

Wikipedia. 2010a. Aviation accidents and incidents. [Online]. Available at: http://en.wikipedia.org/wiki/Aviation_accidents_and_incidents#Statistics [accessed July 5 2010].

Wikipedia. 2010b. Desertion. [Online]. Available at: http://en.wikipedia.org/wiki/Desertion#Absence_without_leave [accessed August 1 2010].

Wikipedia. 2010c. COINTELPRO. [Online]. Available at: http://en.wikipedia.org/wiki/COINTELPRO [accessed August 22 2010].

Williams, W. 2001. The virtue of greed. [Online: *Capitalism Magazine*]. Available at: http://www.capmag.com/article.asp?ID=69 [accessed July 4 2010].

Williams, W. 2008a. Commentary: Greed, need and money. [Online: *The Examiner*]. Available at: http://www.examiner.com/a-1135374~Walter_E__Williams__Greed__need_and_ money.html [accessed July 4 2010].

Williams, W. 2008b. Environmentalists' wild predictions. [Online: *Capitalism Magazine*]. Available at: http://www.capitalismmagazine.com/environment/3432-Environmentalists-Wild-Predictions.html [accessed July 4 2010].

Williams, W. 2009. Lying propaganda. [Online: *Townhall Magazine*]. Available at: http://townhall.com/columnists/WalterEWilliams/2009/09/23/lying_propa ganda/ page/full [accessed July 4 2010].

Williams, W. 2010. Greed and the greater good. [Online: *Frontpage Magazine*]. Available at: http://frontpagemag.com/2010/06/18/greed-and-the-greater-good/ [accessed July 4 2010].

Winders, B. and Nibert, D. 2004. Consuming the surplus: Expanding "meat" consumption and animal oppression. *The International Journal of Sociology and Social Policy* 24(9) 76–96.

Winterfilm 2006. *Winter Soldier: The Film*. [Online: Milliarium Zero]. Available at: http://www.wintersoldierfilm.com/about.htm [accessed October 26 2010].

Wolff, E. 2003. The wealth divide: The growing gap in the United States between the rich and the rest. [Online: *The Multinational Monitor*, 24(5)]. Available at: http://multinationalmonitor.org/mm2003/03may/may03interviewswolff.html [accessed July 15 2010].

Wolff, R. 2010. Why France matters here, too. [Online: *The Independent*]. Available at: http://www.indypendent.org/2010/10/29/why-france-matters-here-too/ [accessed October 31 2010].

Wollstonecraft, M. 2004. *Vindication of the Rights of Women*, edited by M. Brody Kramnick. Harmondsworth: Penguin.

Ya Ya Networks. 2010. What recruiters don't tell you. [Online]. Available at: http://yayanetwork.org/recruiters_lie [accessed August 1 2010].

Zambrana, R.E. and MacDonald, V. 2005. Staggered inequalities in access to higher education by gender, race and ethnicity, in *Emerging Intersections: Race, Class, and Gender in Theory, Policy, and Practice*, edited by B.T. Dill and R.E. Zambrana. Piscataway: Rutgers University Press, 73–100.

Zastrow, C. 1996. *Social Problems: Issues and Solutions*. Chicago: Nelson-Hall Publishers.

Zepezauer, M. 2004. *Take the rich off welfare.* Boston: South End Press.

Zinn, H. 1980. *A People's History of the United States*. New York: Harper & Row Publishers.

# Index

**Bold** page numbers indicate figures.